EPIC GRANDEUR

SUNY Series, The Margins of Literature

Mihai I. Spariosu, Editor

EPIC GRANDEUR

Toward a Comparative Poetics of the Epic

MASAKI MORI

STATE UNIVERSITY OF NEW YORK PRES

Grateful acknowledgment is made for material reprinted from THE
DIALOGIC IMAGINATION: FOUR ESSAYS by M. M. Bakhtin, edited by
Michael Holquist, translated by Michael Holquist and Caryl Emerson,
Copyright © 1981. By permission of the University of Texas Press.

Published by
State University of New York Press, Albany

© 1997 State University of New York

Printed in the United States of America

For information, address State University of New York Press,
State University Plaza, Albany, N.Y. 12246

Production by M. R. Mulholland
'arketing by Nancy Farrell

ʈy of Congress Cataloging-in-Publication Data

saki, 1960–
      ʻrandeur : toward a comparative poetics of world epic /
        ʾri.
          m. — (SUNY series, the margins of literature)
            ʾbliographical references and index.
                 -3201-7 (alk. paper). — ISBN 0-7914-3202-5 (pbk. :

                  ʾ—History and criticism. 2. Literature,
                    ʾse and European. 3. Literature, Comparative-
                      ʾse. I. Title. II. Series.

                                                    96-3486
                                                    CIP

To Eun and Dezsö

CONTENTS

PREFACE

This book attempts a reexamination of the term "epic" as it has come down to us through the ages. Some critics might question the need for reopening the debate around this term, because it points to a dead genre with little relevance to people's lives today. In fact, it is now used to denote almost anything wonderful, spectacular, or large-scale in our everyday life. A new television drama that runs for several hours is an epic, a major football match is referred to as an epic game, companies choose the term for the labels of their merchandise such as bicycles and compact discs. The list goes on. These examples, however, do not indicate that the ubiquitous use of "epic" nowadays is illegitimate or unauthentic. Every age plays its part in changing, augmenting, and expunging the possible denotations and implications of an individual term or concept. What interests me here is twofold: the process of generic transformation by which the term "epic" is now easily detachable from the literary text, and the feasibility of a comparative approach to literary works of different cultures. The examination of these two issues will provide some hints about the future direction of the epic as a genre.

Defining any literary genre is far from simple. Although I do not intend to offer a new, clear-cut definition of the epic, a consideration of the desirability of such definitions is always relevant. Lest it be cast off as obsolete, a definition must adjust itself to the ever changing paradigms of literature as a whole. Furthermore, any attempt to bind a wide variety of works with a single, absolute formula would invariably create countless exceptions and marginal cases, rendering this attempt specious. On the other hand, when a number of literary works appear to exhibit similar features, we need certain criteria both to group them together and to distinguish among them. The need for such criteria is especially obvious when works from different cultures are placed side by side for the purpose of seeking, through them, a basis for mutual cultural understanding. Thus, the concept of a genre has to be globalized so that it can include non-Western texts despite some culture-oriented discrepancies in a broader, nonprovincial framework. This approach assumes that, like other human creations, a literary genre derives its manifestation from a certain common ground of humanity.

Considering the difficulty inherent in defining the epic, I shall propose a few basic elements of the genre as flexible indicators of the partial or total epic quality of a work, and not as mechanical tools for deciding once and for all whether or not a work should be called an epic. By a few basic epic elements, I do not mean specific conventions, such as an invocation to the Muse, extended similes, and a trip to the underworld, because these conventions are often restricted to the Western tradition. Instead, I shall concentrate on other essential elements thematically intrinsic to the experience of reading an epic. Those thematic essentials include coping with one's mortality, communal responsibility, and the double extension of time and space. A sense of mortality is essential here, because an epic primarily concerns humankind with its glories and sufferings, and its sufferings as mortal being hinge on the extinction of life. Moreover, how one faces death with what one has achieved ultimately determines the meaning of an individual's life. What the central figure of an epic accomplishes with his limited span of life must be linked to the security of his people, because his attempt to overcome communal threats magnifies his status and renders his name relevant to the collective memory of the people. Finally, an epic should offer an extensive outlook of time and space, because the world–view thus organized assures people of their existence in the unfathomable universe. Such an outlook is provided by the hero's exploration as well as by the work's total perspective. Taken together, these three thematic essentials of the epic create a sense of human dignity.

There are two points to be noted here. First, I am fully aware of the importance of feminist critical perspectives and of the existence of several central female figures in epic traditions. Since most of the central figures are male, however, I shall refer to an epic hero with the masculine pronoun for the sake of convenience. Second, by "history," I mean not only the recorded memory of the past but also the knowledge of the unfolding present and the prediction of the future. Such an extended concept of history is required to discuss certain epics. Thus, a work can be called "epical" when it deals seriously with the question of death, involves the fate of a large group of people, and explores a vast spatial and temporal expanse. Depending on individual works, there can be qualitative and quantitative differences in each thematic element. Several combinations among the three elements are also possible. Yet only a work that fully satisfies all three thematic conditions should properly be considered an epic.

This approach, while it offers no definitive norms, is an attempt to reevaluate the epic from a global viewpoint, although there are obvious limitations to my argument, such as the number of works and traditions. My view of the epic represents a small, though certain step toward the term's flexible conceptualization and the wider range of applicability within literature and outside it. For example, the generic outlines I propose for the epic have great potential for examining the epic quality of motion pictures. Due to the limited scope of my study, however, I cannot speculate on that possibility.

The demonstration of my thesis requires two stages; therefore, I have divided this study into two parts. Part I will develop the theoretical basis of my argument. In order to provide a historical context for this argument, I shall look at the ways in which influential thinkers have conceived of the epic. Then, I shall apply the proposed three thematic fundamentals to two different epic traditions: European and Japanese. My analysis will show what kind of changes the traditional epic underwent and what similarities and dissimilarities the two traditions have. I shall basically argue that, because of its grand scheme, a traditional epic tends to outgrow its predecessors while its ideal is internalized. Finally, I shall suggest that such grand schematization has often led the epic to the implicit, unacknowledged negation of the cultural values that it openly upholds.

Part II presents two case studies, one English and one Japanese, of what I call transitional epics. By transitional epics, I mean the relatively recent works which, although written after the traditional epic mode lost its impetus, still exhibit the three epic thematic fundamentals. The transition here shows changes in the value systems underlying the epic: from pride in martial exploits to tolerance, from violence to love and friendship, and from subjugation by power to mutual understanding based on equality. This shift from martial to nonmartial motifs should ultimately bring about an epic of peace entirely different from the epics of war that have so far been written.[1] *The Fall of Hyperion* by John Keats and *A Night on the Galaxy Railroad* by Miyazawa Kenji are useful representative works, because they clearly show this transitional phase in the genre as well as its internal problems. For example, I examine *The Fall of Hyperion* as a typical instance of the Romantic works that reflect the changing generic mode in the West after the critically sanctioned traditional epics ceased to be written at the end of the Renaissance. Keats' poem, with its lofty conception of Greek divine warfare, apparently assumes the traditional epic mode, but it certainly possesses the characteristics of a later epic. By contrast, *Galaxy Railroad* varies most from the conventional notion of the genre. With its form of a children's tale and its apparently fantastic nonmilitary content, it relates a story about a boy who dreams of a celestial night trip. But when treated as a new kind of epic in its intended immense scope, Miyazawa's work offers a sharp contrast to the traditional Japanese epic which, like the Western traditional epic, is filled with military motifs and ceased to be written a long time ago.

Through the case studies in part II, I shall reveal the basic similarities that these two works share behind their cultural façades. The features they have in common shall be divided into two groups. The first group includes the gradual generic transformation that has been inherited from the traditional epic: the ever-expanding scope of the three essential thematic elements, the questioning of the conventional warlike mentality, and the search for a principle to harmonize the world. The other shared features, such as fragmentation, dream visions, and a weak central figure, form the second group and intimate the uncertainty that undermines the two works' overt assertions. Because of these limitations, neither *The Fall of Hyperion* nor *Galaxy Railroad* can be regarded as a perfect epic of peace. But, even in their incomplete state, they point to a direction that the epic as a genre might take in the future. It is in this sense that I call them transitional epics.

In fact, it is not certain that an epic of peace will ever be realized. What I shall claim is that, over the ages, the generic transformations of the epic have moved in that direction and that the potential for epic production has remained unimpaired despite great fluctuations in literary modes. Even so, we cannot yet foresee the final outcome of that process of epic transformation. It might even seem that such an epic of high ideals and extreme dimensions is not really feasible. Historically, however, an interval of centuries has always preceded the advent of a critically acclaimed epic, and few literary critics believed that any new work could possibly rival or excel the scope of an older, established epic. Such is the case with the *Aeneid* and *Paradise Lost*. Who can say, then, that we are not in one of those glacial ages of epic creation?

In any case, if an epic of peace is ever actualized, it will mark a new stage of human spiritual attainment and will help both humans and other species to survive and prosper. Today, technological advances have made it possible for the human community to destroy itself forever. Furthermore, as many regional incidents show, when there is a collapse of social stability, human beings can still revert to the brutality glorified in the heroic code of the ancient war epic. In such a situation, we need a strong cultural deterrent to this destructive impulse. What we should hope for is an epic of peace to which people, regardless of cultural orientation, can turn and in which they can find a guiding, inspirational source for their civic activities. Then, the epic will regain its prominence as a pillar of civilization.

ACKNOWLEDGMENTS

I would like to thank the following publishers for permissions to reprint materials from: John Keats, *The Complete Poems*, ed. Miriam Allott, Longman Annotated English Poets, © 1970 by Longman Group Limited; John Milton, *Paradise Lost*, ed. Alastair Fowler, Longman Annotated English Poets, © 1968, 1971 by Longman Group Limited; Edmund Spenser, *The Faerie Qveene*, ed. A. C. Hamilton, Longman Annotated English Poets, © 1977 by Longman Group Limited; Georg Lukács, *The Theory of the Novel: A Historico-Philosophical Essay on the Forms of Great Epic Literature*, trans. Anna Bostock, © 1971 by The MIT Press; William Wordsworth, *The Prelude: 1799, 1805, 1850*, ed. Jonathan Wordsworth, M. H. Abrams, and Stephen Gill, A Norton Critical Edition, © 1979 by W. W. Norton & Company, Inc.; P. B. Shelley, *Shelley's Poetry and Prose*, ed. Donald H. Reiman and Sharon B. Powers, A Norton Critical Edition, © 1977 by W. W. Norton & Company, Inc.; Lord Byron, *Byron*, ed. Jerome J. McGann, The Oxford Authors, © 1986 by Oxford University Press; and Virgil, *The Aeneid*, trans. Robert Fitzgerald, © 1983 by Random House.

I would like to express my gratitude to Drs. Mihai I. Spariosu and Ronald L. Bogue, my colleagues at the University of Georgia, for their valuable comments on, and their unfailing encouragement with this project. I am grateful to Dr. Robert W. Croft at Gainesville College for his stylistic suggestions, to Mr. William and Ms. Leslie Madden at the University of Georgia for their thorough proofreading, and to Prof. Takashi Nakamura at the University of Yamagata for sending me important research materials from Japan. I would also like to thank Ms. Carola F. Sautter, acquisitions editor, and Ms. Megeen R. Mulholland, production editor, at SUNY Press for their expert help as well as Mr. David Hopkins for copyediting my manuscript. Last but not least, my deep gratitude goes to my parents in Japan, who gave me constant moral and emotional support throughout years.

NOTES ON THE TEXT

I originally stated some of my arguments found here in the dissertation I completed at the Pennsylvania State University in the summer of 1990: "The Epic in Transition: John Keats's *Fall of Hyperion* and Miyazawa Kenji's *Gingatetsudō no Yoru*." I had some parts of the dissertation published as two journal articles in Japan with a few changes: "Versatile Calliope: The Generic Transformation of Epic until the Renaissance," *Shiron* 31 (1992): 1–21; "Versatile Calliope (II): The Romantic Epic," *Shiron* 33 (1994): 1–18.

All the English translations of Miyazawa's works, except for the transcription of a character's name, and Japanese-written criticism are mine.

The writing format follows *The Chicago Manual of Style*, 14th ed. (Chicago and London: The University of Chicago Press, 1993), including the romanization of the Japanese language, based on the system used in *Kenkyusha's New Japanese-English Dictionary*. According to this system, an apostrophe is placed after *n* at the end of a syllable that precedes *y* or a vowel. A macron is put over a long vowel except in well-known Japanese city names, such as Tokyo and Kyoto, and words that have become part of the English language (shogunate, etc.). The names of Japanese authors follow the traditional Japanese order, that is, the family name precedes the given name, if they wrote their works in Japanese. If their writings were originally published in English, the order of their names follows the Western practice.

In the notes and the select bibliography, all the writings, the titles of which are listed in romanized Japanese, are published in Tokyo.

I

⌣∴⌣

TOWARD A COMPARATIVE POETICS
OF THE EPIC

1

Theories of the Epic:
A Brief Historical Overview

The term "epic" is associated with the very beginning of Western civilization. It originated in the ancient Greek word ἔπος, which meant simply a word, speech, or song; the larger concept of epic as "heroic poetry" developed later. This last meaning, however, eventually became predominant, and the word now usually denotes, in its narrow, literary sense, a certain type of verse produced until the European Renaissance. In this narrow sense, can the term "epic," so intricately rooted in European culture, apply to literary phenomena outside that culture?

Actually, the problem is even more complicated, because not even within European culture is there a clear sense of what an epic is. The generic term makes one think of certain works such as the Homeric poems,[1] the *Aeneid, The Song of Roland, Beowulf,* the *Lusiads, Jerusalem Delivered,* and *Paradise Lost.* But once a work outside this group is considered, few critics can agree on whether or not the term epic should be applied to the candidate. Furthermore, the major works mentioned above as typical examples of the genre show some inconsistency among themselves. Attempts have been made to justify this inconsistency by classifying them into two groups under somewhat awkward terms, such as oral and literary, or "Primary" and "Secondary."[2] As a result of this lack of agreement, there is a growing tendency to recognize as epics a number of works written after the Renaissance.

This study will seek the essential nature of the epic as a genre in the domain of certain thematic elements. Such a stance is necessary because other approaches, including the philosophical and the poetic, have largely failed to elucidate the generic nature of the epic in its endless variety. By the "poetic approach," I mean the poetics of the epic, that is, speculations on the literary mode intrinsic to the genre, while the "philosophical approach" investigates the extrinsic significance of the epic. Obviously, no clear dividing line exists between the two basic categories, which can often overlap. This classification can, nevertheless, facilitate a brief review of the most important theories of the epic since classical Greece as far as they are relevant to my own thematic method. Plato can be regarded as the originator of philosophical approaches to the epic, while Aristotle provides crucial points of debate for later poetic approaches.

Philosophical Approaches to the Epic

Plato is the first to take up the question of epic poetry in his Socratic dialogues,[3] and his argument has significant bearing on its definition. Plato basically argues against poetry as part of his general argument against writing, as illustrated in the Egyptian myth of Theuth and Thamus in *Phaedrus*.[4] In the *Republic*, however, Plato admits his fascination with poetry, especially with Homer, whom he regards as the best of poets. Thus, while he calls Homer a tragic poet, apparently meaning an author of tragic stories, Plato places the Homeric poems foremost among literary genres. So, when he denounces most poetry as promoting false or inappropriate statements about the gods and the truth, his attack is mainly directed at the epic. More precisely, Plato's denouncement of poetry is based on his idea of mimetic arts as being "at third remove from reality" or "from the truth."[5] Accordingly, he banishes, though courteously, poets from his ideal state, except for the ones "who are severe rather than amusing, who portray the style of the good man" (398b) and follow the laws of the city in their works.

Plato's concern is primarily ethical and political, as he tries to show how to secure peace and security for a community. His ideas reflect his critical view of the Athenian morality of his day and the unstable reality in which city-states frequently waged war against each other, wars in which many of them were actually subjugated or demolished. Thus, at the top of his ideal state, Plato places philosophers as just rulers and specially trained soldiers as faithful guardians. He stresses his motive of founding such a state "not to promote the particular happiness of a single class, but, so far as possible, of the whole community" (420b). Anything that undermines this objective has to be removed from the state or excluded from the education of the guardians. In Plato's opinion, the seductive power of poetry poses the greatest moral threat to the foundation of his imagined state, for poetry charms unsuspecting children and youths to harmful, violent stories of gods and heroes. He argues that the young are prone to imitate characters falsely or inadequately represented in poetry and that their habit will "become second nature" (395d).

The typical examples of those figures are taken from the Homeric poems, including Autolycus who excels everyone "in stealing and lying" (334b) and, above all, Achilles who has "the two contrary maladies of ungenerous meanness about money and excessive arrogance to gods and men" (391c). Plato asserts that poets should not try to make young men, who will become guardian soldiers, believe that "heroes are no better than ordinary mortals" (391e). One should note here that, although Plato does not exclude the military class from his city-state for its self-protection, he does not promote a bellicose mentality in the trained fighters.[6] In fact, as guardians, the soldiers are expected to perform "the voluntary non-violent occupations of peace-time" with "moderation and common sense and willingness to accept the outcome" (399b) as well as "military service or any dangerous undertaking" with "steadfast endurance" (399a). These qualities Plato enumerates as desirable in his warriors (moderation, common sense, willingness to accept the outcome, steadfast endurance) all contrast sharply with what Achilles stands for in the *Iliad*, including the two shortcomings Plato mentions (ungenerosity and excessive arrogance). The contrast is more than a mere coincidence. It follows that, by dispensing with Achilles' two qualities that occasion the entire plot of the *Iliad* and by advancing opposite qualities, Plato implicitly rejects the warlike mentality of the Homeric heroic code as undesirable in a civilized society.

Another instance of Plato's rejection of strife-oriented heroic mentality is found in the myth of Er at the end of the *Republic*. There, the soul of Odysseus, picking up the lot of his next life, happily chooses "the uneventful life of an ordinary man" with careful consideration, because "[t]he memory of his former sufferings had cured him of all ambition" (620c).[7] Plato's attitude toward war and peace is even more overt in the *Laws* where, through the persona of an Athenian engaged in a debate with his fellow travelers, he defines the serious purpose of human life as play. This idea derives from the tragic view of human beings as mere puppets of gods in the Homeric poems. But Plato makes deft use of this view when he states that "each of us should spend the greater part of his life at peace" because he can endear himself to God by accepting his role "as a toy for God" and "engaging in the best possible pastimes" such as "sacrificing, singing, [and] dancing."[8] Plato argues that, when thus favored by the gods, a human being can "protect himself from his enemies and conquer them in battle" (*Laws*, 803). As a result, except for self-defense, people should not pursue war as *the* serious matter of life in the pretext of bringing about peace, because "neither the immediate result nor the eventual consequences of warfare ever turn out to be *real* leisure" (*Laws*, 803).[9]

Another important point Plato offers in his view of the epic is related to his idealism and his concept of divinity as the ultimate good. For the Plato of the *Republic*, "[g]od is the cause, not of all things, but only of good" (380c). He also states that "god and the things of god are entirely perfect" (381b); therefore, a god cannot "wish to change himself" (381c). For instance, Plato disapproves of the representation of Achilles in the *Iliad*, because the hero, born to a goddess (Thetis) by a man of great restraint (Peleus), cannot be such an impossibly defective figure as presented in the epic (391c). In contrast to the perfect, unchangeable divine world, he calls the physical reality the "world of change" (518c, 519b) and the "world of change and decay" (508d). Thus, a philosopher is characterized by "his love of any branch of learning that reveals eternal reality, the realm unaffected by the vicissitudes of change and decay" (485b). While philosophers are capable of "grasp[ing] the eternal and immutable," those who do not possess such a capacity are "lost in multiplicity and change" (484b). Obviously, the epic, which by nature represents the flux of worldly affairs in a wide perspective, is the most remote from what Plato has in mind as the ultimate reality and should, in his eyes, be dismissed from his republic.

In this context, it is interesting to speculate what kind of epic poetry, if any, Plato would allow to be rehearsed in his ideal state. There, an epic would be expected to promote not the conflict-oriented, self-centered, unpredictable mentality represented by Achilles, but a sense of communal cooperation and steadfast determination in maintaining communal peace for the happiness of all citizens. Furthermore, such an epic would not represent the world of change; instead, it ought to give the citizens a hint of transcendental reality from which their spiritual virtue would derive. With the Homeric poems predominantly in mind, Plato himself cannot think of this kind of epic, and he simply bans all epics from his state. With the politically divided Greece of his day, all he can hope for is to preserve the existence of one city-state with an intrepid standing army against external threat. By unintended implication, however, his argument rightly suggests the future direction of the epic, for, as I shall show later on, the epic will increasingly aim at making peace and maintaining it, through some transcendental value, for the sake of an entire community. What Plato would need in order to envision a new kind of epic is a much broader notion of a community, beyond the territory of the *polis*.

Among the few important debates bequeathed to posterity by Plato concerning the epic is the question of whether literature should be taken negatively as an art of imitation. Since the epic is a major form of classical literature, this question is crucial to determine the value of the epic. As we have seen, Plato has an unfavorable opinion of most, if not all, literature because of its supposed harm to society through the misrepresentation of the higher reality he believes in. Thus, Plato in the *Republic* does not hesitate to assert that "the art of representation is something that has no serious value" and that "representative art is . . . inferior" (602b, 603b). Against this view, Aristotle in the *Poetics* takes imitation (mimesis) positively and argues it to be the most important element of poetry. Aristotle does not deny that poets create fiction. For instance, Homer is regarded as the poet "who has chiefly taught other poets the art of telling lies skilfully."[10] According to Aristotle, however, an artistic lie in poetry should not be rejected as unethical, because "the impossible is the higher thing; for the ideal type must surpass the reality."[11] Here, Aristotle introduces the concept of "the higher reality" or higher truth which should be sought not in a Platonic metaphysical sphere but in the "probable impossibilities" of the actual world.[12] And this higher truth, Aristotle argues, can and should be taught through literature.

The change Aristotle brought in assessing the value of literary representation significantly affected literary discourse during the Renaissance, when the epic was considered the most important genre. The debate on the falsity of literature had persisted until then, and many thinkers had recourse to Aristotle's argument in order to defend poetry. For instance, Sir Philip Sidney in *An Apology for Poetry* (1595) claims that although the poet "recount[s] things not true, yet because he telleth them not for true, he lieth not."[13] But Sidney goes beyond merely sounding

like a poet defending his profession when he, as a typical theorist
of the Renaissance, combines the Aristotelian higher truth with
the Horatian purpose of pleasurable teaching and the Longinean
power of sublimity. Sidney asserts that "a feigned example hath
as much force to teach as a true example . . . since the feigned
may be tuned to the highest key of passion"[14] and that, thus
moved, people will perform good deeds. Sidney regards "the Hero-
ical" or the epic as "the best and most accomplished kind of
Poetry," because he thinks, with a kind of Platonic utilitarianism,
that "the lofty image of such worthies" in epic poetry "inflameth
the mind with desire to be worthy, and informs with counsel
how to be worthy."[15] Torquato Tasso holds the same position in
his *Discourses on the Heroic Poem* (1594). Tasso takes the fictionality of literature positively on the ground that what the poet
writes is based "on some true action"; therefore, "his matter is the
verisimilar, which may be true and false, but is generally closer
to true."[16] Continuing, Tasso calls epic poetry "the most excellent
kind of poem" because it is "an imitation of a noble action, great
and perfect, narrated in the loftiest verse, with the purpose of
moving the mind to wonder and thus being useful" for readers "to
raise their own minds to its example."[17] These discourses by
Renaissance theorists including Sidney and Tasso, apart from
the high prominence they give to the epic, are significant in their
articulation of the spiritual values that an epic can propagate.
This high regard for the epic also affirms its possible social role,
a role which Plato could not have granted it due to the political
circumstances of ancient Greece.

Plato's rejection of literature caused another debate regarding the cultural significance of the epic: what kind of audience an
epic should address and what nature it should assume. In this
respect, too, Aristotle refutes Plato's negative view of poetry as a
false or undesirable representation of reality, for, comparing history with poetry, Aristotle points out that "one relates what has
happened, the other what may happen."[18] He considers poetry "a
more philosophical and a higher thing than history,"[19] because
what is possible, unlike the particularity of past occurrences, is
universally applicable. Evidently, what is universal cannot be
dismissed simply as false or easily as inappropriate. During the
Renaissance, Sidney goes beyond Aristotle when he claims that
the poet is superior not only to the historian but also to the
philosopher, because the poet "coupleth the general notion" of
philosophy "with the particular example" of history.[20] Poetry thus

provides more than the accumulated knowledge of what has happened by revealing the inscrutable precepts of what should happen and rendering them comprehensible. Sidney here changes the Aristotelian mood of "may happen" to "should happen" under the critical necessity of his day to moralize poetry. These two points proposed by Aristotle and Sidney (universality and philosophical guidance) are highly relevant to our discussion of the epic, because both of them have the epic in mind as a major form of literature in their arguments. With these views combined, an epic should appeal not only to a people from whose culture it arose but also to a larger audience by presenting its philosophically preferable model of conduct. This notion of the epic basically means the removal of Plato's *polis*-oriented provincialism and the reinstatement of the epic's cultural usefulness that he denied.

Another provocative point originating with Plato is the disapproval of the violent, war-oriented mentality of the Homeric poems. In fact, no later theorist approves of the archaic heroic code that defies social justice and disrupts communal harmony. For instance, Tasso says that readers who have not read the Homeric poems in the original tend to find the ancient warfare "tedious and disagreeable" and avoid it as "obsolete and stale," because they are used to "the gentleness and decorum" of their age.[21] The taste for martial motifs, however, persists even in a supposedly civilized age. Almost in the same breath, Tasso himself states that "epic illustriousness is based on lofty military valour and the magnanimous resolve to die, on piety, religion, and deeds alight with these virtues."[22] He thus admires Ariosto's *Orlando Furioso*, which abounds in combats by knights-errant, and his own *Jerusalem Delivered* is full of military conflicts. Apparently, Tasso believes that one can indulge in endless scenes of gory, exciting battles in the epic as long as the fighting is nobly done, with culturally or religiously sanctioned causes that provide the circumstances necessary for sustained hostility, such as a crusade against invading infidels. Apart from the antagonism to Islamic powers, historically understandable in the Europe of his day, Tasso's unabashed pleasure in the excess of violence and destruction casts serious doubt on his claim that his age is characterized by "gentleness and decorum."

In his *Art of Poetry* (1674), Nicolas Boileau-Despréaux further augments this preference for the bellicose element in the epic when he asserts that a hero in the epic should not be "a commonplace conqueror"; instead, he should be "of the breed of Caesar, Alexander, or Louis."[23] Boileau apparently believes that it is still possible to compose an epic with recent or contemporary military materials. In stating his belief, he promotes imperialism as well as the epic that culturally sanctions large-scale aggression. His view is typical of his time when the European powers were growingly intent on gaining colonies abroad, vying against each other for hegemony. In fact, to acquire literary fame, poets attempted to write the traditional, Virgilian type of epics during the neoclassical period as well as the Renaissance. One might, however, also consider Boileau's remark as representative of the predominant view of the epic as a poetry of war since Greek antiquity.

After the eighteenth century, the epic continued to be perceived as war-oriented. For instance, G. W. F. Hegel in *Aesthetics* (1835) methodologically treats the issue of war, because he views the Homeric poems as the criteria of all epics. One of his main arguments is that the epic should contain a certain national consciousness. Hegel calls the motif of war "the situation most suited to epic,"[24] because in war a whole nation is mobilized in response to a new stimulus. According to him, the kind of war that genuinely suits the epic is more specifically the one between entirely foreign nations, which is serious enough to put national identity and existence at stake, and in which one party claims some high, self-justifying cause against the other, beyond mere territorial expansion.

On one hand, Hegel's idea of war as essential to the thematic dimension of the epic reaffirms Tasso's and Boileau's positions, which shows how persistently the epic of war is accepted as a popular norm of the genre. On the other hand, his argument poses two questions: Does the communal unity at stake have to be limited to a national level? And, can a conflict between nations possibly be the only serious communal crisis suitable as an epic topic? In terms of the size of community, Hegel thinks of a nation larger than Plato's *polis*. Moreover, almost as an effort to include Aristotle, Hegel asserts that, to enjoy acceptance by other peoples and in later periods, "what is *universally* human" should be imprinted "on the particular nation described and on its heroes and their deeds."[25] But even this statement reveals that the community he has in mind for the epic is no larger than a nation. He also contradicts himself when he later discusses the *Divine Comedy* and *Paradise Lost* as examples of religious epics, which are by nature not concerned with national identity.

As to the question of crisis, the epic indeed requires a certain critical situation around which the plot evolves toward a final resolution. Evidently, besides the destruction of war, there are many serious, nonmartial threats to humanity, in physical reality as well as on cultural, spiritual, or philosophical levels. If war can perhaps be justified for self-defense, it certainly should not be tolerated for any other reason as Plato argues. But, as we saw in Tasso's case, even self-defense, or any other justifiable cause, is often used in the epic as an excuse for gratifying the excitement that martial topics arouse. Hegel's argument, which encourages military conflict for some artificial reason as most desirable in the epic, is not an exception. Considering the cultural importance Hegel himself places on the epic, this tolerance of war extends beyond the textual level, whether he intends such implication or not. Thus, Hegel's argument shows the sustained popular acceptance of war-oriented epic while helping us to acquire by reflection a critical viewpoint to such acceptance.

Against this predominant tendency that favors militaristic epic, Giambattista Vico in the *New Science* (1744) is adamant and thorough in denouncing the war mentality of the epic by analyzing the heroic society that the Homeric poems represent as the source of war-glorification. Vico's basic assumption of "the heroic custom" is that all nations took "strangers to be eternal enemies" and that, externally, they "carr[ied] on eternal wars with each other, with continual looting and raiding."[26] Accordingly, he considers the Greek heroic age barbaric, and he calls the early Middle Ages "the returned barbarian times" (636, passim). Vico's detestation of the heroism of violence is evident in his considerably negative view of Achilles, "the greatest of all the Greek heroes" (708), in whom he finds a number of grave shortcomings. For instance, because of his personal grudge against Agamemnon, not only is Achilles shamelessly happy with the slaughter of the Greeks by Hector but also "this man . . . expresses the disgraceful wish to Patroclus that all, Greeks and Trojans alike, may die in the war, leaving only the two of them alive" (667). He comes back to battle "only to satisfy a purely private grief" (786), Hector's killing of Patroclus. Then, "because of a little phrase that does not please him and which has fallen inadvertently" from Priam, Achilles "flies into a rage" and threatens to kill the old, pitiful king in "his bestial wrath" (786). Even in death, his displeasure is not appeased until a daughter of Priam is "sacrificed before his tomb, and his ashes, thirsting for vengeance, have drunk up the last drop of her blood" (786).

Vico's stance completely repudiates Tasso's pedantic assertion that the ancient manner of warfare is horrible only to those ignorant enough to read the Homeric poems in translation. The Achillean heroism can also be repulsive to a scholar like Vico who is most learned in classical literature. Thus, when Vico criticizes Homer, who presents Achilles, "a man so arrogant," as "an example of heroic virtue" (667), he disparages the kind of works Tasso favors: "What he [Homer] preaches is thus the virtue of punctiliousness, on which the duellists of the returned barbarian times based their entire morality, and which gave rise to the proud laws, the lofty duties and the vindictive satisfactions of the knights errant of whom the romancers sing" (667). Such "gallant heroism," Vico argues, is a result of what "post-Homeric poets" either newly fabricated or did to old stories in order "to suit the growing effeminacy of later times" (708) or what Tasso calls the "gentleness and decorum" of his time. Against these two types of heroism of violence, ancient and later, Vico envisions the "heroism of virtue" (708), which only a hero who "devotes himself to justice and the welfare of mankind" (677) embodies. According to Vico, "such a hero . . . is desired by afflicted peoples, conceived by philosophers and imagined by poets" (677). Strictly speaking, however, Vico argues that such heroism "which realizes its highest idea belongs to philosophy and not to poetry" (708).

With Vico's remarks, we come back to a philosophical type of epic which might have been admitted to Plato's republic. Like Plato, Vico's concern is primarily with the security of a community. But, with a subtle twist of Aristotelian universality, what he has in mind is expanded to "the welfare of mankind," and he thereby dispenses with primarily national interests. His concern with humanity as a whole is also obvious when he calls the two forms of polities, "free popular commonwealths and monarchies" which developed later in history, "human" (677). By implied contrast, the ancient society is inhuman with its heroism "now by civil nature impossible" (677). Furthermore, the very fact that he spends an entire book analyzing the system of the ancient heroic society, mainly through the Homeric poems, only to denounce it shows how much cultural significance he assigns to the epic. Otherwise, in his discussion of the authorship of those poems, he would hesitate to state that "the Greek peoples were themselves Homer" (875). Finally, when Vico mentions his idea of the "heroism of virtue," he follows in Sidney's steps by affirming the spiritual value of the epic in promoting peace and justice.

In a word, grafting the Renaissance views of the epic on a humanistic tradition, Vico manifestly suggests what Plato unintentionally implies by the exclusion of literature from his state, that is, the possibility of an epic of peace. But such an epic is unrealizable if, as Vico argues, the literary work is expected to show the moral perfection of philosophy, a goal which is humanly impossible. If the new kind of epic were to be feasible, it should reveal human imperfections as well as the nobility of human spirit with philosophical insight. Such a mixture of imperfections with virtues is very similar to the Aristotelian concept of a tragic flaw. But, unlike the sense of devastation that results from a tragic hero's character failings, a flaw in a new epic hero ought to enhance a sense of belief in humanness through the work's total effect.

Friedrich von Schiller in *Naive and Sentimental Poetry* (1795–96) proposes a kind of poetry in which the poet aspires after what is lacking in reality due to human imperfection. Schiller calls poets naive when they articulate pure nature, which he understands as beautiful without its "crude necessity" and as "an undivided sensuous unity" of perception (sense) and thought (reason).[27] Schiller admires Homer, along with Shakespeare, as a typical naive poet "in his dry truthfulness" of narrating his story without asserting his own self (109). When art develops as a form of civilization, however, the poet expresses himself only "as a *moral* unity, i.e., as striving after unity," because the harmonious unity that "*actually* took place, exists now only *ideally*" (111). Therefore, poets have to strive against the destructive forces of arbitrariness and artificiality within themselves. The poets at this stage are called sentimental because they "*seek* lost nature" (106).

There are two kinds of sentimental poetry, "satirical" and "elegiac," depending on whether the limitation of actuality or the infinitude of ideas becomes predominant in the poet's perception and his representation. Depending on how the poet approaches the basic motif, satire can be further subdivided into two kinds: punitive or pathetic, and playful. Similarly, there are two sorts of elegiac poetry: the elegy proper and the idyll. Schiller intends his classification of poetry to be a transgeneric concept that indicates "*modes of perception*" (145n). Therefore, he states that "individual *genres of composition*," such as the epic, novel, and tragedy, "can be executed in more than one mode of perception, consequently in more than one of the species of poetry" (147n). For instance, he calls Milton's description of the human-inhabited paradise "the most beautiful idyll . . . of the sentimental type" (152).

Schiller's distinction between naive and sentimental poetry is important to our discussion of the epic in several respects. First, it paved the way for the later categorization of the epic into two major kinds, oral and literary. Schiller's influence can be easily detected, for instance, in Hegel, although Hegel gives precedence to naturalness over artificiality whereas Schiller avoids such value codification. Second, Schiller's approach to literature is flexible with his "modes of perception," which are not restrained by conventional generic demarcations, and this method unsettles the authenticity of the conventionally rigidified categorization itself. Just as there can be naive/sentimental, satirical/elegiac, pathetic/playful, and elegiac/idyllic elements in an epic, it is possible to assume the dynamic transgeneric presence of epic elements in other kinds of literature such as drama and the novel. What Schiller says about elegiac poetry is also of some interest: "The elegiac poet seeks nature, but as an idea and in a perfection in which she has never existed, when he bemourns her at once as something having existed and now lost" (127). If so, regardless of whether individual pieces are naive or sentimental, most traditional epics can be considered basically elegiac in their idealized presentation of the lost, bygone glory which they memorialize.

Most significant, however, is Schiller's argument about the nature of sentimental poetry, since naive epic is now impossible to create, and what can be created with the art of civilization is the epic of sentimentality. First of all, he claims that, although the term "sentimental" comes from civilized people's longing for their lost naive nature, it is not appropriate to demean modern poets with a fundamentally different, artistic mode of their ancient counterparts. Schiller thinks that naive poetry attains its end of the perfect representation of actuality "by the absolute achievement of a finite" in nature (113). In contrast, the objective of a sentimental poet is "the elevation of actuality to the ideal or, . . . the *representation of the ideal*" (112), which can be achieved "by approximation to an infinite greatness" in ideas (113). This is essentially a restatement of what the Renaissance

theorists such as Tasso and Sidney regarded as the moral value
of the epic. But, typical of Romantic criticism, Schiller's argument
shows awareness of the limitations that underlie the longing for
an ideal. At the same time, the fact that Schiller assigns this
quality not specifically to the epic but to sentimental poetry in
general signals the epic's waning prominence among kinds of
literature.

In *The Birth of Tragedy* (1872), Friedrich Nietzsche casts
light upon another aspect of the epic's cultural importance. He
argues that Greek tragedy originates in the synthesis of the
Apollinian healing power of dreams and illusions with the
Dionysian impulse for the destruction of individuation and return
to the primordial oneness of existence. Because he focuses on the
early Greek civilization, the epic here designates only the Homeric poems. Following Schiller's notion of naive poetry, Nietzsche
further speculates on it by correlating naive sensibility with the
Apollinian culture. According to him, the Homeric epos exemplifies the Apollinian art before Greece was invaded by the impetu-
ous force of Dionysian rites. As a piece of naive art, it embodies
"the highest effect of Apollinian culture" that must have overcome "an abysmal and terrifying view of the world and the keen-
est susceptibility to suffering" by way of "the most forceful and
pleasurable illusions."[28] Nietzsche thus interprets the Olympian
gods as the reflected images of the Greeks transfigured in a
higher sphere of beauty. He assumes that, through this mirroring, the mortals feel deserving of glory in life; in turn, leaving
life, especially leaving it early, causes real pain to the Homeric
heroes, as we witness in the words of Achilles' shade. Grief here
"becomes a song of praise" of existence worth living through (43).
Homer as "the Apollinian naïve artist" (48) is "unutterably sublime" because of his "consummate immersion in the beauty of
mere appearance" at the moment of the complete victory of "the
Hellenic will" over "its artistically correlative talent for suffering
and for the wisdom of suffering" (44).

In this sense, Nietzsche thinks that, from a collective viewpoint, Homer "bears the same relation to this Apollinian folk culture as the individual dream artist does to the dream faculty of
the people and of nature in general" (44). Accordingly, echoing
Vico, Nietzsche regards "the dreaming Greeks as Homers and
Homer as a dreaming Greek" (39). By this mirroring, the poet is
kept from identifying with his creatures. As a result, "the power
of the epic-Apollinian" is so marvelous that "before our eyes it

transforms the most terrible things by the joy in mere appearance and in redemption through mere appearance" (83). For instance, the angry Achilles remains no more than an image to the poet, and he enjoys the hero's angry expression "with the dreamer's pleasure in illusion" (50). Because Homer "visualizes so much more vividly" than bad poets who "talk so abstractly about poetry" (64), Nietzsche defines the style and form in the Homeric poems with such words as "clarity," "firmness," and "precision" (66, 67, 73).

From this point of view, tragedy is "epic in nature" as far as the chorus "ever anew discharges itself in an Apollinian world of images" and emits "a dream apparition" in the form of the dialogue (65). Objectified thus on the stage, Dionysus wearing a mask of "an erring, striving, suffering individual" speaks "as an epic hero, almost in the language of Homer" (73, 67). As "the objectification of a Dionysian state" of dismemberment causing "the agonies of individuation," however, tragedy "represents not Apollinian redemption through mere appearance but, on the contrary, the shattering of the individual and his fusion with primal being" (65, 73). In this respect, tragedy is "separated, as by a tremendous chasm, from the epic" (65).

In a word, Nietzsche conceives of the epic as a lucid image-product of an Apollinian dream-illusion that disguises the essentially horrible nature of existence, in order to provide a contrast to tragedy that discloses it with the Dionysian "frank, undissembling gaze of truth" through recourse to the projective mediation of Apollinian art (74). Nietzsche also thinks that the spirit of tragedy voiced to perfection by Aeschylus and Sophocles has departed when Euripidean inflammatory drama of "[c]ivic mediocrity" and Socratic cold reasoning of "[o]ptimistic dialectic" took over "Dionysian ecstasies" and "Apollinian contemplation" (77, 92, 83).

The question then is whether the epic can be viewed as a literary form of such a "naïve," cheerful nature totally devoid of Dionysian insight into the mystery of life. Nietzsche's idea of the epic is doubtful even if the discussion concerns only the Homeric poems, not to mention the epic tradition after them. Nietzsche here seems to be philosophizing, to the advantage of tragedy, what Goethe says about the difference between epic and tragic writers: the former appeal to the imagination of the audience whereas the latter should visualize everything, including narrated events, to create far more vivid impressions on the audience. But, reflecting Aristotle, Goethe also says that the epic and tragedy deal with the different aspects of the same topics and worlds, suggesting that, thematically, there can be tragic elements in the epic and vice versa. Furthermore, as we shall see shortly in our discussion of poetic approaches to the epic, Hegel argues the tragic quality in the epic. Although relative optimism might be an element that marks off the epic from tragedy, the epic certainly does not lack the "terrifying view of the world" and the "susceptibility to suffering" in Nietzsche's own terms. His contribution to our discussion of the philosophical nature of the epic, however, lies in his emphasis on the epic's therapeutic power over mortal anxiety *de profundis*.

With the ever growing importance of the novel, it is inevitable for twentieth-century criticism to attempt establishing a generic identity for it in relation to the older, existing genres, especially the epic. *The Theory of the Novel* (1920) by Georg Lukács is a prominent example of such an attempt. Lukács admits the transgeneric nature of contemporary literature, saying that "[a]rtistic genres now cut across one another, with a complexity that cannot be disentangled."[29] Still, he points out the traits of the epic in relation to drama (tragedy), the novel, and the lyric.

According to Lukács, what the epic represents is not simply the Aristotelian unity of action but "the extensive totality of life," in contrast to drama that gives form to "the intensive totality of essence" (46). Because the world functions as "an ultimate principle," the epic cannot go beyond "the breadth and depth, the rounded, sensual, richly ordered nature of life as historically given" (46). Therefore, epic forms "can never of their own accord charm something into life that was not already present in it," and the "indestructible bond with reality *as it is*" decisively distinguishes the epic from drama (47). Lukács here emphasizes the comprehensiveness of life the epic should exhibit as well as the historically circumscribed reality that should bar irrational elements from the epic's subject matter. In terms of character, the character in drama is "the intelligible 'I'" who can psychologically embody the normative force of the "should be," whereas the character in the epic is "the empirical 'I'" in whom "it remains a 'should be'" (47–48). Since "[t]he 'should be' kills life" (48), or in Nietzsche's terms, moral force is "a will to negate life,"[30] the hero in drama carries out "the symbolic ceremony of dying" (48), but the hero in the epic must live to fulfill his given situation. Lukács

thus acknowledges the epic hero's dilemma between moral perfection and human nature that resists it. Echoing Vico's argument
about the epic of virtue as belonging only to philosophy, Lukács
agrees that if an epic hero is created at the dictate of moral force,
he cannot but be "a shadow of the living epic man of historical
reality," and his world "a watered-down copy of reality" (48).

Continuing his comparison between the epic and tragedy,
Lukács says that the subject and the object are clearly distinct
from each other in the epic, as they are not in drama, for the
totality of life can appear only as what the object reveals. On
the one hand, in the great epics, the "life-mastering arrogance" of
the subject is "transformed . . . into humility, contemplation,
speechless wonder at the luminous meaning which . . . has
become visible to him, an ordinary human being in the midst of
ordinary life" (50). On the other hand, because the notion of
totality is not transcendental in the epic, the object of some epic
forms can not be the totality but only an autonomous fragment of
life. In such cases, "the subject confronts the object in a more
dominant and self-sufficient way" (50). Lukács calls such basically lyrical works "minor epic forms" (50), including the short
story and lyric-epic forms. The lyricism of the short story consists
in the "pure selection" of a segment of life (51). The lyric-epic
forms show "not the totality of life but the artist's relationship
with that totality" when "the artist enters the arena of artistic creation as the empirical subject in all its greatness but also with all
its creaturely limitations" (53).

But when the subject alone dominates existence, the objective world collapses while the subject also becomes a fragment
and is "lost in the insubstantiality of its self-created world of
ruins" (53). Exceptionally, such "creative subjectivity" is found in
a great epic (53). The subject is then able to enjoy "the grace of
having the whole revealed to it" as long as it modestly functions
as "a purely receptive organ of the world" (53), because "the totality of life resists any attempt to find a transcendental centre
within it, and refuses any of its constituent cells the right to
dominate it" (54). An obvious example is Dante's trilogy with its
central figure enjoying the providential favor that shows him the
entirety of the universe. But if the subject is far removed from the
empirical reality of life and "becomes enthroned in the pure
heights of essence," an epic cannot be created, for "the epic *is* life,
immanence, the empirical" (54). In this sense, for Lukács,
Dante's *Paradiso* appears as less epical.

As to verse, although Lukács admits it not to be a "decisive genre-defining criterion" (56), he recognizes considerable significance in it as indicative of the true nature of epic and tragedy. In tragedy, verse is "sharp and hard, it isolates, it creates distance," and it places the heroes "in the full depth of their solitude" (56). Tragic verse also exposes any triviality in the writing. Close to the Nietzschean concept of epic cheerfulness through Apollinian mirroring, epic verse contrastingly creates the distance of "happiness and lightness," because the verse lets loose "the bonds that tie men and objects to the ground" (57). Heaviness as a triviality of life is eliminated in the epic, while the triviality of lightness is heterogeneous to tragedy. Therefore, the epic with its verse ought to "sing of the blessedly existent totality of life" (58). Lukács' discussion of the epic and drama is thus distinct in pointing out the presence of lyricism in some epics, recognizing the *Divine Comedy* as a major epic though in a modified sense, and regarding verse as an important, but dispensable element of the epic. His view of epic verse as liberating people from earthly bondage, which is a deliberate contrast to the seriousness of tragic verse, parallels Nietzsche's notion of not only epic cheerfulness but also the therapeutic power of the epic over mortal miseries.

Since verse is not a decisive genre-delimiting factor, Lukács considers the epic and the novel "two major forms of great epic literature" (56). He defines the novel as "the epic of an age in which the extensive totality of life is no longer directly given, in which the immanence of meaning in life has become a problem, yet which still thinks in terms of totality" (56). In relation to this point, Lukács thinks that the detachment created by epic verse is not decisive but tentative as a liberating force. The lightness in the epic is "a positive value and a reality-creating force," only if all the restraints of terrestrial heaviness have already been cast off while people do not forget "their enslavement in the lovely play of a liberated imagination" (58). Lukács thus revises the Nietzschean concept of the epic by laying stress on the severity of mortal existence that underlies the lightness of epic verse as well as on the need to have mortal constraints constantly in mind. When that kind of lightness is no longer provided in the epic, verse is replaced by prose that can take in "the fetters and the freedom, the given heaviness and the conquered lightness" with its plastic flexibility and its rhythm-free austerity (59). For instance, "the disintegration of a reality-become-song led, in Cervantes' prose, to the sorrowful lightness of a great epic, whereas the serene dance of Ariosto's verse remained mere lyrical play" (59). Lukács here considers *Orlando Furioso*, which diverts itself in the frivolity of imagination, less an epic than *Don Quixote*, which, though humorously written in prose, maintains a sad, steady gaze at reality. This criterion that hinges on mortal gravity can be used to distinguish the epic from romance.

Lukács argues that what essentially distinguishes the epic from the novel is how each genre approaches the world that it represents. The epic shows "a totality of life that is rounded from within," whereas the novel attempts "to uncover and construct the concealed totality of life" (60). Therefore, "the fundamental form-determining intention of the novel is objectivised as the psychology of the novel's heroes" who are "seekers" (60). If the goals of the search or the way to them are "given in a psychologically direct and solid manner," this "givenness" implies crime or madness (60–61). In comparison, the epic, along with tragedy, has little to do with crime and madness. The world of the epic is either a "perfect theodicy" or "a purely childlike one" in which a violation of social code entails perpetually exchanged revenge (61). The only insanity the epic comprehends is the "language of a superworld that possesses no other means of expression" (61). It is obvious, then, that what Lukács has in mind as typical of the epic proper does not go much beyond the first two segments of the *Divine Comedy* and the Homeric poems.

In terms of central figures, the individual hero in the novel is "the product of polemical self-contemplation by the lost and lonely personality" (67). He is estranged from the rest of the world because he frames "[t]he autonomous life of interiority" at the time when individuation has made "an unbridgeable chasm" between people (66). In contrast, the epic hero is, "strictly speaking, never an individual," because his world is "internally homogeneous" (66). Therefore, individuality in the epic is a matter of "a balance between the part and the whole, mutually determining one another" (66). Lukács further asserts that, in such a communal organism where one cannot detect sharp, qualitative differences among people, significance is placed quantitatively upon a suprapersonal social unit such as a nation or a family. The epic hero must be a king to bear "the weight of the bonds linking an individual destiny to a totality" (67), and he is never a lonely figure in this linkage. On the one hand, Lukács thus expresses the importance of the communal dimension in the epic. On the other hand, recalling Aristotle's notion of the epic (and tragic) hero as a high-ranked figure, Lukács' idea reveals again its limited scope based on the classical models. At the same time, this idea contradicts his view of the *Divine Comedy*, in which Dante as the central figure is an exile and does not belong to the ruling class, rendering Dante's poem an exceptional case of the epic.

Finally, according to Lukács, the episodic nature of the epic, including the *in medias res* beginning, as well as the inconclusive ending, is symptomatic of the genre's indifference to architectural composition. Loosely related to the central plot, an introduced episode "does not endanger the unity of the whole and yet has obvious organic existence" (68). With his rigorously architectural composition, Dante is once again a great exception. In spite of his work's "perfect immanent distancelessness and completeness of the true epic," his characters are "already individuals, consciously and energetically placing themselves in opposition to a reality that is becoming closed to them" (68). They are no longer "the organic part-unities" of the older epic but "hierarchically ordered, autonomous parts" (68). Because of this integration of epical and novelistic elements, Lukács locates Dante as a transitional writer from the epic proper to the novel, thereby reiterating his view of the *Divine Comedy* as a great epic only in a modified sense.

As a whole, Lukács' discourse on the epic and the novel is significant in four main respects. First, it presents the epic as a category that, defying conventional demarcations, comprehends the novel in the broad sense. Then, the epic can certainly be a transgeneric concept. Because of Lukács' narrow understanding of typical epics, however, the epic is actually contrasted to the novel with such features as the self-enclosed entirety of life and the homogeneity of inner life. This inherent dichotomy foreshadows the reversed comprehension of the epic by the novel, which eventually happens in the general perception of genres as the novel gains enormous popularity. Second, Lukács' consistent stress on "the extensive totality of life" that the epic is supposed to exhibit points to the extremely broad, nonfanciful dimension of the epic world. But the question largely remains how such comprehensive understanding of life should be presented. Third, if the transgeneric epic should present "the extensive totality of life" with an increasingly novelistic mode, this poses a serious problem concerning the central figure: how to reconnect the individuated, lonely figure to the rest of the world without allowing the epic hero to insubstantiate the objective world with his dominant "creative subjectivity." Lastly, unlike most theorists since the Renaissance, Lukács candidly, if reservedly, deals with the epical standing of Dante's trilogy, thereby rendering his definition of the epic more intelligible.

The philosophical debates of the epic thus center on two issues. One is the existence of an epic of war versus an epic of peace. The epic of war has been predominantly foregrounded in both practice and theory, while the epic of peace only remains potential in the arguments that oppose bellicose mentality. At the same time, however, it is generally held that epic production was discontinued a few centuries ago. In effect, this meant a general rejection of war-oriented epic, which had dominated the genre, as unsuitable for modern civilization. I will argue that, in reverse proportion to the decline of war-oriented epic, the urge for realizing an epic of peace has been steadily growing. Second, the debates tend to confer significance of the highest kind upon the epic for presenting a cultural model, providing humans with a remedy for their fundamental anxiety, or revealing a far-reaching view of life in its wholeness. But the legitimacy of such generic prominence cannot go unquestioned when the genre was actually eclipsed by the emergence of other genres, especially the novel. I will try to reestablish the significance of the epic in recent times by proposing a broad concept of the epic that comprehends conventional generic domains.

Poetic Approaches to the Epic

As I stated at the beginning of this chapter, "a poetic approach" implies an analysis of features intrinsic to the epic as a literary mode. By nature, a poetic approach tends to be normative in the specifics of epic creation. The most influential example is found in Aristotle's *Poetics*, in which, while refuting some of Plato's arguments about poetry, Aristotle makes a number of important references to the epic, which he compares with tragedy. Aristotle does not regard verse as an essential element of poetry, and he consigns the elements of rhythm and harmony to a secondary position. Accordingly, he states that "Homer and Empedocles have nothing in common but the metre, so that it would be right to call the one poet, the other physicist rather than poet."[31] Likewise, he argues that "[t]he work of Herodotus might be put into verse, and it would still be a species of history, with metre no less than without it" (9.2).

In terms of the issue of representation, Aristotle states that "the objects of imitation are men in action, and these men must be either of a higher or a lower type" (2.1). He then defines epic poetry as "an imitation in verse of characters of a higher type" like tragedy (5.4). Two issues are involved in this definition: what kind of "characters of a higher type" are meant and what the modal difference between epic and tragedy is if their objects of representation are identical. Out of these two issues, the first concerns a so-called tragic flaw, for what Aristotle means by a character of a higher type is a "highly renowned and prosperous" man who is "not eminently good and just" with "some error or frailty" (13.3). Depicting men who have shortcomings of character such as irascibility and indolence, the poet is expected to "preserve the type and yet ennoble it," as Homer portrays Achilles (15.8). At the same time, Aristotle argues that the poet, in presenting his story, ought to "speak as little as possible in his own person, for it is not this that makes him an imitator" (24.7). He regards Homer as a good example of a self-effacing narrator.

With regard to the modality of representation, Aristotle thinks that, apart from the differences in meter, the narrative mode differentiates the epic from tragedy in two respects. First, the epic has "a great—a special—capacity for enlarging its dimensions," for, "owing to the narrative form, many events simultaneously transacted can be presented" (24.4). Therefore, in the epic, the action "has no limits of time" (5.4). What prolongs epic poetry is its "episodes," as well as the "multiplicity of plots" (17.5, 18.4). In this structure, "each part assumes its proper magnitude" (18.4). Here, we find the first example of the little disputed definition of epic as a long work in the narrative mode. Second, irrational elements have a wider range of use in epic poetry, because "the absurdity passes unnoticed" thanks to the invisibility of the acting figures, for example, the pursuit of Hector by Achilles in the *Iliad* (24.8). Aristotle thus acknowledges the presence of the wonderful that depends on the irrational and can be pleasing in the epic. Such a case contrasts to tragedy, where "[e]verything irrational should, if possible, be excluded" or be placed outside the play proper in preference of "probable impossibilities" over "improbable possibilities" (24.10). While the epic narrative can be extended in these two ways, the "[u]nity of plot" consists not "in the unity of the hero," who has "infinitely various . . . incidents" during his life, but in the unity of action, for "the plot, being an imitation of an action, must imitate one action" (8.1, 4). Aristotle illustrates this point by noting that Homer "made the Odyssey, and likewise the Iliad, to centre round an action that in our sense of the word is one" (8.3).

Aristotle concludes that, as an art, tragedy is superior to the epic because of its use of "all the epic elements," its capability of being appreciated "in reading as well as in representation," and its enhanced unity "within narrower limits," thereby producing "not any chance pleasure, but the pleasure proper to it" (26.4, 5, 7). Although tragedy is the main focus of his treatise, Aristotle provides powerful normative concepts to develop or refute concerning the nature of the epic at the early stage of Western culture. His characterization of the epic protagonist is problematic in assigning the position to a high class. The debate on the use of verse is recurrently important for deciding the range of application of the term "epic." The question of where the unity of the story should be sought is also a much argued point in defining the epic. The tolerance of irrational elements is relevant in discussing the difference between epic and romance. As illustrated by many of the philosophical approaches, the comparison of the epic with other genres often shows its relative, shifting position in the entire literary spectrum of each age.

During Roman antiquity, Horace transformed some Homeric techniques into epic conventions. Far more significant to our discussion, however, is the author of *On the Sublime*, who is traditionally known as Longinus, for he proposes the notion of epic grandeur in the way the epic affects its reader. In opposition to Aristotle, he flatly rejects implausible elements as undesirable in epic poetry. Longinus quotes a number of passages from the Homeric poems in support of his main argument that sublimity derives from inner causes such as the "elevation of mind" and strong passion, as well as from the noble style based on the technical use of language.[32] From this point of view, he considers the *Odyssey* inferior to the *Iliad*, because the *Odyssey*, traditionally held as a later composition, shows "the special token of old age," which is the poet's "love of marvellous tales" in letting a figure tell "the fabulous and incredible."[33] By contrast, the *Iliad* is devoid of such retrospective, internal narration and is filled with action and conflict. Longinus, however, excuses minor flaws in a great poet like Homer by saying that "invariable accuracy incurs the risk of pettiness" and must be "overlooked" in the sublime.[34] Longinus' argument therefore suggests that a great epic in turn inspire the reader with a sense of the sublime that overwhelms ordinary sensibility.

Throughout the Renaissance, some of the points Aristotle raised continued to be debated. For instance, Julius Caesar Scaliger in his *Poetics* (1561) asserts that "[v]erse is the property of the poet."[35] Sidney in *An Apology for Poetry* considers verse "but an ornament and no cause to Poetry," for "the right describing note to know a poet by" is the Aristotelian mimetic skill of "feigning" things.[36] Lodovico Castelvetro basically defends Aristotle in *The "Poetics" of Aristotle Translated and Explained* (1570). Castelvetro, however, notes that "all plots fashioned by tragic and epic poets are and ought to be based upon events that can be called historical."[37] By "historical," he means "possibilities that have never happened," which differentiates poetry from history that deals with "things that have actually happened."[38] Here, by changing the tense of "may happen" in Aristotle's *Poetics* (9.2) to "might have happened," Castelvetro infuses historicity into the Aristotelian universality of poetry. The past-ness of subject matter is emphasized after Castelvetro to the extent that it almost becomes a fixed epic norm. At the same time, while he lays stress on the three unities in drama, he asserts that "an epic poem may contain a number of very long actions and need not limit itself to one country" as long as the poem forms "a complete whole . . . of a suitably moderate length."[39] The multiplicity of action thus tolerated means a modification of the Aristotelian unity of action in epic poetry. In this way, Aristotle's postulates are challenged, altered, or supported by the Renaissance theorists.

During the neoclassical period, critics followed and codified the Renaissance theories, and placed great importance upon reason and the orderliness of nature. Thus, Boileau in *The Art of Poetry* considers rhyme "a slave, whose duty it is to obey" good sense.[40] When he discusses kinds of poetry in a hierarchical order, he places the epic in a penultimate position between tragedy and comedy. The epic is written "[i]n an even grander strain" than tragedy.[41] But comedy is better because, unlike its Greek predecessor, later comedy, supposedly French, "learned to laugh without ill-feeling, learned how to instruct and reprove without bile or venom."[42] In terms of the unity of action, Boileau understands well what Aristotle means when he points out: "Do not offer us a subject too full of incident. The wrath of Achilles alone, skillfully managed, abundantly satisfies what is required for an entire *Iliad*. Abundance in excess of need is likely to impoverish the whole."[43] This notion is effective in curbing the length of the epic. Otherwise, if multiplicity of actions is not somehow contained, an epic can be virtually endless without offering coherence and the central focus of the plot. Following Aristotle, Boileau also says that the epic "carries on its vast narrative of long-continued action" and that "[f]able is its support."⁴⁴ As a teacher of poetical art, Boileau highly recommends the Homeric poems as good examples for epic poets to follow. But he also prefers Ariosto, whose style is at once "impressive and pleasant . . . with his comic fables," to "those cold and melancholy authors" who, despising such pleasantry, try to write their epic poems in grave, serious style.⁴⁵ This taste is not surprising, because Boileau advances Aristotle's position on irrational elements, saying that the epic "lives by the marvelous."⁴⁶ At the same time, his argument, which is primarily concerned with style, suggests that, though often appropriate, the solemnity of expression is not necessarily essential to the sublimity of the epic.

Before we go into the nineteenth century, it is interesting to note what Henry Fielding attempted with the definition of the novel. As an artist of the kind of writing that has been "hitherto unattempted" in English,⁴⁷ Fielding apparently felt the need to authenticate what he created by formulating a generic identity. Relying heavily on neoclassical criticism, he proposes, in the preface to *Joseph Andrews* (1742), two appellations: "a comic Romance," and more elaborately "a comic Epic-Poem in Prose" (4). These interesting coinages have several significant implications. First, the middle part of the second definition, "comic Epic," is based on Aristotle's statement in *Poetics*. Following Aristotle, Fielding thinks that a lost piece called *Margites,* which is ascribed to Homer, held "the same relation to Comedy which his *Iliad* bears to Tragedy" (3). Accordingly, as in drama, Fielding classifies the epic into two kinds, the tragedy (tragic or serious epic) and the comedy (comic epic). Second, he offers an alternative, longer definition of "a comic romance," because he wants to distinguish his work from *"Romances"* that have "very little Instruction or Entertainment" (4). It follows that, although Fielding needs for his novel the concept of comic epic, which historically does not exist unless we take "comic" in the Dantean sense, he nevertheless rejects romance as an undesirable alternative to the epic. His point becomes clear when he explains that, by "comic," he means "Ridiculous" as opposed to "Burlesque," for the former, in which "the just Imitation" of "Nature" produces pleasure, is superior to the latter that dwells on "unnatural" absurdity and monstrosity (4, 5).

Third, the fact that Fielding's writing of the new kind is not composed in verse does not pose a problem for referring to it as an epic, because, except for meter, his work possesses "all its [epic's] other Parts" (3). Thus, we find the phrase "Poem in Prose" at the end of his second definition. From this point of view, then, an epic does not necessarily have to be written in verse. Fourth, his "comic" writing is different from "the serious Romance," because "its Fable and Action" are "light and ridiculous" while its characters are "Persons of inferiour Rank, and consequently of inferiour Manners" (4). In terms of "its Sentiments and Diction," it exhibits "the Ludicrous instead of the Sublime" (4). Last, Fielding's writing is as different from comedy, "as the serious Epic from Tragedy," because of "its Action being more extended and comprehensive" with "a much larger Circle of Incidents" and "a greater Variety of Characters" (4). Apparently having the debate on the multiplicity of actions in mind, Fielding attempts to reaffirm both the unity of action and the multiplicity of plots by extending the scope of occurrences and characters in the epic.

By having recourse to the two terms "romance" and "epic," Fielding means a story in the narrative mode. By "Epic-Poem" specifically, he indicates a long, complex metrical piece with many episodes and characters. Again, the idea is Aristotelian. At the same time, the full titles of Fielding's novels contain the word "history," such as *The History of the Adventures of Joseph Andrews, and of his Friend Mr. Abraham Adams*. With the playfully feigned veracity of the described events, this Cervantic assertion of historicity indicates that the events of a "comic Romance" or a "comic Epic-Poem in Prose" are supposed to have taken place in the past. It follows that Fielding's idea of epic itself, outside the distinction of comedy and tragedy, implies a long, complex narrative piece of fiction, not necessarily written in verse, but representing incidents of the past without preposterous invention. In fact, this is a basic definition of the epic that has resulted from more than two thousand years of debate. Later theorists either speculate on part of the definition even further or use it to elucidate the nature of some other genre in contrast to the epic. Furthermore, Fielding's argument demonstrates the predominant generic position the epic still enjoys during the eighteenth century, because he relies on the epic in order to justify his own fledging genre.

In "On Epic and Dramatic Poetry" (1827), Johann Wolfgang von Goethe, allegedly the actual writer of the brief treatise even though he co-signs it with Schiller, compares the epic with tragedy. He finds many fundamental similarities between the two genres as far as topics, structural devices, and the general laws of poetry are concerned. As to the epic, Goethe mainly thinks of the Homeric models. He asserts that the characters should be taken, if possible, from "a cultural period when spontaneous actions are still possible," that is, "when human beings do not act from moral, political or social motives, but from purely personal ones."[48] He also says that "the Greek myths from the heroic era were especially suitable material" (193). Furthermore, Goethe explains the epic writer as a wise rhapsodist "who recites events which lie completely in the past and surveys them with serene detachment" (194). Emphasizing, like Castelvetro, the pastness of epic subject matter, Goethe thus renders it a norm in his definition of the epic.

Goethe's other points are mostly conventional. For instance, he says that the epic poet should not present himself as a figure of authority in his poem so that the audience "will not associate any particular personality with what they hear" (194). As far as topics go, human issues of sublimity and significance ought to be the concern of both epic poetry and tragedy although the two genres pick up two different aspects. The epic depicts the individual's "physical interaction with the world . . . which requires broad, descriptive treatment" (193). In contrast, tragedy portrays the suffering of an individual who is "interacting with himself" (193), as a result of which a limited scope of action is possible. Although this view is basically Aristotelian with a tinge of Longinus, the contrast of the epic hero's extrovert orientation with the tragic hero's introversion is new. As to the worlds represented in the two genres, although Goethe considers them the same, he specifically points out the geographical dimension of the epic world. He says that, on the immediate, physical plane of the characters, "the dramatist normally restricts himself to one locale, whereas the epic poet ranges more freely over a larger area" (193). When the world further away is at stake, including "all of nature," the epic writer "makes this world more accessible through imagery, which the dramatist uses more sparingly" (193).

Goethe's contribution to the present discussion of the epic thus lies in his argument about the double dimension of time and space. This point has been latently present in the topical variety or comprehensibility of the epic, but it has never been so clearly articulated. In addition, since both epic and tragedy essentially deal with the same topics and identical worlds, Goethe's argument suggests the intermingling of mutual generic elements.

In *Aesthetics*, Hegel, basing his discussion on the etymology of the Greek word *epos*, defines epic in general as what has been transcribed into words with an autonomous meaning. Accordingly, the epic includes such literary forms as the epigraph, the maxim, some philosophical exposition, cosmology, and theogony, from which Hegel then distinguishes the epic proper. Hegel thinks that the creation of an epic requires the "immediate unity of feeling with action,"[49] which can take place only during a "heroic past" of a national culture when the freedom of individual will is not yet circumscribed by rigidly organized, social institutions (1047). To keep an epic from falling into a cold, superstitious, poetically decorated yet hollow piece, the poet should be totally immersed in that old situation. Hegel thus does not approve of the intrusion of any contemporary value into the poet's material of the pure past. At the same time, because the epic objectively shows occurrences in marked contrast to the outburst of subjective feelings and expressions in the lyric and to the totally inner-oriented complication and denouement in drama, the poet is not supposed to assert his subjectivity. Nevertheless, as a spiritual work, an epic should be taken not as a production of collective authorship but as that of an individual poet, which gives the piece "a genuine, inwardly organic, epic whole" (1050).

Hegel is obviously influenced by Goethe in his theory of the epic, and his theory in turn affects Lukács' in diverse ways including historically given materials and the rejection of imposed morality. Like Goethe's, Hegel's argument largely points to the Homeric poems. He frankly admits that, to avoid expected confusion, he derives from the two poems "a proof of what can be established as the true fundamental character of epic proper" (1051). Later, he emphasizes the necessity to "keep to the primitive epics" because an epic survives and stays fresh as long as it unfailingly shows "primitive life and work in a primitive way" (1077). In the primitive life, individual epic characters feel immediate intimacy with their particular surroundings through a particular world–view, which leads to the idea of a nation as the subject matter in both its physicality and its spirituality. The emphasis on nationality necessarily leads to the motif of collision, especially to war, as we have already seen in the philosophical debates on the epic. The hero of an epic should be endowed with "an entirety of characteristics," especially "the national disposition and manner of acting" (1067), so that he can assume a position preeminent enough to affect a national undertaking. As we have seen, Lukács rephrases Hegel's idea of an epic hero as the king of a community.

Hegel sounds Aristotelian when he dwells on the action of an individual as a source of unity in the epic. He argues that objectively described occurrences can take vital shape only if they are interlaced most closely with an individual. But this does not mean that the epic appears as a biographical account of a hero, because the events in his life may disintegrate into separate entities. Therefore, "[b]oth the unity of the individual and the unity of the occurrence must meet and be conjoined" (1066). The rejection of biographical description, which accords with Aristotle's argument for the unity of action, is essential to keep the epic from falling into the often inconsistent details of a life's ramification. But Hegel modifies the Aristotelian position by asserting that an epic should describe "not an action as such, but an event" (1069). What counts is not the heroes' "devotion of activity to their own end but what meets them in their pursuit of it" (1069). For instance, all of Odysseus' experiences during his wandering are not "the result of one action, but occur as incidents . . . mostly without the hero's contributing anything to them" (1069). Moreover, Achilles' anger triggers all that follows, and from the beginning it manifests "not a purpose or aim at all but a situation" (1069).

But Hegel later remodifies his position, for he asserts that the epic can achieve its integral unity of an epic event with either "[a]n inherently determinate aim" or "the satisfaction of a particular passion" (1088). He thus admits that, at the center, there always has to be a heroic figure who executes his aim or acts on his emotion and that the hero's action presupposes and entails a wide range of linked incidents. In fact, Hegel's emphasis on the circumstances of a central action, which derives again from his view of the Homeric poems as the generic paradigm, obviously does not apply as well to other epics. In the *Aeneid*, for example, Virgil's hero has a specific aim, a mission to accomplish, around which his action is formed. As a compromise, Hegel explains the episodic nature of the epic by stating that an additional sphere that encompasses the individual main event must be related to that event, while each of the two aspects maintains the independence needed to claim a realistic existence. He thinks that the loose connection of the individual parts makes the epic receptive of later changes, rearranging "single sagas previously polished up to a certain artistic height . . . into a new comprehensive whole" (1082).

With regard to the unity of the epic, Hegel also argues that "the poetry of human existence" should stand on the equipoise between "inner life and outer reality" in order to reveal "the entirety of a world in which an individual action happens" (1078). Hegel thus repudiates the Goethean externality of the epic hero's existence. For this reason, the epic hero "can seem to yield to external circumstances without detriment to his poetic individuality" (1082). Hegel also notes that, along with the detailed delineation of outer circumstances and inner conditions, the use of obstacles is another way to show the wholeness of a world and that it is permissible only if the obstacles appear to arise out of the circumstances without artificiality. Hegel's dwelling on the entirety of the epic world evidently influences Lukács' notion of the epic totality of life. Hegel then specifies the external reality as the actual, geographical world viewed by a people as well as the broader world with gods and nature, thereby stressing like Goethe the spatial dimension of the epic. As to the internal life, he says that feelings and reflections can be expressed by the occasional shift to lyrical and dramatic modes as long as these modes do not disrupt "the smoothly flowing epic tone" of objective narration (1079). Here, Hegel is not necessarily rigid with conventional genres and, similar to Schiller, he tolerates generic crossovers in representational modes to a certain degree.

At the same time, because of his emphasis on the circumstances which impede the epic hero's pursuit of his objective, Hegel thinks that the central, heroic figure should be bound to many constraints that are beyond his control, which can be called fate or "the element of an inherently necessary total state of affairs" (1071). The fate turns tragic "in the epic sense in which the individual is judged in his whole situation" (1071). In Lukács' words, the epic hero has to live through his given situation to its fulfillment because of, and despite of, the moral force that denies life. Hegel thinks that because the situation is too great for individuals who are just "clay" in the hands of destiny, the epic takes "an air of mourning" (1071). In this case, too, what he has in mind is obviously the Homeric poems in which humans are little more than game pieces for deities, although he points out that human figures are independent enough of the gods not to be their "obedient servants" in those poems (1072). The tragic quality of the epic, resulting from the fact that there is little the hero can do in face of overwhelming difficulties, is indeed important to induce a sense of humanness in its limitation. But the tragic quality of the epic, which should differ from that of tragedy proper, calls for an affirmation of humanity even in its frailty and limited power.

Finally, Hegel divides the epic into three kinds by stages of historical development: (1) oriental epic, (2) Greek classical epic and its Roman imitation, and (3) "romantically-epic poetry" that appeared in Europe after the Roman period (1094). The oriental epic in general does not gain much esteem because the individual lacks independence from a schematic universe. With his aforementioned high regard for the Homeric poems, Hegel considers the *Aeneid* and its kind, which he calls "the artistic epic proper" (1099), devoid of primitive freshness and secondary in aesthetic importance. He asserts that it required a new ethos of peoples for the epic to regain its vitality. Hegel subdivides what he calls the romantic epic into three kinds: pre-Christian pieces, works of the Christian (Catholic) Middle Ages, and those of the Renaissance. The pre-Christian pieces, represented by the poem ascribed to Ossian, the older *Edda*, and the Nordic myths, are considered "partly misshapen and barbaric ideas" and are rejected on the basis of their severance from the national sensibility of Hegel's modern Germanic culture (1102).

The medieval epic is again divided into three kinds: secular, religious, and chivalric. *The Poem of the Cid* is first mentioned as a good example of the first of these kinds, because it has "genuinely epic materials" with "still purely *national* medieval interests, deeds, and characters" (1102). The *Nibelungenlied* as another example of the medieval secular epic is not so well viewed because of its rather un-epical collision, shortage of individuals, lack of lifelike immediacy, and tendency to be "lost in what is harsh, wild, and gruesome" (1103). The medieval religious epic is predominantly represented by Dante's *Divine Comedy*. Hegel admits that this poem can be called an epic not in the usual sense of the term but due to its "firmest articulation and rounded completeness" in the description of "the entirety of objective life" from a Christian, theological perspective (1103, 1104). As to the chivalric tales with their pursuit of honor in knighthood, love affairs, and Christian mysticism, Hegel is reluctant to include them fully in the category of the epic. He then offers a critique of romance in light of its weak sense of national character and circumstances, its strong subjectivity, and its lack of "fundamental realism" due to its fantastic presentation (1105).

Predictably, Hegel does not approve of the Renaissance epic that ardently emulates classical literature at the sacrifice of "original creativity" (1107). At the same time, he points out the variety in form and subject matter that the epic developed during this period. He first recognizes two directions in relation to the Middle Ages. The first direction consists in the caricature of chivalric tales. This type is best illustrated by Ariosto for his "incredible buffooneries" of chivalric fantasy and by Cervantes for his depiction of the genuinely admirable aspects of the knightly code through illusions and madness against the background of prosaic, deficient reality (1107). Tasso's *Jerusalem Delivered* is representative of the second direction that does not treat the chivalric tradition comically. With the motif of the crusade placed at the center, this work possesses "a real and sacred interest, national too in part, a kind of unity, development, and rounded completion of the whole" (1108). Still, Hegel does not regard Tasso's poem favorably, because, as "a poetically manufactured event," it lacks "the primitiveness which alone could make it the bible of a whole nation" (1108). He disapproves of the *Lusiads* by Camoens for the same reason. In the field of religious epic that was newly vitalized by the Protestant movements, Hegel acknowledges Milton's classical knowledge and elegant expression in *Paradise Lost.* Nevertheless, he places the English poet below Dante mainly in terms of diffused epic objectivity (1109): the conflict and catastrophe is rather dramatically structured while lyrical outpourings and moral didacticism are rampant. In the end, Hegel states that the highly artificial nature of Renaissance epic renders its subject "clearly unsuitable for the primitive type of epic" (1109).

Hegel's concept of the epic in general is, then, consistently biased by his high regard of the Homeric poems. His admiration of the Homeric poems is such that he makes a clear distinction between them and other works of oral origin by labelling the latter as barbaric. In his insistence on the primitive nature of the epic, it is not surprising to find Hegel say at the end that today's entire world situation has become "diametrically opposed in its prosaic organization to the requirements . . . irremissible for

genuine epic" (1109). Truly epic works from the most recent periods can be found only in a nonconventional sphere that includes
"an unlimited field of romances, tales, and novels" (1110), but
Hegel avoids undertaking the explanation of its historical development. It should also be noted that, although he usually means
epic poems by "epic," the distinction between verse and prose is
apparently not significant to Hegel, as it is clear from his discussion of *Don Quixote* as well as from his reference to novels as
a new sphere of the epic. At the same time, Hegel's classification
of the epic suggests the possibility of grouping epic works, whose
tradition extends far before and after the Homeric poems, sys-
tematically by some historical perspective. His argument is also
significant in articulating the cultural role of the epic as a communal bible.

In the twentieth century, M. M. Bakhtin in the *Dialogic
Imagination* (1975) tries, as did Lukács, to reveal the unique
nature of the novel by contrasting it to the epic. His argument
can be considered, in many respects, an important achievement
of the poetic approach to the epic, although his marked preference for the novel problematizes it. Simply put, Bakhtin asserts
that, along with the other genres, the epic is an old, fixed form
whose development has long been completed, whereas the novel
is the only literary phenomenon that continues to develop.
Bakhtin mentions three features of the novel: "(1) its stylistic
three-dimensionality, which is linked with the multi-languaged
consciousness . . . ; (2) the radical change it effects in the temporal coordinates of the literary images; (3) the new zone . . . of
maximal contact with the present (with contemporary reality) in
all its openendedness."[50] According to him, all of the three characteristics, which are related to one another, have been brought
about by the historical shift of European civilization from
"monoglossia" to "polyglossia" (12), or from the isolation of a
"culturally deaf semipatriarchal society" to the active awareness
of "international and interlingual contacts and relationships"
(11). This is especially the case with the first feature. The shift to
a "polyglot" world requires "a process of active, mutual cause-
and-effect and interillumination" of languages (12). Because of
this new consciousness, a language becomes qualitatively different even if its linguistic fundamentals remain the same. In
contrast to the epic and other old genres that derive from a culture of monoglossia, the novel, the origin of which Bakhtin traces
back to the Hellenistic period, appeared and developed "precisely

when intense activization of external and internal polyglossia was at the peak of its activity" (12). Therefore, Bakhtin thinks that the novel has played a major role in renovating literature stylistically.

Although highly persuasive in the case of the novel, Bakhtin's argument remains problematical as far as the epic is concerned. On the one hand, it seems that, by relating the epic to monoglossia or a culture of "semipatriarchal society," Bakhtin, like many other theorists, mainly thinks of the Homeric poems as a generic model. If so, his notion of the Greek *epos* is obviously oversimplified to suit his discussion of the novel, for the Homeric world is not based on pure monoglossia, though it might be quite patriarchal. The Homeric poems, especially the *Odyssey*, reveal the frequent contact the ancient Greeks had with other, hetero-lingual peoples including the Egyptians for whose culture and learning the Greeks had deep respect and the Phoenicians to whom the Greeks were greatly indebted in navigational skill and overseas trade. It should also be recalled that the Homeric poems themselves are composed not in a monolithic language but in multiethnic dialects that will later be integrated as Greek. We can therefore apply what Bakhtin says about the novel to the epic as well: Because of the appearance of the Homeric poems, the Greek language became qualitatively different even though its linguistic fundamentals remained the same. On the other hand, by epic, Bakhtin possibly understands an even more primitive production of a "culturally deaf," linguistically closed society. In this case, however, the problem is more serious, because, although such epics certainly exist, they essentially belong to the sphere of anthropology. In other words, Bakhtin's argument would exclude all the major epic works in the West, including *Beowulf* which, in spite of its monoglot appearance, shows complex, international relations among the peoples around the North Sea. In any case, Bakhtin apparently conceives of the epic of monoglossia as representative of all other epics, and he bases his discussion of the epic on this unidentified, probably purely conceptual example.

To explain the other two features of the novel by contrast, Bakhtin then enumerates the three characteristics of the epic, which are closely interrelated: (1) a national epic past—"absolute past" after Goethe's (and Schiller's) terminology; (2) normative national tradition; and (3) an absolute epic distance that separates the epic world from the contemporary reality of the singer or the author and his audience. Bakhtin first claims that the

epic has always been about a nation's heroic past, about its
"'beginnings' and 'peak times,'" its great founders, its "'firsts' and
'bests'" (13). In this case, the heroic age is not simply the subject
matter of the epic. The represented world is transferred into a
remote time inaccessible to the poet, who sings of his people's
ancient history with great reverence. This means that "epic discourse is infinitely far removed from discourse of a contemporary
about a contemporary addressed to contemporaries" (13–14). In
this process, the epic past is hierarchically "valorized to an
extreme degree" because of the sacred, creative importance of
memory in ancient literature (15). According to this view, "everything is good" in the past; "all the really good things . . . occur
only in this past," and this past is also "the single source and
beginning of everything good for all later times" (15). The epic
past is thus called "absolute," because it is "both monochronic
and valorized" and "lacks any relativity" of the "gradual, purely
temporal progressions" that might link it to the present of the
poet and his audience (15). In this "[a]bsolute conclusiveness
and closedness," the epic world has neither "any openendedness, indecision, indeterminacy" nor any "loopholes in it through
which we glimpse the future," thereby denying any "potential for
a real continuation" (16). Bakhtin accordingly calls the epic
"already completely finished, a congealed and half-moribund
genre" with an "ossified generic skeleton" (14, 8).

Bakhtin then claims that only a national tradition filling
the space between the valorized plane of the sung heroes and the
plane of the singer and his audience can preserve and manifest
the epic past. The reliance on tradition is "immanent in the very
form of the epic," because the world of the absolute epic past is
"given solely as tradition, sacred and sacrosanct, evaluated in the
same way by all and demanding a pious attitude toward itself"
and the traditional language used to describe it (16). Finally,
Bakhtin claims that the third element, epic distance, is determined by the first two features: the absolute past impenetrably
walled off from the perpetually developing present of the singer
and his audience, and the national tradition that detaches the
world of the epic from any personal experience and initiative in
understanding and interpretation in order to provide new
insights. As "an utterly finished thing," the epic world stands
"not only as an authentic event of the distant past but also on its
own terms and by its own standards" (17). With such an inter-
vening distance, one cannot really touch the world of the epic,

because it is "beyond the realm of human activity" (17). According to Bakhtin, the epic distance thus consists in the language as well as in the material of the valorized past, for the dead who are taken away from the sphere of contact must be spoken of in a different style.

In contrast, the novel has "contact with the spontaneity of the inconclusive present," which "keeps the genre from congealing" (27). Both the author and the represented world are "subject to the same temporally valorized measurements" (27), because the author's language now stays on the same plane as the hero's. The novel is also capable of providing "an authentically objective portrayal of the past as the past" with current reality kept as a point of view (29). Time and the world progress "as becoming, . . . as a unified, all-embracing and unconcluded process" (30). The novel's most direct contact with what the author and the readers are directly engaged in contemporary life makes the represented object "attracted to the incomplete process of a world-in-the-making" and "stamped with the seal of inconclusiveness" (30). As a result, the novel involves the danger of "substitut[ing] for our own life an obsessive reading of novels, or dreams based on novelistic models" (32), but this is not the case with the epic and other genres, unless they are novelized.

In terms of the absolute epic past, what is great is always known to the offspring only in the form of memory. The present is "something transitory . . . without beginning or end" (20). The future counts as long as it is "the future memory of a past . . . a world that is always opposed in principle to any *merely transitory* past" (19). Beyond that, the future is conceived of "either as an essentially indifferent continuation of the present, or as an end, a final destruction, a catastrophe" (20). In this temporal scheme, "[t]he beginning is idealized, the end is darkened" (20). In the novel, the world unfolds "as an uninterrupted movement into a real future" (30), and the relationship of the artistic image with the ongoing event of life also entails a close contact between the represented object and the future. Accordingly, Bakhtin considers prophecy typical of epic foresight, and prediction akin to novelistic foresight: "Epic prophecy is realized wholly within the limits of the absolute past (if not in a given epic, then within the limits of the tradition it encompasses); it does not touch the reader and his real time. The novel might wish to prophesize facts, to predict and influence the real future, the future of the author and his readers" (31).

It is obvious again that Bakhtin manipulates the epic in order to offer an insight into the nature of the novel. In fact, each of his points concerning the epic involves a problem. First, although some epics solely treat of the past, many others also concern the present and the future of the singing poet and his audience at least allusively. For instance, the *Aeneid* is written exclusively in implicit and explicit reference to the future (that is, Virgil's contemporaneity and beyond) of Rome. The *Lusiads* deals with the poet's recent situation with much intended implication for his people's present and future. Such poems as the *Divine Comedy* and the *Faerie Queene* are also strongly committed to the poets' contemporary situations. And religious epics such as *Paradise Lost* and the *Divine Comedy* are by nature concerned with afterlife and the distant future. It is true that, beyond the poet's present, the epic's perspective on the future has to be more like prophecy compared with the novel's, which is more like prediction. As the instances above prove, however, epic prophecy is circumscribed neither "wholly within the limits of the absolute past" nor "within the limits of the tradition" of an epic. Therefore, Bakhtin's assertion that the epic past has no continuity with the unfolding present and the future is inaccurate.

Furthermore, it is hardly possible for any literary work, including the Homeric poems, to look back at the past without projecting, implicitly or explicitly, an awareness of a new reality on the historical material from the viewpoint of the author's present. In this case, what Schiller says about idyllic, sentimental poetry is useful to explain the possibility of such projection. Schiller's notion of idyll that depicts idealized nature in a seemingly self-enclosed literary world is similar to Bakhtin's concept of the epic that seeks perfection in the past. Schiller contends that, in the idyll, the poet does not explicitly show the opposition between nature and art, or the ideal and actuality, in his description of pure pastoral life. Even so, the poet's language betrays the contrary, because it carries "the spirit of the age and has undergone the influence of art,"[51] and the unintended, yet underlying dichotomy renders the mode of perception in the idyll elegiac. Since Schiller's modes of perception cross generic boundaries, this idyllic mode also applies to the epic unless its subject matter is taken from the author's present or a very recent past. While Schiller's argument explains a sentimental longing for what is lost, it also suggests that, in the same unintentional manner, the epic poet might cast a critical look at the heroic period that he depicts. It is obvious, then, that what Bakhtin attempts is a theoretical mythopoeia of the *absoluteness* of the epic past.

As to the bright beginning and the gloomy end that Bakhtin refers to, it is possible to find an epic with either of these plot elements. For example, *Beowulf* has a disastrous view of the future while *Paradise Lost* offers an idealized beginning. But we cannot find an epic with the completion of Bakhtin's simplified temporal scheme. *Beowulf* does not provide any idealized view of either its own past or even its present fraught with constant danger. *Paradise Lost* refers to the end of the world as Christianity's final victory over evil. Moreover, such pieces as the *Aeneid* and the *Lusiads* notably show the troublesome beginnings of empires and their bright future.

In relation to the supposedly bright beginning, it is likely that Bakhtin uses the word "idealized" with the same sense as "valorized" about what he calls "the absolute past" of the epic. But his notion of the epic valorized past is problematic, too. First of all, "the absolute past" he means does not point to the genuine beginning of society or the world, unless he only has in mind works like the *Aeneid* and *Paradise Lost*. The Homeric poems, for instance, are not about the beginning of Greek society but about a certain developed social and cultural stage. When Bakhtin talks about the "valorized" or "idealized" past, he only looks at part of the past, that is, the heroic figures. The situations that surround the heroes, however, are almost always hard and far from peace and serenity. The Homeric poems exemplify this point very well. There, the heroes, who belong to a Hesiodic time between the bronze and the iron ages, are racially superior to present humankind, and are certainly idealized in terms of both physical size and conduct, despite some behavioral flaws. But, as Achilles' words to Priam clearly illustrate, the Homeric heroes find themselves in the midst of harsh reality. They might be slaughtered as an entertainment for the gods or die miserably in decrepitude, like Odysseus' dog Argos. Accompanied by such hard circumstances, of which not only the heroes but also the poet and his audience are aware, the epic past refuses simple valorization.

One should also point out that the world of the epic is not "opposed in principle to any *merely transitory* past." In fact, the epic is always concerned with mortality and mutability, that is, the transient nature of the world, and such a world cannot remain a frozen status quo with mere idealization. The heroes grieve over their changing situations. Such is the case with Achilles, for instance, who grimly anticipates his early death in the *Iliad* and laments it in the world of the dead in the *Odyssey*. Charlemagne literally cries over his hard fate of ceaseless campaigning at the end of *The Song of Roland*. In this light, the epic past is not isolated with total stability as Bakhtin claims. The epic world does *not* have "[a]bsolute conclusiveness and closedness," but does have some "openendedness, indecision, indeterminacy" and some "loopholes in it through which we glimpse the future." Therefore, the epic past is not absolutely set apart but is only relatively removed from our contemporaneity.

As to the national tradition Bakhtin mentions, the epic generally depends on a strenuous tradition that has a sense of history as many theorists speculate. But the concept of a nation ranges too widely in the epic. In the Homeric poems, there is no nation in the modern sense of the word: it can refer to a tribal unit or a loose assembly of such units. In an imperialistic epic like the *Aeneid*, the envisioned empire controls many small nations. And a religious epic like *Paradise Lost* has no interest in national identity, unless the Christian community is metaphorically called a nation in a secularized sense. There is no reason why the epic tradition should be a national one. It follows that the concept of nation in the epic is no more than a useful indicator of a large communal group.

As far as plot is concerned, Bakhtin states that the novel, lacking in "internal conclusiveness and exhaustiveness," calls for "an *external* and *formal* completeness and exhaustiveness, especially in regard to plot-line" with a clear awareness of "a beginning, an end, and 'fullness'" (31). By contrast, the epic has no concern for formal beginnings and can stay incomplete, because "[t]he absolute past is closed and completed in the whole as well as in any of its parts" so that "[o]ne may begin the story at almost any moment, and finish at almost any moment" (31). Here, Bakhtin shares Lukács' belief that the epic lacks architectural structure. In addition, he thinks that, because everyone in the culture already knows the story, "[t]he specific 'impulse to end' . . . is absolutely excluded from the epic" (32). On the other hand, the novel is characterized by the impulse both to continue and to end. Thus, Bakhtin believes that, while the novel holds the audience's interest by manipulating unknown events, the epic cannot hold this interest because its plot is already familiar to the audience.

Evidently, here, Bakhtin is thinking of epics of oral origin, the stories of which, along with their historical background, are already known to the audience because the poems have been rehearsed many times before by generations of bards. His notion of the epic, however, ill applies to epics by individual poets who blend their inventions with historical materials. In this case, the audience or the readers do expect new storylines, and therefore are very much interested in the plot itself. The inconclusive beginnings as well as the similar endings in most of the post-Homeric epics can be largely ascribed not to the epic's lack of concern for structure as Bakhtin claims, but to the normative force of what Horace recommends as a poetic technique. At the same time, works like *Beowulf* and the *Nibelungenlied* have quite definite beginnings and conclusive endings. Furthermore, Bakhtin's argument totally ignores the Aristotelian definition of an epic action that, centering on the protagonist, unifies the story in terms of a beginning, a middle, and an end.

Even more problematic to the nature of the epic is the fact that Bakhtin, who places so much emphasis on the novel's contact with the inconclusive present, disregards the significance of an inconclusive plot, which is naturally akin to reality. In fact, the endings in epics such as the *Aeneid* and *Paradise Lost* are not only incomplete but also ambiguous in implication. The inconclusiveness of the epic plot as well as its ambiguity is related to the epic's fundamental concern with the vicissitudes of the world that cannot be complete, perfect, and permanent as Plato's negative view of the epic indicates. This point is best demonstrated by the changing mode of the novel itself. Against Bakhtin's claim that the novel alone possesses the impulse to continue and to end, an increasing number of novels have open endings rich in ambiguity, unfulfilled middles, and beginnings that are not well defined in a traditional manner. In addition, the order of these three basic plot segments is dislocated in many novels that explore their narratological potentiality. As far as the plot is concerned, then, the novel is becoming like the epic rather than the other way around.

Another difference Bakhtin finds between epic and novel concerns the representation of the individual. In the epic, the individual is "a fully finished and completed being," which indicates "something hopelessly ready-made" (34). Bakhtin believes that an epic hero cannot be anything more than what he appears, because, in the idealized presentation of his figure, there is no gap between his inner self and its outer manifestation. Bakhtin here modifies and expands what Goethe says about the extrovert interaction of an epic hero with the world. Moreover, the epic hero as well as the author does not have any initiative in ideology to affect individual images due to their "single and unified world view" (35). Epic figures are determined "by their various situations and destinies, but not by varying 'truths'" (35). In this context, there is no confession to make, no self to expose. These features account not only for "the exclusive beauty, wholeness, crystal clarity and artistic completedness" of the image of the epic character, but also for "his obvious woodenness" (35). This part of Bakhtin's argument essentially corresponds to Lukács' discussion of the internal homogeneity of the epic world, the totality of which is "rounded from within."

Bakhtin claims that, by contrast, the novel exposes the individual's inconsistency between surface and center, between potential and reality. People cannot be "exhausted entirely by the plots that contain them" (35). Unlike the epic or tragic figure, a novelistic character possesses "unrealized potential and unrealized demands," or "an unrealized surplus of humanness" and "a need for the future" (37). Therefore, one of the essential themes of the novel is "precisely the theme of the inadequacy of a hero's fate and situation" (37). In this sense, reality in the novel is "only one of many possible realities," because "it bears within itself other possibilities" (37). The incongruity in a novelistic individual leads to the disintegration of the epic and tragic hero who is replaced by "a new, complex wholeness on a higher level of human development" (38). The individual also acquires "the ideological and linguistic initiative necessary to change the nature of his own image" to a higher degree of individualization (38). Here, Bakhtin rephrases Lukács' argument about novelistic individuals, who psychologically become "seekers," even of their own "concealed totality of life."

As Bakhtin points out, many epic heroes lack flexibility in their characterization because they are fully realized externally, and there is not much room for their inner change. This is due to the fact that, as I have already discussed, these figures, but not their environment, are idealized. Other epic heroes, however, show the possibility of internal transformation. In fact, one of the main themes of the *Divine Comedy* is the spiritual regeneration of Dante the poet-narrator through his supernatural journey. But, even in the case of Achilles, despite Vico's vehement criticism, one can detect an inner metamorphosis in his final sympathetic conversation with Priam. This reconciliation cannot be expected to come from Achilles who initially argues with Agamemnon, but it is based on Achilles' deep-rooted doubt of his way of life in battle and plunder which, as an embodiment of martial strength, he is supposed to pursue unscrupulously. Furthermore, as Hegel points out, there can be occasional shifts to the lyrical or dramatic mode of narration in the epic, which allows the heroic figure to explore the potentiality of the inner self. An obvious example is found in the Satan of *Paradise Lost*, although Hegel mentions Milton's poem as a bad case of excessive outpourings of internal thought.

Bakhtin oversimplifies the image of the epic individual. In a word, unlike Hegel who scrutinizes the diversity of epic phenomena, Bakhtin constructs his concept of a typical epic out of various kinds, and he does not look at the variety itself. He develops his biased argument of the epic, based on his idea of the typical, but in fact hypothetical work, in such a way that he can proclaim the novel's great influence over all the other genres. He asserts that the novel "could never be merely one genre among others" once it appeared, because "the future of all literature" is inherent in it, and all other genres have been more or less novelized (39). Because the novel possesses self-questioning plasticity through a zone of contact with the reality of the ever developing present, this novelization of other genres implies not "their subjection to an alien generic canon" but "their liberation from . . . some sort of stylization of forms that have outlived themselves" (39). There is no denying that the novel is a major genre in modern literature and that other genres are significantly affected by it. But Bakhtin's argument assigns the novel an excessive role. It is easy to round up all the elements which he considers un-epical, such as the contact with contemporaneity and the inner complexity of a character, and to call epics with such elements "novelized." But the fact is that such elements often exist inherently in the epic. Without refusing the due significance the novel occupies in the development of literature, we ought to have a modified look at Bakhtin's argument.

By drawing a sharp contrast between epic and novel, Bakhtin relegates the epic to a secondary position as an obsolete genre. Because of "its hopelessly finished quality" (30), the epic has no future, unless it is novelized to allow freedom of forms and adapt to the ever changing modes of literature. Through his low esteem of the epic, Bakhtin exemplifies the current view that gives this genre a minor, lusterless role in the making of literature, or even in the whole establishment of literature. Bakhtin's theory is significant, however, because, even in the present climate of critical indifference to the epic, it indirectly suggests the future survival, possibly the potential growth, of the genre. As Bakhtin rightly claims, any genre has little chance of remaining creatively vigorous without self-examining its relevance to the rest of literature. This argument dictates that, since the novel is a growingly dominant literary form, it affects and will affect the epic in style and characterization. Such violations of generic borders appear "considerably more often in the novel," because the novel is "a developing genre" and is "in the vanguard of change" (33). But this does not exclude the possibility that the epic will contribute to the development of the novel in other aspects such as theme and plot. After all, generic influence cannot be one-directional in the organic dynamism of literary transformation.

Recent scholars who write on the epic have also been far from unanimous in defining it as a genre. For instance, Brian Wilkie points out that scholars in the last three hundred years have agreed on only the two most basic criteria: "an epic must be long" and "narrative."[52] This definition liberates the epic from the formal constraints of verse form and accepts the growing tendency to perceive as epics nonverse works written after the Renaissance. Such a transgeneric concept thus nullifies the distinction that separates the novel from the epic; consequently, many long novels in the narrative mode would have to be considered epics. Most novels, however, concern themselves with the very limited daily scope of people's lives, a characteristic which our expectation of the epic does not accept. Conversely, the notion of the epic as a long narrative might also be reinforced by equating an epic with a long poem, as William Calin does in his book on the French epic tradition.[53] Yet this definition would produce too much generic circumscription.

One can avoid the circular problem, however, by placing more importance on other properties of the epic. For instance, Paul Merchant maintains that two major elements constitute our experience of the epic: its creation of dimensions beyond everyday realism, and its close relation to history, with its two "most important original functions" as "a chronicle" and "a storybook for general entertainment."[54] Accordingly, Merchant mentions *War and Peace*, along with the *Iliad* and the *Prelude*, as typical examples of the epic. There is arguably little problem about including the large-scale Russian novel in the genre. But Merchant also mentions works like the *Canterbury Tales* and *Piers Plowman*, although he reservedly admits that these English medieval poems "would not be placed in the central line of epic."[55] The two poems "of the open, all-embracing narrative" might be regarded as works of an *epical* scale,[56] but, as epics, they remain marginal at best. The question then arises as to what degree and with what criteria a work can be called "epical" even if it might not be generally recognized as an epic. Nevertheless, Merchant's definition is useful in proposing a nonpoetic method of approaching the epic.

One might also be tempted to try a detailed, comprehensive list of epic generic features. Calin provides one example of such a list:

> [I]t is normally in verse, of some length, in the narrative mode, fictional but based on history or legend; . . . [I]t treats on a grand scale a martial, heroic subject, manifests artistic coherence because it concentrates on a single central hero or event of national significance, contains stylized "episodes," and is grounded in the supernatural. . . . [T]o adhere to the mode a poem ought to be a narrative, a good story well told; be based on history, the primary subject-matter "real"; have a hero larger than life; treat martial feats; give a "heroic impression" or "epic awe"; manifest grandeur, largeness, high quality and seriousness, a sense of amplitude, breadth, inclusiveness, and general significance; testify to human achievement and the dignity of man; represent a "choric voice," a collective, community point of view; and, in strictly esthetic terms, be composed in the "grand style," benefit from the author's control, and perhaps use traditional stock motifs.[57]

Calin's eclectic definition seems at first sight to be fairly complete. Still, even here, difficulties arise. One significant question is again whether the epic should always involve war. If so, the *Divine Comedy* has to be precluded from our consideration, which leaves our potential list of epics awkward and disputable. Some works like *The Song of Roland* and the *Nibelungenlied* contain more than one "single central hero," and an "event of national significance" is not necessarily found in *Paradise Lost,* or even in the two Homeric poems. Above all, because of the diverse sources from which Calin's description is compiled, it sounds rather tautological.

Finally, we have seen that the poetic approaches concerning the definition of the epic differ widely in such issues as the use of epic verse, the significance of epic action, and the relation of the epic to other genres. The philosophical approaches show the same lack of agreement regarding the cultural function of the epic. One fundamental problem is that many critics have explicitly or implicitly based their views of the epic on the Homeric poems mainly for two reasons: the two works evidently offer the safest way to deal with the generic notion in terms of the Greek origin of the word "epic," and the two poems occupy initial positions in the epic tradition. This emphasis on the Homeric poems inevitably places many other works in an awkward position. Most typically, post-Dantean critics feel uncomfortable or even reluctant to discuss the *Divine Comedy* as an epic. In temporal terms, critics generally locate the subject matter of the epic in a remote past, although such temporal specifications are of little concern to several important scholars, including Plato and Aristotle. In the particular cases of Nietzsche and Bakhtin, the critics' ideas are evidently biased against the epic in favor of some other genres. Since all of the approaches discussed so far have been unable to offer a unified concept of the epic, I shall propose, in the next chapter, a thematic approach that will go a long way toward achieving this goal. This approach will not only take into consideration the issues discussed in the present chapter, but will also open the possibility of considering the epic from a comparative, world-wide perspective.

2

Epic Grandeur:
A Thematic Approach to the Epic

Western theories and criticism offer little agreement in defining the epic through poetic and philosophical approaches. Nevertheless, we can employ elements of these approaches to sketch a thematic outline that would place the epic in a global perspective. Such an outline would not be provincially circumscribed and would comprehend various instances from many parts of the world. Even though developing a clear-cut definition that might satisfy everyone seems to be an impossible task, we can nevertheless search for a few basic elements found in most (if not all) of the works that are usually considered epics. First, we can hypothetically accept the two elements everyone has agreed on: an epic is long and is composed in a narrative mode. To these two elements, one might add that of grandeur.[1] Still, a new question immediately emerges. How can an epic be great? How does a work of this kind enable us to feel the greatness of humanity and the world?

I assume that epic grandeur stems mainly from three thematic elements: the hero's attitude toward his mortality, his communal responsibility, and the dual dimension of time and space he and the entire work must cope with. The first element, human mortality, is best explained through Northrop Frye's modes of fictional literature. Frye locates "most epic" in "the *high mimetic* mode," where the hero is "superior in degree to other men but not to his natural environment" as far as his "conventional power of action" goes.[2] In other words, an epic is, after all, a story about a human destined to be baffled by nature, however excellent that person might be. Thus, the hero's human limitations ultimately center on the problem of mortality. From an extended perspective, mutability, that is, change in the way things are, takes the place of mortality, not as a creative force which regenerates itself out of its own ashes, but as a destructive force that can by no means be withstood in the passage of time.

The hero's mortality becomes especially noticeable when the high mimetic mode is compared with the two higher modes of "myth" and "romance" that Frye postulates. In romance, the hero is "superior in *degree* to other men and to his environment."[3] Although a human being, he can more or less bend the order of the natural surroundings to his will with his special powers. Additionally, the hero's environment, itself inhabited by such beings as "talking animals, terrifying ogres and witches," is beyond "the ordinary laws of nature."[4] In a word, the hero in romance is superhuman, and his environment supernatural. The contrast with the high mimetic mode is sharper in myth, where, "superior in *kind* both to other men and to the environment of other men, the hero is a divine being."[5] The hero in myth is an immortal god, whereas the central figure in the high mimetic mode is a mortal being, no matter how superior the hero proves himself to other people. As Nietzsche says, "the god is typically different from the hero" in the sense that "[l]aboriousness is an objection" and "light feet are the first attribute of divinity."[6] It would seem that the ultimate question that awaits a mortal, great or not, is how to deal with death. How the protagonist comes to terms with the end of his life and what he can achieve within a limited life span determine his status as an epic hero.

Furthermore, the epic protagonist, or in some cases a central group of people,[7] has to solve a grave problem of the community to which he or it belongs. The communal size need not necessarily be of national dimension. It might range from a family with all its human and economic resources, as in the *Odyssey*, to a huge totality, such as the whole of humanity prefiguratively manifest in *Paradise Lost*. The point is that, although the hero faces a communal problem which appears beyond his capacity, he somehow overcomes the difficulty in the end. From this point of view, a protagonist who is preoccupied solely with his own personal troubles can hardly be called an epic hero.[8] The gravity of the issue, which stems from the communal dimension, together with the hero's devotion to the task of overcoming the problem, constitutes one major factor of epic grandeur.

A dynamic double expanse of time and space is a third source of epic grandeur.[9] The temporal expanse is usually expressed by references to a people's history, either annalistically or through recollections and prophesies. The latter two devices, which combine the retelling of the past, after beginning *in medias res*, with a prophesy or prophetic vision of the future, are common in many European epics. In some cases, such a prophetic perspective even extends beyond the actual history that precedes the composition of the epic. In this broad sense, the epic contains a strong sense of history in which the troublesome present of the hero or the author contrasts with the time already gone and sometimes also with the time yet to be realized.

The spatial expanse is presented through reference to contemporary geographical circumference. In the world–view of the ancient Greeks and Romans, this meant the Mediterranean Sea and the lands surrounding it. The northern part of Europe, including the British Isles and the Danish and Scandinavian peninsulas, formed the world for those whose culture produced *Beowulf*. But, in the imagination that creates the epic, "the world" known to people cannot be limited to the regions actually traveled. It can also mean mythic foreign lands, like the pagan Middle East and Africa in *The Song of Roland*, and, more broadly, heaven and hell, as in *Paradise Lost*. Sometimes, physical wandering consciously overlaps a spiritual journey. The multiple meaning of the hero's travel typically happens in allegorical works such as the *Divine Comedy* and the *Faerie Queene*. In many epic instances, the spatial expanse extends to the entire universe, and this cosmology naturally introduces supernatural elements such as celestial and subterranean deities. Because of the comprehensiveness of the dual dimension of time and space, the epic involves multicultural contact and has "the tendency . . . to be etiological" about objects, customs, events, names, communal groups, and the world itself,[10] thereby often leading to the display of encyclopedic knowledge.[11]

In Pascal's famous words, a human being, although "the weakest thing in nature," possesses dignity as "a thinking reed," and we ought to look to thought, "not to space or time which we can never fill," in order to be elevated in moral life.[12] Nevertheless, we do have to face the vastness of time and space, "which we can never fill." Because of being weak thinking reeds, we cannot help experiencing ontological anxiety about our place within the boundless cosmos, as well as within the interminable stretch of time. Our fascination with scientific enterprises to expand the horizon of our knowledge, such as the exploration of the outer space and the archaeological search for the first human species, belies this anxiety of existence in a modern guise. As Nietzsche notes, our "resolve to be so scientific about everything" is "perhaps a kind of fear of, an escape from, pessimism" at the exact time when we are "more and more ardent for logic and logicizing the world and thus more 'cheerful.'"[13]

People at a primitive stage of society invent myths and populate every corner of their surroundings with supernatural beings in order to render every phenomenon related to their lives intelligible. Otherwise, the world would be a frighteningly inexplicable place. As the human capability of perception and understanding grows, however, the supernatural framework that myths offer becomes labile and inadequate to alleviate people's anxiety. As M. I. Finley explains: "A human society without myth has never been known, and indeed it is doubtful whether such a society is at all possible. One measure of man's advance from his most primitive beginnings to something we call civilization is the way in which he controls his myths, his ability to distinguish between the areas of behavior, the extent to which he can bring more and more of his activity under the rule of reason."[14] When mythology no longer provides a sufficient means to systematize the world, one significant, alternative answer to the ontological problem is the epic, especially in its extensive exploratory mode.[15] The epic shows human dignity, not only because it covers a vast expanse of time and space, but also because human thought organizes those incomprehensible dimensions into a meaningful system and reassures people about their existence in an unfathomable universe. For this reason, the narratorial viewpoint gauges the dual dimension of the universe without sharing physicality with its protagonist. More importantly, whether he wishes it or not, the epic hero explores, with mortal gravity, the known and unknown expanse of time and space as far as the exploration is relevant to him and his people. A literary figure who is bound to a specific moment without a clear vision of past and future, or who roams within a small circle no farther than his native town or village, does not deserve the name of an epic hero.

We have listed three elements (the hero's attitude toward his mortality, his relation to the community, and the dual dimension of time and space) as the main sources of epic grandeur. In a typical epic, these three elements do not function independently of each other. Rather, they are inextricably intertwined. For instance, a serious, communal problem occurs when the safety of the group is somehow threatened by an external force. Such a threat usually requires a member or members of the community to cross the boundaries of the ancestral territory in order to find a solution. In this scenario, the three elements of epic grandeur are of little consequence unless they are integrated into one totality of action through the central figure or people. The central figure assumes the extremely difficult duty of overcoming a community-oriented problem. Aware of his own mortality, he challenges the limit of human achievements. Often, in the course of his full or even partial success in the external world, he experiences a maturation of his inner self. Through his laborious wandering, physical and spiritual, his (and our) scope of the universe, imaginary or not, expands significantly while his (and our) understanding of life also greatly deepens. Only after he has carried out these tasks is he fully qualified for the title of epic hero as an embodiment of human dignity.[16] Heroism is manifested in the manner in which the protagonist deals with the problem. Even the incompleteness of the hero's deeds enhances the total effect of epic grandeur, because it gives us a distinct sense of humanness in which the hero suffers from his mortal handicaps.

Hercules, for instance, is not an epic hero, even if we disregard the absence of a literary work in which he plays a principal role. This archetype of an extraordinarily powerful man struggles with his fate only to succumb to it and die in the end. The locations where he performs his famous twelve labors are dispersed through the geography of the Greek mythological world. The story of Hercules thus claims two of the proposed epic elements (struggle with mortality and geographical exploration). He overcomes his physical trials, however, out of personal necessity, with little relevance to the fate of a community. Moreover, his prospect of time does not extend beyond his life either to the past or to the future, while his deeds, not locked to a semi-historical event like the Trojan War, are perceived to have taken place in a vague, mythic past. The lack of the other two elements (commitment to society and an extended sense of history) disqualifies him as an epic hero of full standing, and perhaps this is the reason why no epic has ever been written about him.

Ovid's *Metamorphoses* might also serve as an example of a half-epical piece. With a chronological account of the world's history from its inception, the poem clearly exhibits sufficient spatial and temporal dimensions, dealing, as it does, with the reversed evolution of humankind and its natural environment from the golden to the iron ages. But, as the title clearly shows, the work finds its main interest in the continuity of life through transformation into another form of life (e.g., Daphne into a laurel, Syrinx into a reed) rather than in the discontinuity of life through death. The theme of such myriad transformations does not allow the presence of a central figure with earthly gravity. Ovid's poem thus does not meet a basic requirement of epic grandeur in the sense that, in its expedient rhetoric of perpetual becoming, the work eludes the stern reality of being and ceasing.

When irony is pursued for the sake of ridiculing the solemnity of epic grandeur, it produces mock epic. The three thematic elements of the epic are distorted while the serious tone is retained, although often in an exaggerated style. In Alexander Pope's "The Rape of the Lock," for example, the style is consistently lofty, but death is found only in the table battlefield of a card game. The seriousness of mortality is replaced by the frivolity of the main topic (the prankish theft of a lady's hair) and is dissipated by the ineffectual presence of the aerial guarding spirits. Communally, the poem concerns a handful of the leisured class. The scenes are limited to those of their social gathering and of a lady's private room, and the space is suddenly extended to heaven by the supernatural lift of the lost tuft at the end. Except for the lock jokingly hung in the air forever, there is no sense of historical continuity, with temporal duration compressed to a few days. Such sustained distortion of the three thematic elements, together with stylistic overrigidity, creates the tonal discrepancy essential to the parodic nature of mock epic. It is obvious, then, that the serious style which can stand by itself apart from the epic proper is not a generic essential but a derivation from the graveness that the genre's thematic elements produce.

The three elements of epic grandeur can also create an ironical effect when a writer makes conscious use of their reversed dimensions without holding to the serious style. For instance, in James Joyce's *Ulysses*, the protagonist Leopold Bloom has his own risks and worries as a common man. Yet his life is never really endangered, and he is not disturbed by the idea of imminent death. Unlike his heroic doppelgänger Odysseus, Bloom is a typical, novelistic hero or, rather, anti-hero in the sense that he represents ordinary lonely individuals who cannot help themselves, let alone their community. The double expanse is limited within the city of Dublin and within one specific day. Joyce's novel thus manipulates its overlaid Homeric substratum and reveals the paltriness of modern life by implied contrast.

Given the postulate of epic grandeur, one might question the "humanness" of epic heroes, especially those whose origins are partially divine, and who, accordingly, perform marvelous deeds beyond normal human abilities. Achilles, who is the son of the Nereid mother Thetis and the human father Peleus, immediately comes to mind. Likewise, Aeneas, although modified in prowess, has the same kind of mixed parentage. Similarly, the people of the heroic age, which Hesiodic chronology dates between the bronze and iron ages, were reportedly twice as large in physical size as present humankind. Because all these figures are superhuman by nature, it often might not seem appropriate to call them "men" like us. But their seeming unhumanness is nullified by their inability to overcome their mortality. Gilgamesh, the protagonist of the excavated Mesopotamian narrative, provides an illuminating case as an archetypal epic hero.

Gilgamesh can be regarded as the world's oldest extant epic, for it dates back to the third millennium BCE and clearly exhibits the three basic elements of epic grandeur: the hero's great concern with his mortality, the community for whose security he fights, and the wide, mythological space which he traverses. The story's sense of temporal dimension alone is weak. Still, it is told retrospectively as a kind of chronicle of the hero's achievements. Among its epic elements, the search for immortality in face of death forms a central theme.

The opening of the story relates how the gods produced Gilgamesh as a perfect creature. By endowing him with an excellent body and qualities such as beauty and courage, they made him "[t]wo thirds . . . god and one third man."[17] Compared with Gilgamesh, even Achilles is more bound to human limitations and less able to exert godly powers. Gilgamesh, the king of the walled city Uruk, is so strong that he fears nothing. Even his creators eventually relinquish their attempts to vanquish him with might. With his incomparable power, Gilgamesh successfully protects his city and people for a long time from all external threats, including the raging Bull and the wild man Enkidu, sent by the gods to destroy Gilgamesh. But when death destroys the life of Enkidu, who has become Gilgamesh's close friend and is second only to him in power, the mighty hero realizes the fate common to every mortal being:

He [Gilgamesh] touched his [Enkidu's] heart but it did not beat, nor did he lift his eyes again. When Gilgamesh

touched his heart it did not beat. . . . Bitterly Gilgamesh
wept for his friend Enkidu; he wandered over the wilderness
as a hunter, he roamed over the plains; in his bitterness he
cried, "How can I rest, how can I be at peace? Despair is in
my heart. What my brother is now, that shall I be when I
am dead."[18]

Gilgamesh then undertakes a long journey in search of everlasting life. After having traveled through many lands and almost
attaining his goal, his quest nevertheless ends in failure. In spite
of his more than half divinity, this strongest of all men dies lan-
guishing over his unavoidable mortality in the end. Thus, the
unsolved question *Gilgamesh* poses is how to deal with one's
eventual death. Other heroes in later epics, whether they boast of
their divine origin or not, and no matter what incredible deeds
they perform, can never avoid this question, either. Each has to
face the same problem in his own way. In this respect, he is no
different from ordinary people, and the epic, therefore, concerns
all humans.

   The hero's struggle with his mortality is also essential in
discussing the tenuous distinction between epic and romance.
The blurred demarcation occurs because the two genres have
many features in common. In the epic, even without partial divinity, a hero usually has some kind of extraordinary power, physical (e.g., Beowulf's martial excellence) or mental (e.g., Odysseus'
cunning and resourcefulness). Moreover, a hero often has a
supernatural guide and protector, either a divine parent (e.g.,
Venus for Aeneas) or a patron deity or spirit (e.g., Athena for
Odysseus). Some heroes are equipped with objects of miraculous power (e.g., Roland's horn and Odysseus' herb). And, in
many cases, the world of the epic is full of supernatural beings,
such as Achilles' speaking horse Xanthus, the Cyclopes, the
Harpies, Grendel, and the dragon, not to mention numerous
gods and goddesses. All of these are indeed the elements that
constitute romance.[19]

   But epic and romance differ markedly in the extent of the
hero's concern about mortality. The hero of a romance, greatly
endowed with special powers, via a magician and/or personal
belongings of miraculous power, survives many seemingly fatal
incidents. After foiling death a number of times with such magi-
cal helps, he does not appear really concerned about the immediacy of death. In contrast, an epic hero accepts the possibility of

death as an important fact of his life. He might survive as many life-threatening situations as the hero of a romance. But every time he navigates successfully through trouble, whether he relies solely on his own merit or receives some external assistance, death remains a grave likelihood. His serious attitude toward death is not diminished even if someone has predicted he will have a long life. In fact, many epic heroes die by the end of the narrative or soon thereafter, while heroes in the romance, especially good ones, often live to see a happy ending to their story and are guaranteed to have a happy life thereafter. It is clear, then, that Frye's description of a romance hero as "superior in *degree* to other men and to his environment" indicates not only that the world of romance is immersed in magic but also that the hero of romance faces his human limitations, including his mortality, with apparent aplomb. On the other hand, Frye's description of the epic hero as "superior in degree to other men but not to his natural environment" directly points to his mortality as one of his chief human handicaps that are insurmountable in physical reality.

The topical treatment of love also distinguishes the epic from romance. In general, love between the two genders almost always provides one of the main motifs in romance. A romance can occur with a weakened emphasis on magic and battles, but it is hardly possible to conceive of it without a strong interest in amorous affairs. In sharp contrast, in the epic, any devoted relationship between a man and a woman seems, at best, of secondary importance. The *Iliad* does not show much interest in the topic of love except for a few, minor occasions such as Hector's parting from Andromache. In the *Odyssey*, a divulged love affair between Ares and Aphrodite is used as laughing-stock for a feast song by the bard Demodokos. And, although Odysseus often thinks of Penelope during his twenty years of absence from Ithaca, his affection for his wife is not his only motivation for homecoming. His affair with Circe is meant to be temporary and does not involve serious commitment on either side, while his relation with Calypso is a forced one. *The Song of Roland* contains practically no element of love. This topical irrelevance of love can be ascribed to the communal significance in the epic, for a topic that focuses on the privately closed relation between a small number of individuals is thematically unsuitable for the epic.[20] Love in the epic, however, sometimes has a broader relevance beyond personal sexuality. Such is the case with Aeneas' famous broken "marriage" with Dido in the *Aeneid*. But in this case, too, the importance of their love affair is secondary to the poem's overall scheme, because it is introduced as a minor subplot to explain the origin of the Punic Wars that loom in the future course of the state Aeneas germinates. Love gains major significance in the epic only if it is elevated even higher and is translated into nonsexual causes with broad communal concern, such as patriotism, humanitarianism, and a providential favor.

With regard to the communal element of epic grandeur, along with Lukács' postulate, Thomas Greene describes the relationship between individual and community as follows: "The hero must be acting for the community, the City; he may incarnate the City, but he must be nonetheless an individual with a name. What he does must be dangerous, not only for other people but for him."[21] This idea obviously comes from such works as *Gilgamesh*, in which the hero is the king of a walled city, and the *Aeneid*, which concerns the fate of the future Rome. But there are many significant exceptions to the correlation of the "City" to the community. In the *Iliad*, this definition applies perfectly to Hector as the defending pillar of Troy, but not to the principal figure, Achilles. Infuriated by Agamemnon's conduct, Achilles keeps himself from the battlefield and even wishes a military disaster to befall the Greeks so that his fighting presence should be desperately needed. With such a motive based on personal interests, he is certainly not defending any community.

Even so, Achilles is tied to some group interests. On a smaller scale, he is the leader of the Myrmidons. On a larger scale, his heroic life means little outside the arena of the Trojan War, in which two communities seek mutual destruction. He has deliberately chosen to acquire fame as the greatest warrior during a short life, instead of having a long peaceful life at home. His power is such that, with some divine intervention, his mere withdrawal from battle puts the Greeks in danger of defeat and of a shameful retreat from the Trojan shore. At the same time, Achilles' sulking and inertia from active fighting jeopardizes his hope for illustrious fame. In this sense, the latter half of Greene's definition above fits Achilles' case very well, because "what he does" is "dangerous, not only for other people but for him." Even without caring for a community or a city, in his passivity Achilles indirectly, but closely relates to the communal dimension. Thus, even if the communal problem might not be located at the very center of a hero's concern, the work can properly be felt to be an epic if the hero is involved with an issue of suprapersonal dimension in an indirect, circumstantial way.

In the case of the *Iliad*, one might also question its very limited scope of time and space as unepical. As I observed earlier, the sense of dimension in time and space depends on a people's perception of *their* world and *their* history. No absolute standard determines which world–view is broad enough or which time-span is long enough for the physical dimensionality of an epic. But, one may still argue that, in the *Iliad*, the sense of time and space remains very limited by all reasonable standards. Achilles, grumbling over Agamemnon's unfairness toward him, does not budge from his ship most of the time. Even when he does, the area which his onslaught covers is no more than a mere strip of land between the beach, where the Achaean boats are secured, and the circumference outside the city wall. This area has to be called "a mere strip of land," compared with, for instance, the "world," including the underworld, which Odysseus explores in the other Homeric poem. Moreover, in the *Iliad*, the duration of time is limited to just a few days between Achilles' argument with Agamemnon and the burial of Hector.

But here one should take into account the spatial and temporal dimension that lies in the background. The Argives have journeyed over the perilous stretch of the sea, which is vastness itself to them, and they will take the same marine route to their homeland after their victory over the Trojans. Furthermore, by taking sides, the Olympian gods show direct interest and actively participate in the war. Because of their activities that encompass the sky, the earth, and the sea, the spatial dimension of the poem far exceeds the plain of Ilium where the battle takes place. As to the aspect of time, the whole story is narrated as an important repository of the glorious, "heroic" past of the tribes that were to become the Greeks. A heavy sense of history thereby permeates the work. These factors make us feel the epic expanse in the *Iliad*, even if the main hero explores little of the world during the limited time of the story. Although the *Iliad* is a rather special case, it is not exceptional in terms of the dual magnitude of the background. To a smaller degree, *The Song of Roland* shares similar features.

The requirement of a military motif may constitute another problem in defining the epic thematically. The description of war and combat is so common to epics that it naturally appears to be an integral component of the genre. Thematically, however, the description of martial scenes is not central to most seemingly war-oriented epics, although it provides many of their most exciting episodes. In *Gilgamesh*, for example, the violent episodes that prove the hero's extraordinary might are used to illustrate the main point we have examined: even the strongest men must eventually die. The *Iliad* shows an abundance of both gruesome and exciting war scenes, but it is obvious from the very first line that the poem is not about the Trojan War itself but about the rage of its principal hero and the consequences of that wrath. More remarkably, *Paradise Lost*, where extensive war scenes between rebel angels and loyal ones occupy the entire sixth book, advocates not excellence in martial competition but the bravery of patience and heroic fortitude of mind. Internal, spiritual virtues over the external, physical ones are stressed even in the case of Satan. Despite his Achillean stance, the scenes in which the fallen angel personally engages in battle are few. His major encounter with Death results in nonfighting and a new alliance. No matter how false it might be, Satan's heroism lies not in his external, martial achievements but in the inner strength, indomitable courage, and endurance with which he accomplishes his end. Otherwise, Satan would not have been regarded as *the* hero of Milton's major work by Romantic poets like Byron and Shelley.[22]

The dubious case of the *Divine Comedy* as an epic has much to do with its lack of actual battle scenes and the absence of a strong hero who distinguishes himself on such occasions. At the same time, Dante's trilogy never fails to fill us with awe and admiration at the magnificent view of the universe that it offers. Accordingly, as we have seen in the previous chapter, both Hegel and Lukács consider the poem exceptional as an epic. Hegel seeks the epic nature of Dante's trilogy in the poet's articulate, complete description of life in its totality. Lukács, in turn, considers it an epic in terms of the central figure's pure receptivity to the vision of the world that is granted him.

Presumably, as Hegel points out, military confrontations are often used in the epic because such scenes can easily introduce the national dimension. A conflict of nations topically conforms to our concept of the epic, for it naturally involves communal interests, puts many lives at stake, and often occurs over an extended stretch of time and space. The question, however, is again whether military strife of a national scale is the only element that jeopardizes or problematizes the way of life of a large group of people. Hegel himself says that a martial motif involving nations is the most suitable topic for the epic, thereby acknowledging the possibility of topical alternatives. At the same time, what he calls the greatest suitability of a martial motif is actually tantamount to the greatest facility with which authors can place their works into the zone of epic dimension through thematic treatment. Then, some nonmilitary topic might as well be used in an epic. But, in creating a work of epic dimensions, such a noncombative topic obviously demands at once an imagination that defies the fetters of convention and a schematic elaboration that gives the work coherence of form and meaning. The *Divine Comedy* represents such a thematic possibility of the epic. And if we approach Dante's poem from the viewpoint of epic grandeur, the poem can easily be regarded as a full-fledged epic. I shall discuss the epic nature of Dante's work more closely in the next chapter.

From the perspective of epic grandeur, one might be rightly inclined to consider some religious scriptures instances of the epic of peace. For example, the Bible, especially the New Testament, provides a humanity that suffers from mortal miseries with hope of salvation, and it strongly discourages the use of violence. The Bible also exhibits a distinct sense of geographical magnitude even though its events take place mainly in a small area of the Middle East. And there is a strong sense of historical continuity from the genesis of the world to the apocalyptic vision of the future. But, along with the other scriptures, I will not treat the Bible as an epic in my argument, because it is essentially an object of religious faith. Moreover, in part II, I shall argue that the later, nontraditional epic tends to either dispense with the religious element or avoid exhibiting it too explicitly even if the work contains religious ideas.

In the context of thematic significance, formal differences and conventional, generic distinctions are not essential in qualifying or disqualifying a literary piece as an epic. An epic can be written in prose as well as in verse, and a novel can be called an epic if it meets the conditions of epic grandeur. Furthermore, the only points that have been unanimously accepted as generic norms of the epic (length and the narrative mode) are not necessarily definitive. Although an epic cannot be composed of just a few lines, it does not always have to be as extensive as, say, the Homeric poems. The work can even be fragmentary as long as it shows a sense of human greatness through the three epic elements. It is also possible to assume that an epic can be actualized not only as a narrative but also in some other representational form. A play or a movie, for instance, can equally bear the name of epic, for what I am suggesting is a reorganization of generic fundamentals into a small number of thematic items centering on epic grandeur. Instead of deciding once and for all if a work should be called an epic, my thematic approach determines which epic elements a work possesses and the extent to which the work is epic-like. Thus, my three fundamental thematic elements do not offer a single, definite, inflexible definition, but pliable outlines for broadly circumscribing the nature of epic grandeur.

3

The Transformation of Traditional Epic

This chapter will examine the changing nature of the epic tradition. If the epic metamorphoses in the course of time, I would like to suggest that the fluctuation must be due to the shifts in the meaning and significance of the three thematic elements of epic grandeur—attitude toward death, communal relevance, and the dual dimension of time and space. Rather than external factors (social, political, economic, etc.), two main internal tendencies can explain the mechanism by which the change takes place. One is the gradual magnification of the three epic elements, the other is the internalization of the epic ideal. In other words, intrinsic changes are indispensable for the production of epics. On the one hand, many talented poets failed their contemporaries' expectations in bringing forth a great epic representative of the age, because they held too rigidly to the epic conventions. Their efforts produced nothing but the skeleton of the epic spirit.[1] On the other hand, each great epic involved some kind of renovation which allowed it to surpass its predecessors; thus, although based on the old model, the epic tradition was maintained by each poet's efforts to bring a new dimension to his work.[2] Harold Bloom ascribes these laborious efforts to the poets' "persistence to wrestle with their strong precursors," because "self-appropriation involves the immense anxieties of indebtedness."[3] Change, then, is beneficial and necessary to sustain the tradition. Through its own metamorphoses, the epic tradition continuously adapts to the changing needs of each age.[4]

Western Traditional Epic

The European epic until the Renaissance serves as an example of a tradition with a long, diachronic perspective. In light of the three thematic elements, the traditional European epics can be classified into three kinds: archaic, imperial, and religious. The archaic type is best illustrated by the Homeric poems. The imperial type is represented by such works as the *Aeneid* and the *Lusiads*, the religious type by the *Divine Comedy* and *Paradise Lost*. In each of these epic types, the problem of mortality, or of mutability as an extended aspect of mortality, weighs most heavily. As we have seen, the archetypal epic *Gilgamesh* already shows a human being's desperate struggle with death. Ever since, epic heroes have struggled to find a way not to succumb vainly to death, but rather to triumph somehow over it.

The archaic type, which C. S. Lewis calls the "Primary Epic," is characterized not only formally, by its oral performance, but also thematically, by the "background of meaningless flux" in which the hero finds himself.[5] In the famous passage in book 24 of the *Iliad*, Achilles tells Priam about his pessimistic view of the world although he enjoys fame as the mightiest soldier in the Homeric world. He accuses the gods of forcing pains and misery on human lives "while they / feel no affliction."[6] By comparison, the *Odyssey* offers a less pessimistic view of the world, and Odysseus is more fortunate than other heroes with a goddess' favor and his homecoming. Nevertheless, the world he goes through is a dangerous one, constantly threatening his life with snares, seductions, cannibals, monstrous giants, and divine displeasure. Moreover, Odysseus knows from Tiresias' prophecy that human miseries, such as deadly strife, old age, further wandering, and death, will befall him once he is out of Calypso's island. The Homeric poems thus illustrate an archaic epic in which, as Arthur W. H. Adkins observes, "over death the gods can have no control, since even kings, whom the gods must love, . . . prosper, die, and may die as miserably as Agamemnon died."[7] The hero of the archaic epic, therefore, is apparently overburdened with the problem of mortality.

Yet one can detect a kind of positivism that resists a totally nihilistic view of the world in the two works. In the *Iliad*, after ten years of war on a foreign soil, Achilles learns to emerge, however momentarily, from his rigorous heroic code of personal glory and sympathize with Priam, the enemy king humbled to beg for his son's body. In the *Odyssey*, Calypso's island, as well as Circe's, becomes a kind of earthly paradise where even immortality is promised to Odysseus. But his desire to escape from the fabulous island suggests his awareness that human nature is not compatible with immortality. Physically, Odysseus, with his daring spirit, would hardly be able to endure an eternal life on a tiny island. More importantly, alone, away from his fellow beings and his *oikos* or "aristocratic rural estate,"[8] his life has no other meaning than to satisfy a nymph's carnal desires. Confirming Achilles' view of humanity, Odysseus becomes little more than a plaything of a deity. For this ontological reason, Odysseus risks his life to go back home to Ithaca after twenty years despite the human miseries awaiting him there.[9]

What is truly heroic about the Homeric heroes is that, although their actions are mortally limited, they find the meaning of their existence by themselves, through hard experience, in the midst of a hopeless world. They have neither mission nor hope, since no external agent directs their lives toward a logical purpose, as in later branches of the epic tradition. Yet this sense of the value of life, acquired at great cost, distinguishes these works from *Gilgamesh*, in which the hero merely resists death in vain and does not acquire much meaning from his life. At the same time, both Achilles and Odysseus are fully conscious that the individually oriented values of their lives are destined to be temporal and do not supersede the inevitability of death. As the *Iliad* and the *Odyssey* illustrate, the view of life in the archaic epic is overwhelmingly tragic, while human resistance to the fate of mortality remains very frail.

The communal aspect seems of little significance in the archaic type of epic because of its individual-oriented heroism.[10] Nevertheless, Odysseus cares for his family-based social unit as well as for his Ithacan comrades. Similarly, Achilles, despite his refusal to fight with the Trojans, has a certain responsibility for a group. As the leader of the Myrmidons, whom he has brought from his homeland, he has a duty to his men, although he might not be a very caring commander except for Patroclus. The communal size of the archaic epic tends to be little larger than tribal, and the hero does not have a strong sense of responsibility to his tribal community in pursuit of his personal glory. In a larger perspective, Achilles and Odysseus are situated against the background of the Trojan War, in which two communities seek mutual destruction. In this respect, the hero's relation to the community is external and circumstantial.

Excluding imaginary locations, the spatial dimension in archaic epic is small, compared with the spatial dimension in later types. The world of the Homeric poems is basically limited to the regions in and around the Mediterranean. Including imaginary places such as heaven, sea, and the world of the dead, the

Homeric universe still seems more two-dimensional than three-dimensional. The principal deities reside not in a celestial sphere but on Mount Olympus. The sun, drawn on a chariot, hangs so low that an unexperienced chariot driver like Phaëthon can bring it close to the ground. To reach the world of the dead, Odysseus does not really descend to the subterranean domain. Instead, he sails on the ocean with the help of the north wind. In Vico's description of the archaic cosmography, the sky is located at "no higher than the summits of the mountains" while the underworld is "no deeper than a ditch."[11] It should be recalled, however, that what matters in the epic sense of geographical expansiveness is that the people whose culture created the archaic epic considered it immense. The temporal dimension is likewise comparatively short. The *Iliad* devotes its main story to no more than several days before the burial of Hector, and the duration of time in the main plot of the *Odyssey* does not seem much longer. But both poems exhibit a longer perspective in the background of the story. The *Iliad* is intricately related to the ten-year Trojan War. In the case of the *Odyssey*, Odysseus' narration provides flashbacks into his troubled past, and Tiresias' prophecy extends to the end of the hero's life. Furthermore, the archaic type of epic in general employs the sense of history by narrating the story as a glorious, yet limited part of a specific tribe's distant past.

The heroic code of the archaic epic, which tends to focus on the pursuit of personal fame, becomes incompatible with social needs when a society develops in complexity and requires strong control and an elaborate system to sustain itself.[12] Although a conscious modification of the archaic type, imperial epic is characterized by the increased importance of the communal aspect as well as by its more distinctive and purposeful answer to the problem of mortality. In the *Aeneid*, to convince Aeneas of the meaning of his toilsome migration, the shade of Anchises tells him in the underworld:

> "Come," he said,
> "What glories follow Dardan generations
> In after years, and from Italian blood
> What famous children in your line will come,
> Souls of the future, living in our name,
> I shall tell clearly now, and in the telling
> Teach you your destiny."[13]

This progeny will eventually bring forth an unprecedentedly mighty empire on earth. With established fame as the founder of this empire, Aeneas will acquire a kind of immortality, which is symbolically expressed by Jupiter's promise to his divine mother Venus. The problem here is not, as in *Gilgamesh*, how to avoid death, but what to do in the face of mortality. The solution is to devote oneself to a great cause. The promised "empire without end" will not only bestow glory on the race which has built it, but will also bring bountiful peace to the entire world.[14] Heroism lies in the attempt to overcome the difficulties which oppose this goal; consequently, the hero is expected to survive any dangers and resist any temptations until, guided by a divine power, he finally accomplishes his mission. With the ascendancy of a great empire as its essential theme, imperial epic centers on the fate of nations and thus has a wider scope of mortality than the archaic type.

Many later epics, intended to inspire nationalism and justify colonialism, belong to this category. Luis Vaz de Camoens' *Lusiads* (1572) is the most remarkable instance, in which Portuguese explorers "founded a new kingdom among distant peoples, and made it great."[15] This type of epic intentionally instructs the members of a nation about how to maintain an empire, and from this instructional point of view, the sense of communal duty is very important. Not only does *pius* Aeneas assume responsibility for the welfare of his people during their migration or expedition, but he is also expected to subordinate everything personal to the cause of founding a mighty empire for posterity, because, as Ernst Robert Curtius notes, "the great theme of the *Aeneid* is not Aeneas, but the destiny of Rome."[16] Thus, the hero in an imperial epic is not allowed to think about his own life in personal terms, apart from the significance it bears on his community. The hero's strong sense of responsibility for the security of his people as well as his insemination of the empire's future glory greatly enhances the communal dimension of imperial epic. Aeneas' instance shows that the imperial hero's relation to the community is direct and partially internal. In sharp contrast to Aeneas, Achilles as a typical archaic hero takes the freedom of choosing not to flee death in order to gain personal, soldierly fame.

As in the archaic type, the space presented in the imperial epic is sometimes actual and sometimes imaginary. The actual, nonfabulous space here, however, tends to be wider, not only because of increased geographical knowledge, but also because of its territorial expansionism. The universe as a whole also further expands into three-dimensionality. Unlike Odysseus, Aeneas goes *down* to visit the realm of the dead. And, according to Vico, "the heavens rose ever higher" with the growth of the analytical faculty of the human mind.[17] Manipulated for politics, time is also more ample in scope. The beginning of an empire is sought in an ancient past. Furthermore, in order to enhance artificially the sense of communal glory, imperial epic often provides an extensive perspective of time by means of a prophetic vision of the future, which some divine power reveals as a favor, and also by means of the scenes depicted on a shield or a city-wall. As Bakhtin points out, the epic prophecy in this case is possible only within the traditionally circumscribed future of a given epic.

To the writers of religious epic, however, even an empire is too frail an object, when they witness not only imperialism entailing mundane evils but also the collapse of one empire after another in the course of history. Not finding anything permanently stable in the world and searching for the spiritual fulfillment that no worldly values provide, they turn their attention to another world as well as to the interiority of life. Obviously, the *Divine Comedy* (1307–21) and *Paradise Lost* (1667) are typical examples. They persuade us to follow Christian principles in our lifetime, since our efforts will be requited in the afterlife. To the question of "what a human can do in the face of coming death?," the answer is no longer devotion to any worldly value but devotion to religious faith. Heroism means living with a firm faith in providence, and martial excellence as a virtue is characteristically renounced. Satan, who is the embodiment of archaic martial excellence, is depicted as a false hero in Milton's poem. The ideal of the religious epic is internalized into such virtues as love and mental fortitude in faith.

By its nature, religious epic seeks to comprehend the fate not only of Christians, but also of nonbelievers. *Paradise Lost* sees the history of all human beings as prefigured in the first parents. Similarly, the *Divine Comedy* supposedly records the destiny of all people after their deaths. Dante's journey as a representative, frail man shows every human a possible way for salvation. In a word, the community in religious epic is no less than all humanity, and the hero's relation to the community is symbolic and wholly internal. Religious epic, which comprises such a huge congregation of people, is very close to exhibiting the mutability of the world. In fact, *Paradise Lost* ascribes the beginning of the mutable world to the trespass of Adam and Eve, and describes in detail how, after the first humans are made mortal, the "changes in the heavens" ordained by God "produced / Like change on sea and land."[18] In Dante's poem, the dimension of mortality is widened even further by directly connecting the afterlife with Hell, Purgatory, and Heaven.

In relation to the vast community, the importance of history is obvious. In *Paradise Lost*, Christ's creation of the universe is retold by Raphael in book 7, and God's prophecy of His Son's final victory over Sin and Death is found in book 10 (633–39). Within the framework of immortal affairs, these temporal references stretch from the beginning of the world until its ultimate end. History is not exploited for a worldly purpose. Instead, the duration of cosmological time is explained from a religious viewpoint, at once cosmogonical and eschatological. Here, time is ultimately extensive, and the prophetic outlook goes far beyond the author's present or the limitation of a tradition.

On one level, the inclusive nature of religious epic tends to require for its setting the entire spatial expanse of the known world, as illustrated by Satan's temptation of Christ in *Paradise Regained* and Dante's characterization of Ulysses in *Inferno*. The latter is no longer the Homeric hero who roams the Mediterranean world, often against his will, but an uncompromising explorer who pursues geographical knowledge beyond mortal bounds. On another level, the spaces in the *Divine Comedy* and *Paradise Lost* are mostly imaginary and are infinitely expanded to the full scale of the universe. The spatial expanse of *Paradise Lost* is plastically dynamic with the rough, unfathomable tri-part of Hell, Chaos, and Heaven. In the midst of that universe, the earth floats as a tiny, fragile particle. As Paul Sherwin notes, "Milton's theocentric universe demands a muse whose voice is unmediated by time or place."[19] In contrast, Dante's universe is fixedly static with another three components—Hell, Purgatory, and Heaven— each of which is meticulously subdivided in a hierarchically numerical order. Milton's universe achieves the vitality of a living organism, while Dante's universe makes us feel the full weight of an edifice. Several reasons account for the difference: the prevalent astronomical view of the universe, the stage of universal history each poet sings of, and his attitude toward the political, religious establishment. In any case, one element remains constant: the spatial expanse is three-dimensionally enhanced far more than in imperial epic. Dante's poem is essentially a massive, structurally systematic attempt to give a coherent meaning to the universe, while Milton's poem reveals the meaningfulness of the universe through an etiological perspective. On the other side of such epistemological persistence to understand the universe lies an immense uncertainty about our existence.

One *topos* that typically shows the shift through the three types of traditional epic is the world of the dead. Because the need to cope with one's mortality has prompted the development of this epic tradition, the world that supposedly exists on the other side of death provides us with the negative picture of each particular view of this world. First, the world of the dead which Odysseus finds in book 11 of the *Odyssey* is no more than a repository of lost souls. There, those powerless, obscure shades, including the ghost of Achilles, perpetually wander in the darkness and bewail their fate, which, according to Nietzsche, suggests the praise of life worth living before death. The meaninglessness of their shadowy existence, however, apparently reflects the pessimistic view of mortal life that Achilles expresses in the *Iliad*. The purposeless roaming of the shades, individually or in categorized groups, stems from the absence of a supernatural scheme that consistently motivates communal unity in the Homeric world. Horizontally located somewhere in the west, this gloomy abode of ghosts does not appear spatially very large. Furthermore, the passage of time holds little significance except that, led by Hermes, the new souls of the dead are daily sent to the dumping site of human spirits in the shape of screeching bats. This trait probably develops from the Homeric view of history in which days gone by have no direct bearing on the living.

In book 6 of the *Aeneid*, the similar world that Aeneas visits with the Sibyl nevertheless refuses to be a mere convention taken from the *Odyssey*. It is true that Aeneas too meets many ghosts. Along with the fact that the place is now definitely an underworld, however, one essential difference is that it is also a place where some souls are purified and prepared for reincarnation, as Anchises indicates. In a word, the underworld Aeneas witnesses is no longer a mere repository of lost souls but a temporary depository where death becomes a part of the regenerative process for a specific communal purpose in the world to come. Each of the three epic elements converges here. Death is endowed with a meaning, now that life has a designated meaning. The community is specified and greatly increases its significance. This underworld is so wide and far away that Aeneas needs guides to reach and go through it. Thus, the history that has been made is wedged into the history to be made through the process of reincarnation.

In Dante's poem as well as Milton's, the meaning of the afterlife is even more closely related to the meaning of life, and the community is immense. Because Dante and Milton are greatly indebted to Virgil for poetic inspiration, the *Divine Comedy* and *Paradise Lost* are similar to the *Aeneid* in the sense that they place the damned in the subterranean region. Unlike Virgil's underworld, however, the spaces for the souls of the dead in these religious epics include not only Hell but also Heaven and Purgatory. Furthermore, these spaces do not serve as utilitarian means for facilitating the worldly matters of the living. Instead, life on earth is subordinated, through death, to afterlife in these spaces.[20] Consequently, the revived souls do not return to the world of the living, and the history of the past has no direct relevance through afterlife to the history to be unfolded.

Specifically, the underworld of religious epic is distinctive because the place is meant to be Hell where sinners undergo symbolic, eternal retributions. By comparison, the world of the dead in the *Odyssey* is not exactly a hell, because, except for a few exceptions like Ixion, Sisyphus, Tantalus, and Tityos, all the ghosts purposelessly roam the place in loose groups based not on the sins they committed but on the gender and social status they held in life. The *Aeneid* basically follows the same format, although its underworld also operates as a place of regeneration. As the types of traditional epic shift from archaic through imperial to religious, the sense of morality penetrates more deeply into the world of the dead. Thus, the motif of the world of the dead alone can metonymically illustrate the generic change of the epic in terms of the three elements of epic grandeur.

The different combinations of the three thematic elements also account for epics that do not exactly belong to any of the preceding types. For instance, *Beowulf* has many of the features of an archaic epic, such as the oral origin, tribal contentions, and the relatively small spatial and temporal dimension. Above all, this Old English piece is characterized by a strong sense of people's helplessness in an unstable world that does not justify their life. Like Achilles and Odysseus, Beowulf finds himself in hostile circumstances. Represented by such threatening supernatural beings as Grendel and the dragon, the world is dark and baneful by nature, and it incessantly encroaches on human life. At the

end, Beowulf embraces a sudden and harsh death after a right-
teous reign over the Geats for half a century. The poem also
repeatedly suggests the imminent genocide of the tribe after the
death of their good king. As W. P. Ker puts it, it is "Chaos and
Unreason," not gods and human beings, who are on "[t]he winning side" in the world of *Beowulf*.[21]

But, in spite of the overwhelming pessimism, a marked difference between *Beowulf* and the Homeric poems occurs in terms
of the hero's commitment to the welfare of the community. Not
despairing in the tragic circumstances and believing in his power,
Beowulf, within his capacity, does what he can to protect the
Danes and his own people, a trait that clearly distinguishes him
from Achilles, who sulks in his ship, or Odysseus, who cares
only for his immediate circle of people. With all his lifelong duty
and struggle, Beowulf feels greatly satisfied with himself at his
death, far more than Achilles feels temporarily when giving Hector's body back to Priam and with a far larger communal concern
than that which prompts Odysseus' homecoming. Beowulf's final
contentment with his life and death is a mixture of the archaic
human pride in strength with the imperial devotion to one's society even though a mission is not externally provided.[22] Without
this positive value, *Beowulf* would be no more than a gruesome,
gory story teeming with monsters, as Hegel describes the Nordic
myths. Therefore, although very close to an archaic epic in many
respects, *Beowulf* should be considered an intermediate piece
between archaic and imperial epic types.

In the case of Edmund Spenser's *Faerie Queene* (1590–96),
the imperial and religious types are combined, since one important message of the work is the sustenance of the Christian
world through the hands of powerful British monarchs. Like the
Divine Comedy, however, Spenser's poem is essentially a major
attempt to restructure the universe with an ethical paradigm at
the time when the European notion of the world was increasingly
shaken by various factors such as geographical expansion, astronomical discoveries, and religious turmoil. Episodes such as the
Garden of Adonis, Calidore's vision of the nymphs, and the Mutabilitie Cantos reveal Spenser's main concern with cosmic reorganization. Allegory and numerology facilitate the reorganization on multiple levels. Especially important are the words of
personified Nature at the end of the Mutabilitie Cantos. When
Mutabilitie claims her sovereignty over the universe, maintaining
that "[n]othing doth firme and permanent appeare, / But all

things tost and turned by transuerse,"[23] the judge Nature sub-
dues her presumption with the explanation of circularity inherent
in changes:

> They [all things] are not changed from their first estate;
> But by their change their being doe dilate:
> And turning to themselues at length againe,
> Doe worke their owne perfection so by fate:
> Then ouer them Change doth not rule and raigne;
> But they raigne ouer change, and doe their states maintaine.[24]

Transcendence over mutability rather than over mere mortality is
the main theme of the poem. The poem's community is no less
than the universe itself, entailing the immensity of the double
dimension in time and space. In this sense, the *Faerie Queene* is
representative of all European epics up to the Renaissance.
Behind the attempt at orderly reorganization there lies again a
huge anxiety about a boundless, chaotic, meaningless world,
which leads Gilgamesh to total desperation and Achilles to
valiant nihilism.

A steady magnification of each of the three epic elements is
discernible in the generic development from the archaic, to the
imperial, to the religious type. The traditional European epics
do not necessarily appear in this chronological order, but the
magnification of the three elements culminates in the religious
type. At the same time, the virtue promoted in each of the three
types becomes more and more internalized. In archaic epic, especially with an Achillean figure, *aretē* or "virtue" means "manly
power" or "valor," and largely denotes excellence in martial
affairs. In imperial epic, while the word is still charged with the
same outer quality, a significant proportion of the semantic range
is placed on such inner qualities as endurance and responsibility. Finally, in religious epic, where a Satanic figure embodies
martial bravery which is not a determinant in the war of angels,
the same word assumes an ethical tone and points to spiritual
qualities like faith and elevated love. I call these two tendencies
the aggrandizement of the three epic elements and the internalization of the epic ideal.

Two points should be noted in these two major tendencies
that occur gradually along with the development of the traditional epic types. One is the weakening strength of the central figures. At the center of the story, there is always a hero (or heroes)

whose actions synthesize the three epic elements into one totality of meaning. This does not imply, however, the uniformity of
the physical and spiritual qualities of the central epic heroes.
In the Homeric poems, Achilles and Odysseus are robust in both
mind and body. In the *Aeneid*, although he is a strong figure,
Aeneas' might is not so impressive. Less fierce and bloodthirsty
in fighting than Achilles, Virgil's hero is not the strongest soldier
in the Trojan War. In fact, during a single combat with Diomedes
in the *Iliad*, he is taken away from certain death by his mother,
the goddess Venus, who cares for his life. During his voyage and
campaigns in the *Aeneid*, he is more wavering in his determination than Odysseus, who is intent on homecoming. And, unlike
Odysseus, Aeneas needs the Sibyl to guide him on his journey
into the underworld. In the case of the two religious epics, Dante,
the literary figure in the *Divine Comedy*, is so weak, physically
and spiritually, that he always needs someone to guide and protect him during his journey through the three spaces of afterlife.
In *Paradise Lost*, Adam is also presented as no more than an
ordinary man with a vulnerable mind and body.

The other point concerning the aggrandizement and internalization inherent in the epic's generic transformation is the
central figure's strengthening tie to the community, along the
gradual enlargement of the communal dimension. The Homeric
heroes do not have much sense of communal responsibility,
whereas self-sacrificial devotion to the community is what characterizes Aeneas most. In the case of the two religious epics,
Dante and Adam do not have the sense of communal duty that
Aeneas does. Unknowingly, however, they bear a far heavier burden, because each of them symbolically stands for all
humankind. As a representative of frail humanity, Dante is
expected to report all he witnesses during his journey to his fellow beings in order to promote the Christian faith. In Adam's
case, the fate of all people is prefigured in his actions in the garden of Eden. In sum, the hero's relation to the community is
external and circumstantial in the archaic type, direct and partially internal in the imperial type, and symbolic and purely
internal in the religious type.

It follows that the central epic figure becomes weaker in
reverse proportion to the intensity of his tie to the community
and the aggrandizement of the three epic elements. The greater
the sublimation of the ideal becomes, the greater the magnification of the epic setting. In such circumstances, the hero who

stands at the center of the epic as a mere mortal cannot bear the weight of huge significance imposed on him and sees his physical and spiritual powers decline. If he can endure such an immense weight upon his single self, he emerges as something more than an inhabitant of the natural world, probably a resident of myth or romance who is endowed with supernatural power.

Exhibiting the heroic code of behavior, the epic affects people's view of the world and can function as a vital instrument to maintain an ethical society. This is why Renaissance critics like Sidney highly regarded the genre as the polar star of a culture. The epic then bears a special communal importance. In retrospect, *Gilgamesh* may have been once buried and forgotten when its culture was destroyed, because it provided no answer to the problem of humanity's existence. Without a lasting appeal to humankind, it could not survive historical turmoils. In light of the ideal, the three types of traditional Western epic might indeed appear as illusory products of Apollinian dreams. In one way or another, they are designed to "make life possible and worth living."[25] Against what Nietzsche postulates, however, the epic means more, because, being fully aware of the tragic nature of mortal existence, it has the power to move us toward the making of a better future. Thus, one can argue that the epic came into being in the West in order to provide people with a constructive view of the world. We will next look at another culture in order to examine the nature of traditional epic from a comparative viewpoint.

Japanese Traditional Epic

The viewpoint of the three constituents of epic grandeur also applies to the Japanese literary tradition, although the Japanese epic displays two additional features: lyricism and an ethical code that embraces death. The Japanese term that corresponds to "epic" is *jojishi*, which literally means "a poem or poetry describing things or incidents." Although an epic trend has long existed in classical Japanese literature, *jojishi* is a recently coined word to translate the Western counterpart that has an older origin. No elaborate, normative theory of the epic exists in Japan, because, despite the objectivity that the term *jojishi* suggests, classical Japanese literature is heavily lyric-oriented.

The first vernacular work of literature in the middle of the eighth century, known as *Man'yōshū* (The collection of ten thousand leaves), is an anthology comprised mostly of poems called *tanka* (short song).[26] *Tanka* is a form of Japanese lyrical poetry with thirty-one syllables. A definitively influential literary theory appeared as a preface to the next important anthology of *tanka* poetry, *Kokin(waka)shū* (The collection of Japanese poetry past and present) (905). The central ideas of Ki no Tsurayuki, who wrote the preface as one of the compilers, are found at the beginning:

> The seeds of Japanese poetry lie in the human heart and grow into leaves of ten thousand words. Many things happen to the people of this world, and all that they think and feel is given expression in description of things they see and hear. When we hear the warbling of the mountain thrush in the blossoms or the voice of the frog in the water, we know every living being has its song.
>
> It is poetry which, without effort, moves heaven and earth, stirs the feelings of the invisible gods and spirits, smooths the relations of men and women, and calms the hearts of fierce warriors.[27]

Somewhat reminiscent of Wordsworth's "spontaneous overflow of powerful feelings" of those who also think "long and deeply,"[28] the first paragraph speaks of the inherent nature of all creatures to express themselves in song. A *tanka* poem therefore refers to a spontaneous expression of emotions regulated in the format of thirty-one syllables. The second paragraph discusses the poetic power that irresistibly affects other beings, and of their capability of being affected by that power. The two ideas, the spontaneity of expression and the affectivity of poetry, considerably influenced Japanese classical literature in general.

Tsurayuki's preface is comparable to Aristotle's *Poetics* in the sense that both works set the generic criteria by which an entire literature was largely defined for centuries: the former by means of the lyric, the latter by means of drama (tragedy).[29] Apart from the completely analytical approach of the Greek philosopher, the main difference between the two writers lies in the fact that Tsurayuki does not refer to any epic piece because there was none before his time, whereas Aristotle discusses the nature of other genres, especially the epic, in relation to the tragedy because the Homeric poems constituted too monumental a heritage in Greek literature to ignore.

The problem of mortality, which always looms large in the Western epic tradition, has great significance in the Japanese tradition as well. In the case of Japan, however, writers did not seek a solution to overcoming mortality by upholding an ideal, as is largely the case with the European tradition. Instead, because of a national characteristic that tends to honor the defeated or weaker party, rather than the victorious or the stronger one, a completely different solution was proposed, one which might be called the uplifting of death. Generally speaking, admiration for the defeated side is not exclusive to Japanese culture. The *Nibelungenlied*, for example, presents the glory of a defeated, yet proud Germanic people from Burgundy. The first half of *The Song of Roland* shows the end of the proud Frank hero after whom the work is titled. At the close of *Beowulf*, the old warrior-hero dies while it is repeatedly intimated that all his toils to keep his people secure will come to nothing. Still, the preference for the defeated over the victorious has been so strong in Japanese culture that it has led to a kind of aesthetic of the tragic loser.[30]

This tendency has left unmistakable traces in Japanese literature and is visible in *Kojiki* (The record of ancient matters) (712), which is the officially compiled history of the Japanese mythological past. In Japanese mythology, one of the most popular figures is Prince Yamato Takeru. The main reason for his popularity is his tragic, early death. In spite of his divine lineage from the sun-goddess, his young life is exhausted because he has been ordered by his emperor father, who is afraid of his extraordinary might and bravery, to make repeated expeditions against several rebellious tribes on the four corners of the expanding, dynastic frontiers. Similarly to Gilgamesh, Yamato Takeru can be considered an archetypal epic hero in terms of his powerlessness before death, his devotion to the security of his community, and his wide-ranging expeditions. But his limited presence in a small part of the mythology as well as his failure to provide a solution to mortal limitations prevents him from being a full-fledged epic hero.

During the Heian era (794–1192), a deep sympathy for people of disadvantaged standing was an important general feature of court literature. During that period, aristocratic men promoted their status in the court mainly by marrying their daughters to influential families. As a result, Heian aristocratic women were expected to be highly accomplished in various arts, including the skill of reading and writing literature in Japanese, because refinement in those arts was a socially required condition to entice good, prospective candidates for their marriages. Meanwhile, although similarly active in composing *tanka* poems, their male protectors pursued the study of Chinese literature, which was regarded as a male domain. Consequently, most of the prose works in Japanese were written by women around the Heian court, and the authors' attention was very often turned to the sufferings of women in a male-dominated society.

There are basically two kinds of court literature: tales and diaries. In Earl Miner's terminology, the "affective-expressive" poetics Tsurayuki formulated for lyrical poetry earlier in the same period also characterizes these prose pieces.[31] In the diaries, the spontaneity of expression is typically manifested with descriptions of overflowing emotions. Affectivity often appears in the tales, where the literary figures are easily moved to tears for such reasons as poetry, seasonal signs, and human affairs. Furthermore, the spontaneity of expression takes the more direct form of *tanka* poetry both in tales and diaries. Social customs required Heian aristocrats, male or female, to compose poems on various occasions, often impromptu. This custom is reflected not only in the anthologies of *tanka* poetry, such as *Kokin(waka)shū*, but in the prose works that also include many poems. The two trends of Heian prose literature merge and culminate in *Genji monogatari* (*The Tale of Genji*) (approximately 1007) by Murasaki Shikibu. The piece is written on a grand scale in length and scope. But, along with the other prose works, it is far from the world of the epic because of its passive acceptance of mortal life, its very narrow, unchallenged circle of aristocracy, and its limited sense of temporal and spatial expanse. *The Tale of Genji* more closely resembles a novel in terms of its keen psychological insight into the private lives of aristocratic men and women.

In a totally different way, the preference for the weak appears conspicuously in chronicles of battles and rebellions, which began to be written around the tenth century. These chronicles are categorized as *gunkimono(gatari)* (martial stories), where emphasis is put on describing the tragic bravery of the defeated, rather than mere weakness. Although there are earlier examples of the *gunkimono* tradition, the most typical and important work is *Heike monogatari* (*The Tale of the Heike*, henceforth referred to as the *Heike*), which developed in the thirteenth century.[32] The work draws its main materials from a war which took place on a national scale between two mighty military clans, the Genji and the Heike, toward the end of the Heian era. The contention between the two families, both of whom prided themselves on their imperial lineage, was a struggle for hegemony over the nation. The struggle ultimately ended quite dramatically. After incomparable prosperity for about twenty years, the Heike were suddenly challenged by the rebellion of the Genji, who had been severely oppressed during that period. Within a few years (1180–85), the Heike were completely annihilated. The *Heike* treats this historical event with some fictional elements mixed in. As the title clearly indicates, the work does not celebrate the victory of the Genji. It is written mainly from the viewpoint of the defeated Heike, with whom it sympathizes. The work also shows sympathy with an outstanding Genji general called Yoshinaka, who, soon after having successfully driven away the Heike from the capital of Heian-kyō (Kyoto), dies due to factional strife within the winning clan.

The national predilection for the vanquished, which the title clearly illustrates, is essential to understanding it as an epic. In fact, Kenneth Dean Butler calls it "a true epic of major proportions."[33] Although the initial author has not been identified, scholars believe that the work was originally a written composition. At the same time, it is not unlike the two Homeric poems, because the entire work was recited thereafter by blind bards playing a lute-like instrument called a *biwa*.[34] It has reached the present length of thirteen books after a few centuries of textual evolution by multiple authorship, probably including those blind bards.[35] Thus, the *Heike* possesses the textual qualities of both an oral and a literary epic.

More importantly, the Japanese work fully satisfies the three thematic epic requirements I have outlined. In terms of temporal dimension, a sense of history permeates the work. Although supplemented later with a number of episodes, the *Heike* originally developed from an annalistic chronicle form and is dotted with the specific dates of factual, historical events. It chronologically evidences the ascendancy and decline of the Heike clan. One segment, which is a record of the shifts of the capital, also displays the nation's history from its mythological origin up to the contemporary period of the work's subject matter (book 5). Finally, the story as a whole is narrated as a turbulent, but glorious part of the nation's history, just as in the case of the archaic European epic. The *Heike* omits only the prospect of a glorious future, a characteristic often found in the European imperial and religious epic with its temporal extension through prophecy. This is partly because of the lack of the supernatural machinery that watchfully tends the growth of a community from the past through the future. Moreover, as in the case of the *Nibelungenlied*, which does not present a panorama of the bright future of a particular Germanic tribe, the omission is inevitable in a work that depicts the process of the complete destruction of a politically powerful group.

With regard to the other physical element of epic grandeur, the spatial setting of the work is limited to the Japanese islands except for a few occasional references to China and India that marked the limitation of the people's geographical knowledge abroad. This insularity is obviously due to Japan's separation from the Asian continent by the hostile sea. Japan was virtually a whole world for the Japanese people of those days. The idea is well expressed by the word *tenka*, which literally means "(the entire world) under the heaven" and actually refers to the Japanese nation. One should remember that what counts in the spatial dimension of the epic is how the people who produced the work regarded the meaning of "the world." *Beowulf*, as mentioned earlier, well exemplifies this point.

On one level, the communal dimension clearly manifests itself in the story's concern with the annihilation of a powerful family that ruled one nation for many years by another equally powerful family that succeeds to power. This motif of two large groups seeking mutual destruction is very similar to the Trojan War in the Homeric poems, and the destruction of a whole clan is obviously related to the problem of mortality. More precisely, the annihilation of such a prominent, influential group of people is indicative of human limitations on a large scale. In fact, the community which concerns the *Heike* on another level is the Japanese nation itself, because the story involves all kinds of people, including emperors, aristocrats, noble women, monks, courtesans, a huge number of soldiers, and the unmentioned common people who make up the rest of the population. The courses of all these people's lives are greatly affected by the military and political strife between the Heike and the Genji. In this larger sense of the community, the problem of mortality assumes the extended dimension of mutability.

The central theme of the *Heike* concerns the mutability of this world, and the fate of the Heike clan is presented as a typical example of the fragility of people's lives and the instability of their fortune. Even a powerful man like Kiyomori, who establishes and maintains the prosperity of the Heike clan, has to perish in the end, even though he unabashedly clings to life. The emphasis on the changeful nature of the world is deeply rooted in Buddhism, which does not acknowledge any mundane value. In this case, the *Heike* corresponds to a new Buddhist movement that occurred in Japan some time before the main historical events in the work took place. The new, religious movement is called *Jōdo-shū* (*Jōdo* = Pure Land, *shū* = sect), in which the present world is regarded as *Edo* (Dirty Land). The point of its doctrine is as follows:

> It was Amida, the Buddha of Boundless Light, who eons ago vowed that all should be saved who called on his name, . . . It was to the Pure Land, a special place prepared by Amida, that the Buddha welcomed those who had won eternal bliss by calling on his name, . . . [T]his faith aimed at rebirth in a land of bliss. At the same time there was a shift in emphasis away from the individual's efforts to achieve enlightenment toward an exclusive reliance on the saving power of the Buddha.[36]

In Buddhism, human life is considered just one cycle of the eternally repeated transmigration of the soul from one shape of life to another. Life is pain, because, in each span of life, we cannot avoid experiencing many kinds of agonies and sufferings, including birth and death. To be freed from the endless cycles of painful life is the Buddhist ideal, known as nirvana. According to the teaching of the Pure Land sect, one can achieve the self-effacement of existence from eternal metempsychosis by praying to the Amida Buddha with his divine name and being accepted by the god into the Pure Land.

The new religious belief, as well as the general Buddhist world–view, permeates the *Heike* from the very first lines to the last chapter. The opening lines of this work are familiar to most well-educated Japanese:

> The sound of the Gion Shōja bells echoes the impermanence of all things; the color of the *śāla* flowers reveals the

truth that the prosperous must decline. The proud do not
endure, they are like a dream on a spring night; the mighty
fall at last, they are as dust before the wind.[37]

The hint of retribution for excessive pride and arrogance here
probably has as much to do with Confucianism as with Buddhism, because, a little later, one finds a short list of the Chinese
despots and Japanese rebels who fell out of power shortly after
having gained it by force or guile. Nonetheless, the main tone of
these lines evidently depends on the Buddhist notion that nothing stays the same in this world. This strong sense of transience,
which is called *mujōkan*, stands for the ethos of medieval Japan.
In the last chapter of the *Heike*, the cloistered empress, who is
the sole survivor of the Heike clan, compares her painful life to
the six cycles of rebirth found in Buddhism. Often in the story,
someone decides to spend a lifetime in praying to Amida, living
as a monk or a hermit, after he or she realizes the unreliability of
worldly values. Other people are reported to be in heaven since
they, sentenced to death, called on the god just before execution.

Two inseparably intertwined factors produce spiritual values
in the *Heike*. First, because of the Buddhist influence, the work
impresses us with a strong sense of the fragility of life and prosperity, similar to Achilles' and Beowulf's feelings about the world
around them. To continue the comparison, the world is mutable
and meaningless, a world–view which is especially prominent in
the archaic type of Western epic. This view is also ever latent in
the imperial and religious types, and dominates the thematic
background of the traditional epic in Japan as well. In the *Heike*,
this pessimistic world–view itself is the integral theme of the
entire work, which consists of thirteen books and focuses on
several heroes. In this respect, the ultimate community which the
Japanese work supposes is the whole of humankind, and the
Japanese people in the story represent all human beings who are
subject to the ever changing state of life.

Possibly, the *Heike* was originally created to illustrate the
Buddhist view of a mutable world. Such a work, which does not
offer a solution in dealing with the acute sense of mortality or
mutability, would be no more than a piece of religious propa-
ganda. In fact, the book does propose one solution, which forms
the second factor of its spiritual value. This spiritual aspect is
related to the *samurai*, the warrior class of feudal Japan, who
constitute the central figures of the *Heike*.[38] As soldiers, they

have the potential to become heroes. But, in the book, there is no hero in the Western sense, no single figure who occupies a position of central importance in the story, because the story's theme deals with the vicissitudes of a great many people. Rather, many instances of individual heroism appear. Heroism in the *Heike* differs from that of Western epic heroes, because the work reflects a Buddhist view of the world and presents the practical side of *samurai* life.

Although the *samurai* lived in a society strongly influenced by Buddhism, they were not expected to run away from the battlefield, arguing that war is the vilest and vainest of all human activities. On the contrary, the religious view about the fragility of the worldly values worked with them in an opposite direction because of their strong sense of personal honor. Because they viewed the world as unstable and meaningless, they did not avoid a death that brought their mundane life to an end. They might even wish for death, a glorious death in battle, which would bring fame and honor to the brave soldier's name. An honorable death was considered to be a transcendental value over the extinction of life. And, since the social structure of the *samurai* was based on feudalism, loyalty to their lord was considered of primary significance.[39]

A typical instance of *samurai* loyalty and their code of honorable death can be found in the words of a dying warrior named Tsuginobu who fought for Yoshitsune, a young illustrious commander of the Genji, in the battle of Yashima. Yoshitsune asks his weakening soldier if there is anything which makes him unwilling to pass away, and Tsuginobu answers:

> There is nothing. I regret only that I must die without seeing my lord rise to prominence. For the rest, he who wields bow and arrow must expect to perish by an enemy shaft. And for a warrior to have it told in later generations, "During the fighting between the Minamoto [Genji] and the Taira [Heike], a man from Ōshū, Satō Saburōbyōe Tsuginobu, exchanged his life for his master's on Yashima beach in Sanuki"—that will be an honor in this world and a memory for the next.[40]

For this soldier, loyalty and honor are more important than continued existence. Like many other *samurai*, he wants an honorable death unstained with any shame, a death that will be preserved in the memory of his class. The soldier consciously wills his own death, not reluctantly and submissively as in the Heian court literature. Even when another *samurai* figure faces a death sentence and, following a religious custom, calls on the Buddha's name, his soldierly ethic influences him. When Shigehira, one of Kiyomori's sons captured in battle, is about to be beheaded in Nara, he extends his neck without showing any fear while reciting Amida's name ten times. The influence of religion is evident, but Shigehira's unflinching attitude toward immediate death also comes from the soldier's ethical sense that any show of cowardice is a great disgrace. Such an attitude is acknowledged as admirable, since Shigehira's fortitude is reported to have moved several thousands of spectators to tears.[41]

Indeed, many tears are shed on such occasions. This kind of sentimentality, which shows one aspect of the sympathy toward the defeated in the *gunkimono* stories, comes largely from the affective quality of the Heian court literature. The *Heike* also exhibits the expressive side of court literature through the many *tanka* poems with which it is interspersed. The affective and expressive qualities are often combined when a poem composed on an important occasion moves the audience to admiration. In terms of lyricism in the epic, it should be remembered that Hegel allows an epic to assume lyrical and dramatic modes occasionally if the objective tone is not interrupted to delineate emotional life. He likes to mention Hector's parting from Andromache as an example. In that scene, despite its being a tense, lyrical moment, excessive emotions are objectively portrayed with great restraint. In addition, one of the reasons Hegel places *Paradise Lost* below the *Divine Comedy* is the former poem's intense outpourings of internal thought. Thus, as long as the Homeric poems set the generic criteria of the epic, epic objectivity might have to be upheld at the expense of lyrical elements. The Japanese epic as well as Western instances like Milton's poem, however, poses a premise contrary to Hegel's postulates about lyricism and epic objectivity. The Japanese story generally has "epic objectivity" in describing people's feelings, and yet it also contains many instances of lyrical affectivity. Such evidence from both West and East suggest that, in some cases, lyricism can be an essential part of the epic nature.

In the *Heike*, several *samurai*-figures flee in face of death and leave a reputation stained with dishonor. Apart from the sense of realism which this kind of behavior helps to produce, however, these examples of cowardice contribute to the *samurai*'s ethical code of death with honor, because they are always found to be coupled closely with an episode of someone who shows the expected nonchalance toward death; thus they enhance virtue by contrast. One exception might be Kiyomori. As the daring head of the mighty Heike clan, he never shows any sign of cowardice. But his personal courage does not contribute to the ethics of the warrior class, for he clings to life to the very end and still wishes to fulfill his revenge on Yoritomo, the leader of the rebelling Genji. Kiyomori's case is thus presented as an example never to be followed. What soldiers should aspire to is readiness to die at the right moment. With such a display of fortitude and bravery, the *samurai* attitude should be regarded as one style of heroism. Like heroism in the Western epic, the ethical code of warriors manifests itself as a spiritual value for the *samurai* society outside of the literary work.

In both Japan and the West, then, the epic holds some kind of ideal. One crucial difference, however, must be noted. In the European epic tradition, the epic ideal fundamentally lies in life, and each hero holds to a certain meaning of life in the particular circumstances where he finds himself. In spite of great navigational difficulties, Odysseus willingly leaves Calypso's island, where he could be eternally at ease, with the sole intention of returning to his native Ithaca. Likewise, Aeneas, the imperial epic hero, does not choose death in the burning palace of Troy, nor does he choose to stay with Andromache in "Troy in miniature"[42] or with infatuated Dido in Carthage. The Trojan leader's concern is to survive until he settles his people in the promised land of Latium. It is the same even with the religious type of epic in which worldly values are subordinated to the significance of the world to come after death. By going through the triple phase of afterlife, including every frightening circle of Hell, Dante, as a Christian hero, experiences a spiritual rebirth and brings back the total view of the Christian universe to induce the spiritual rebirth of the rest of the living.

Certain heroes of the basically archaic type, such as Beowulf, Roland, and Achilles, seem to be different, because, in the world of ceaseless change, they do not hesitate to die for martial honor. As Mihai I. Spariosu puts it, their heroic code similarly "brings about a kind of negative justice whose logic demands that those who live by the sword must also die by it."[43] Despite the helplessness they might feel about their surroundings, however, these figures at least believe firmly in one thing:

their heroic power. This strong belief gives them pride and a reason to live, at least for the time being. Beowulf's case has already been discussed, but other epic heroes illustrate this point as well. For example, Roland, in addition to the Christian framework that validates his end against the Moslem aggression, does not blow his horn, that is, he does not choose to die until he thoroughly proves his soldierly merit against the unmatched, huge enemy forces. A more typical example is Achilles. He does not flee his predicted, imminent death precisely because he believes in his power as an unparalleled, mighty soldier and wants to make it permanent in people's memory after his death. In a word, his great pride as the strongest soldier gives his life meaning and makes him stay in battle as much as possible.

In contrast, the underlying principle of conduct for the warriors in the *Heike* is oriented toward death. They also seek worldly fame and success. But, unlike their Western counterparts, the *samurai* figures do not try to find the meaning of life in life itself. Nor do they embody meaning, except feudalistic loyalty and the behavioral code that encourages them not to survive a situation which would bring ignominy upon them. In such a situation, they characteristically choose a voluntary death. Sometimes, this death takes a ritualized form of suicide, usually known as *harakiri* in English, in which a warrior cuts open his belly with a short sword and often has someone else chop off his head. At other times, in a final moment of a losing battle when he does not have time to commit the ritualized suicide, a warrior thrusts his long sword into his mouth and jumps off his horse headlong to the ground. Or, before the rest of the troops are engaged in a major battle, a single warrior charges into the front of the enemy army. All these forms of suicidal behavior are sought by the *samurai* figures in order to prove their bravery and gain soldierly fame. Ironically, such fame is accomplished not by what they achieve in life but by the very act that brings their life to an end. The *samurai* view death neither as a fact that should be delayed as much as possible nor as a way out that brings early relief to pain-stricken life. Death thus achieves a positive value.

In relation to this *samurai* code of behavior that is oriented toward death, their soldierly pride differs slightly from that of the Western epic heroes. Individually, the Japanese warriors are weaker mortals than their Western counterparts. Unlike Beowulf, they do not demonstrate their power by fighting with supernatural forces such as Grendel and the dragon. In contrast to Roland, none of them can single-handedly turn back an overwhelming number of enemy troops. Unlike Achilles, no *samurai* figure is convincedly and acknowledgedly proud of himself as the strongest soldier. In short, none of them epitomizes the type of hero often found in a Western epic: a hero who assumes single, unrivaled prominence in the story *and* is fully aware of his importance. The superiority of a *samurai* figure over others is always within credible mortal limits. Unlike a Western epic hero, *samurai* figures can at most be powerful and important in the story only collectively. The confidence they realistically place in their human strength is considerably weaker than their Western counterparts; consequently, the meaning they find in life by way of their strength is significantly less. By readily choosing to commit a ritualized suicide or die in the battlefield instead of resisting their fate to the utmost, they give place, one after another, to other figures who equally do not claim single prominence. This easy shift of the central position in the *Heike* explains the book's large number of heroic characters.

So greatly enhanced is the significance of mortality that, in the Japanese work, a soldier often wishes good luck to his opponent in the battlefield. On many of such occasions, a high-ranked soldier tells his apparently stronger enemy of inferior prestige that he is someone good to kill for a reward and promotion. In comparison, although Hector would be unhappy to be killed by someone of lesser standing, he is evidently not willing to be killed by Achilles, although Achilles is acknowledgedly the strongest soldier in the Trojan War. At the same time, both in the East and in the West, it is a great shame for a soldier of important status to be killed by one of the nameless ranks. In the *Heike*, such is the fate that befalls Yoshinaka, who was once officially called the "Morning Sun Commander."[44] Yoshinaka's ignominious death, which occurs shortly after his brilliant rise to power, thus illustrates the theme of impermanence succinctly. By contrast, in a Western epic, it is hardly conceivable for a central hero to be killed by a lowest-ranked soldier.

The fundamental question which concerns the *Heike* is how to deal with death, a problem common to all human beings. As we have discussed earlier, the traditional epics in Europe propose three solutions to the problem: a belief in power, the foundation of an empire, and religious faith amidst the ebb and flow of life. Each of these solutions is supposed to provide a transcendental value above mortality. No matter how desperate the hero might look, the principle of his heroic conduct derives from the meaning of life. Similar elements are found in the *Heike,* in the forms of a soldier's pride, his loyalty to a lord, and his religious yearning for heaven. But the emphasis on the mutable nature of the world, not on the humanity that resists it, brings a completely different consequence in the medieval Japanese work, since these three elements are integrated into the ethical code of the warrior class and make the *samurai* consider a suicidal death the most desirable end. The essential difference resides in culturally encoded epistemology, that is, in different ways of perceiving a given world. Traditionally in the West, emphasis is placed on *logos,* the Aristotelian will that attempts to construct life into a meaningful system as it analytically conceives the world. In the traditional Japanese perception of the world, however, because of the strong Buddhist influence, people accept life as it is and do not strive to find a consistent affirmation of existence.

The Japanese tradition therefore looks upon a defeated person as more heroic than a victor, and this tradition is still felt in modern Japan. With its strong emphasis on the heroic nature of vanquished people, as well as its literary influence over the nation because of its popularity,[45] the *Heike* has elevated this tradition until it has become a major component of Japanese ethos. Thus, because of its three elements of epic grandeur and its warrior code of death with honor, *The Tale of the Heike* well deserves its literary position as a major Japanese epic.

After the initial composition of the *Heike,* the *gunkimono* tradition persisted for about two centuries and produced a few more voluminous books, all of which treat the Genji-Heike war or similar medieval conflicts. In other words, as Helen Craig McCullough claims, the *Heike* "served as a model for medieval chronicles of later military campaigns."[46] Those later stories carried on the tradition of a sympathetic interest in the defeated side. Among those works, the most popular figure by far was Yoshitsune. In the middle of the fifteenth century, *Gikeiki* (The chronicle of Yoshitsune) was written along this tradition. Although, as the title indicates, it is a lifetime story of the Genji general, the work primarily recounts his biographical segments not already covered in the *Heike.* That is to say, Yoshitsune is presented not as a young, spirited Genji general ever-victorious against the Heike, but as a dejected fugitive who has to be brought up obscurely as a beleaguered son of a lost clan leader and is finally driven to death by his suspicious, politically powerful brother Yoritomo.

Before Yoshitsune is given troops by Yoritomo to march against the Heike in the capital, his early life contains quite a few romance-like elements. Despite his beautiful, nonmasculine appearance, the young Yoshitsune always emerges victorious from small battles with his wit and might. After he reads a Chinese book of military strategy that legendarily endowed past readers with special powers, Yoshitsune also exerts extraordinary prowess. For instance, when he successfully fights with Benkei, who is an unruly, powerful monk-soldier, he jumps "blithely back onto the wall while he was still three feet in the air."[47] After he is estranged from his brother, however, Yoshitsune never shows any sign of superhuman prowess and is reduced to a very vulnerable figure who roams about the country to escape his brother's relentless pursuit. So great is his mortal downfall that, in the latter half of the story, the focus of the narrative shifts to Benkei, who has become one of his ever-present retainers. In his resourcefulness, Benkei helps his crestfallen lord to go through a number of dangerous situations. In the end, Yoshitsune commits the expected suicide. The hero's manner of life and death does not set a distinctive model for others to follow, and the emphasis on his individual achievements hardly relates to the fate of a large community. Because of the hero's mortality, his traveled space, and the distance of his time from ours, however, *Gikeiki* can be regarded as a traditional epic work.

Another example of post-*Heike gunkimono* stories is *Taiheiki* (The chronicle of great peace) (completed around 1370). This book concerns the actual warfare that broke out and lasted for decades in the middle of the fourteenth century (1318–68). The strife, similar to that between Genji and Heike in the *Heike*, was caused by the last resurgence of the controlled Kyoto aristocracy against the Kamakura shogunate, the ruling government of the *samurai* class. After a few years of frustrated imperial reign by Emperor Godaigo, the political initiative was quickly regained by Ashikaga Takauji, who was the leader of an illustrious Genji clan. Splitting the nation in two, the war dragged on between the northern dynasty propped up by the Ashikaga shogunate and the southern dynasty of Godaigo's line that fled from the capital. *Taiheiki* annalistically records all of the major and minor events that happened in the process. Consequently, the work involves the lives, downfalls, and deaths of many people, and there are many heroic *samurai* figures. The heroic behavior of the *samurai* figures based on their ethical code of death, however, is stylized from the examples of the *Heike*. Furthermore, *Taiheiki* lacks the great thematic appeal the *Heike* enjoys, because the work extends its historical scope too far by recording every notable incident that occurred during the long warfare. In other words, the *Heike* achieves a kind of Aristotelian unity of action with its theme centering on the relatively swift annihilation of the Heike clan. *Taiheiki*, by contrast, lacks such a thematic focus, because its size is inflated with too many incidents and episodes that are not well integrated into a meaningful whole. But because all of the three epic elements are fully present, this work possesses the grandeur of a major epic.

Other *gunkimono* works include *Soga monogatari* (The tale of the Soga brothers) and *Genpei seisuiki* (The rise and fall of the Genji and the Heike), which are both from the early fourteenth century. Similarly to *Gikeiki* which centers on one individual's life, *Soga monogatari* narrates the story of two brothers' lifelong pursuit of their father's assassin. This work thus idealizes what Lukács calls "a purely childlike" world of *samurai* vendetta based, in Vico's terms, on "the virtue of punctiliousness."[48] As the title reveals, *Genpei seisuiki* which stretches through forty-eight chapters basically extends the *Heike* motif of the Genji-Heike warfare with chronological detail as in *Taiheiki*.

After the fifteenth century, *gunkimono* stories which treat of medieval warfare ceased to be produced. Possible reasons might be the introduction of guns into battle in the sixteenth century and the rise of the merchant class in the seventeenth century when the nation's political center shifted from Kyoto to Edo (latter-day Tokyo). But martial, epic-like stories continued to be written. A typical example is a long, narrative story called *Nansō Satomi Hakken den* (The legend of eight heroes in Nansō) (1814–41) by Takizawa Bakin. This story resembles the *Faerie Queene* in its numerological allegory. In *Hakken-den*, there are eight heroes, and each of them stands for one of the eight cardinal Confucian virtues. *Hakken-den*, however, is more like a romance than an epic in terms of its often supernatural content, which is best exemplified by the origin of the eight heroes. They are fathered by a dog on a human princess (*hakken* actually means eight dogs). For this reason, *Hakken-den* is classified as one of *yomihon* (reading books) which exhibit imaginary, "romantic" motifs. Furthermore, *Hakken den* shows poetic justice called *kanzen chōaku*, in which good is promoted after hard trials while evil is always subdued in the end. This world is far from that of the *Heike*, where many good people embrace unmerited deaths because of historical upheaval beyond individual control.

Since Japan discarded its isolationist policy and its feudal system in the middle of the nineteenth century, however, no work that can be considered epical in the traditional sense has been produced. There are at least two possible reasons, external and internal. On the one hand, when the nation was opened to the West, various Western ideas suddenly flooded the country as it was rapidly industrialized. For decades, it kept many intellectuals busy to introduce those new ideas in translation to catch up with what was going on in the West. As a result, Western movements, such as Romanticism, realism, and naturalism, left their imprint all mingled on the history of the nation's recent literature. In one way or another, all these movements encouraged writers to concern themselves with modern private life. On the other hand, apart from the *samurai* ethical code and the Buddhist religious belief that urges people to renounce impermanent worldly values, the traditional Japanese culture failed to find a transcendental idea that concerns a great many people under the same destiny. Instead, many Japanese prose works, continuing the tradition of Heian court literature outside the *gunkimono* group, tend to be autobiographical and show a strong interest in personal affairs within a small circle of people. Due to these external and internal reasons, a kind of novel called *shi-shōsetsu* or *watakushi-shōsetsu* ("I"-novel) typically occupies a significant position in modern Japanese literature. *Shi-shōsetsu* treats autobiographical materials that are taken almost unchanged from the author's personal life.

Thus, the Japanese epic tradition that exalts the heroic code of a warrior society shows a distinctive cultural severance from a post-isolationist period when the nation adapted to modern Western civilization. In this sense, classical Japanese literature provides us with a perfectly comparative viewpoint precisely because it was bred in the local soil without any influence from the West. At the same time, if the epic is to survive as a genre in modern, cultural environments both in Japan and in the West, it must be revitalized through an imaginative will that approaches our troubled world with renewed enthusiasm. I find examples of such an imaginative will in certain European Romantic poems and in a Japanese work from the early twentieth century. In part II, I shall discuss these works as belonging to a new kind of epic that prefigures the full emergence of an epic of peace.

II

᷍

THE FALL OF HYPERION AND A NIGHT ON THE GALAXY RAILROAD: TWO CASES OF TRANSITIONAL EPICS

4

The Cultural and Historical Background of
The Fall of Hyperion and
A Night on the Galaxy Railroad

In part I, I examined the generic usefulness of the three thematic elements of epic grandeur; the nature of the generic transformations in the traditional Western epic, with its two major tendencies of external aggrandizement and internalization of values; and the main features of the Japanese epic tradition from a comparative standpoint. I have also shown, from a dual cultural perspective, the direction of the generic development of the traditional epic in general. It is now generally held, however, that the epic tradition ceased to evolve after the culmination of the religious type in the West and after the discontinuity of the martial story tradition in Japan. In Europe, many authors have attempted to write traditional types of epic after the Renaissance, but none of these attempts has been considered successful, because they are, in form and spirit, little more than superannuated imitations of their predecessors: either the kind of values presented in the traditional types (archaic, imperial, religious) did not answer the needs of the community, or the reading public could fulfill these needs with works already extant. In any case, the conventionalized works stagnated the generic development of the epic rather than bringing a new dimension to it. From this point of view, the epic seems to have died off.

In opposition to this generally accepted idea of generic extinction, I propose the notion of epic continuity. Central to this premise is the constant self-transformation of the epic that searches for a new identity as a peace-promoting genre. As we have seen, although war mentality became gradually weaker in Europe, as reflected in the three types of traditional epic, that shift of values has always been overshadowed by an indulgence in the excitement that military conflict or any other kind of violent strife provides. In Japan, the war mentality never faded in the martial story tradition. In contrast to such traditional cases, I suggest the possibility of an epic that encourages people to think in non-confrontational terms, making peace and harmony its utmost priority and concern. This type of epic should relinquish any self-righteous excuse for entertaining war themes while keeping a distinct sense of epic grandeur.

Such an epic of peace, however, has so far not been actualized and might never be. But the traditional epic's tendency to doubt its own value system and to disengage itself from being a medium of war has constantly been pointing in that direction. To prove this ongoing generic movement, I would now like to examine two relatively recent works, one from the West, the other from the East, which possess all the traits of epic grandeur and exhibit a nonviolent stance far more clearly than the traditional epic. I shall approach them with the same comparative method that I employed in part I. But because they are both left incomplete and contain unresolved problems, I shall call them transitional epics, only foreshadowing the possibility of a full-fledged epic of peace.

The two works which I shall analyze are *The Fall of Hyperion* (1819) by John Keats (1795–1821) and *Gingatetsudō no Yoru* (*A Night on the Galaxy Railroad*, henceforth referred to as *Galaxy Railroad*) by Miyazawa Kenji (1896–1933). At first, it might seem odd to compare two such diverse works, apparently so unrelated to each other. One is a British poem from the Romantic period. Fragmentary as it is, the poem, written in blank verse, is an inheritor of the English and European epic tradition. In contrast, the Japanese piece is a prose work produced on the other side of the earth, in a completely different cultural environment, more than a hundred years after Keats' poem. The Japanese work seems a curious mixture of Märchen-like fantasy and science fiction. In terms of their motifs, no two works could be more divergent. One describes the generational warfare of the ancient Greek gods, whereas the other concerns a small boy who dreams of a trip in the night sky. Above all, no direct literary influence has so far been documented between Keats and Miyazawa.[1] Although Miyazawa read, wrote, and even taught English and was familiar with European literature in general, no reference to Keats or his works has been detected in Miyazawa's writing. Apparently, the two works show little resemblance to each other, except for the obvious fact that they both remain unfinished.[2]

Nonetheless, it would be instructive to compare *The Fall of Hyperion* and *Galaxy Railroad* from the viewpoint of their unfinished condition. The immediate question is why these pieces are incomplete. Apparently, the two writers had to give up their major works, not just because of external factors such as their unfortunate ill health and premature deaths, but also because of the internal conflict inherent in the very grand schemes of their projects. In Keats' case, the entire Western epic tradition weighed heavily on his shoulders. In Miyazawa's case, his refusal to take easy recourse in the Japanese literary tradition deprived him of a stable basis on which to build his literary world. Above all, the fundamental affinity between the two works concerns the manner in which their structural edifices broke off under the sheer pressure of their authors' overblown idealism.

The Fall of Hyperion and *Galaxy Railroad* share certain traits that inspire us with a sense of human greatness, pertaining to the thematic elements of epic grandeur. Despite their utter difference in cultural backgrounds, they most clearly embody the dynamics of the changing nature of the epic in their incomplete status. I have chosen *The Fall of Hyperion* out of a number of Romantic epic attempts because, despite its surface similarity to the traditional epic, Keats' poem certainly possesses the characteristics of a transitional epic and proves itself a creation of its age. The poem's internal contrast facilitates an explanation of the new features of the epic. *Galaxy Railroad,* on the other hand, may not seem very appropriate as an epic because of its prose form and its apparently fantastic content. Nevertheless, Miyazawa's work is useful as a new kind of epic because its unconventional generic mode offers sharp contrast with the traditional Japanese kind. The external contrast will also make clear the features of a transitional epic.

Before undertaking a comparative analysis of the two works, we must first review their basic cultural and historical background. Keats' poem will be discussed in the context of the other British Romantic works because, sharing many features with them, it proves not to be an isolated phenomenon as a transitional epic. Miyazawa's work, however, needs a detailed introduction because it has only recently become known in the West.[3] Most importantly, transitional epic derives its self-consciousness, which is one of its important characteristics, from traditional epic, and this feature cannot be explained outside a historical perspective.

The Self-Consciousness of Traditional Epic

Along with the three elements of epic grandeur, I have
assumed that the epic should be constructive, that is, that it
should exhibit an epic ideal which can serve as an elevated moral
and spiritual standard. But when the ideal proposed in the epic
is extremely noble and apparently impracticable, some doubt
about its feasibility and justifiability in the form of covert, internal statements can often undermine the openly held, positive
argument of the work.[4] Just as self-consciousness is manifested
in many forms of modern literature, doubt about the epic ideal
applies to transitional epics as well.

Of course, self-doubt finds its subtle inception in the traditional epic itself. By nature, the epic epitomizes the noblest spirit
of an age and a culture, and that spirit is most heavily circumscribed by societal connotations in the most extended dimensions of time and space. Such superlative attributes necessarily
tend to make an epic work a strained structure, overcharged
with the ideality of humanness. In the West, frictions symptomatic of the generically inherent strain are already perceptible
in the Homeric poems. One typical example is the initial conflict between Achilles and Agamemnon in the *Iliad*. In this case,
the slave girl Briseis, for whom the two men contend, is not a real
issue. What causes Achilles' mighty rage is his severely wounded
pride as the most prominent hero because, as Spariosu puts it,
"the war booty (*moira*) is no longer distributed according to the
old standard of prowess in battle, but according to political and
economic expediency."[5] The supposedly absolute value of
Achilles' heroic code is easily violated by Agamemnon. As the
leader of the entire Greek camp, the Mycenaean king is by necessity more used to the give-and-take of favors and objects for
their practical value without necessarily considering the super-
imposed value of honor. He thus treats the heroic code as no
more than something to bargain with. Achilles' belief in his own
power is successfully challenged from the very beginning by a
force that denies the centrality of its importance.

Later in the story, Achilles' ideality is further put into question, when he invokes a disaster on the Greek troops with the
sole purpose of having them entreat his return to the battlefield,
and also when he mistreats Hector's corpse. The problem here is
not just that these actions are unseemly and egotistical. By taking these actions, Achilles declares his heroism indisputably

superior to the collective interest of society as well as to the minimum respect that the fear of the dead and the gods traditionally commands. Such "excessive arrogance to gods and men," as Plato puts it,[6] is hardly possible for a single self to maintain, unless he becomes a supernatural presence, a trait which the norm of the epic prohibits.[7] What saves Achilles from degenerating into such an impossible figure is his tragic awareness of the certainty of his early death and the compassion he shows to the beseeching Priam. Moreover, his words to the Trojan king imply his fundamental doubt of the heroic code of destruction he publicly professes.

The *Odyssey* shows the ambivalence of the heroic ideal as well. Odysseus' yearning for homecoming loses its innocence as a basic, sincere, human wish when he is repeatedly called "raider of cities" and destroys with his fellow soldiers other people's homes on his way back from Troy, the city they also sacked.[8] His eventual homecoming brings about the carnage of the suitors before peace is restored. Even his resourceful ability to disguise himself and deceive others is obviously a double-edged, somewhat questionable virtue. Cunning is a heroic quality insofar as it promotes survival in a hostile world. But it becomes such a part of Odysseus' personality that he uses it even when the situation does not demand it. For example, he unnecessarily torments his aged father Laertes by pretending to be a total stranger at their long-waited reunion. In such an indirect way, the archaic type of epic implies the problematic nature of the ideal it promotes.

Because its conception is fraught with political manipulation, imperial epic points to the fissure of its ideal in a more subtle, symbolic way. A classical example is found in the *Aeneid*. A pioneer of imperial epics, the poem advocates the expansion of the Roman empire and tries to justify the empire's rule over the Mediterranean world. According to a famous legend, Virgil on his deathbed wanted the manuscript of the uncompleted work to be destroyed.[9] Perhaps Virgil as a perfectionist wanted to annihilate his epic for purely aesthetic reasons, since he was "[c]onscious of many imperfections" in the work.[10] Although his actual reasons cannot be ascertained, perhaps he was unwilling to have his poem exploited for its ostensibly political purpose. Commissioned by Augustus to produce a work expressive of the ethos of the newly founded empire, the poet undertook the literary enterprise, but his original reluctance may have surfaced again as he neared death.

At least one internal piece of evidence seems to indicate Virgil's doubt about promoting Roman imperialism. It is the puzzling passage at the end of book 6, where Aeneas and the Sibyl take their leave of Anchises in the underworld. There are two gates by which dreams can issue forth from the world of the shades, and the unborn to the world of the living. One is made of horn through which "the true shades pass with ease," while the other is an ivory gate from which "false dreams are sent . . . to the upper world." After having given all his instructions, Anchises "[t]ook [his] son and Sibyl there and let them go / By the Ivory Gate."[11] The passage is very important to the meaning of the entire work, since it is at this point that Aeneas becomes fully prepared to undertake the destined landing on Latium. He has been inspired by the ghost of his father with "love / Of glory in the years to come," and taught about "Laurentines, / And . . . Latinus' city," as well as about "how / He might avoid or bear each toil to come."[12] The whole project of germinating the coming empire in the promised land, which forms the theme of the following six books, virtually begins here with Aeneas' readiness for that toilsome enterprise. With the Trojan hero led through the Ivory Gate, however, the whole ideal of imperialism, which the *Aeneid* is supposed to represent, appears to be dismissed as a mere false dream at the very beginning of the ideal's enactment.

This symbolic description of the beginning of the imperial ideal is no more than a slight and indirect deviation from the work's political scheme. Yet the scene of the two gates seems to imply a latent, but strong distrust of Roman imperialism, which the work supposedly intends to propagate as a certain way to peace and prosperity. The suspicion seems to be confirmed by several other episodes. Aeneas' desertion of Dido implies the justification of treachery for the great cause. The hero's violent slaughter of Turnus, with which the poem abruptly ends, does not promise peaceful means of achieving the imperial goal, suggesting that, after all, prosperity for the Romans comes at the sacrifice of other peoples. At the same time, the supposedly perfect image of Aeneas as the hero who does not fail to be faithful to his duty is actually often humanized by his lament, as well as by his reluctance to follow his divinely imposed mission.

A similar implication of self-consciousness can be found in the *Faerie Queene*. In this allegorical work, the Blatant Beast, which harms society with calumny, is still at large even after the poem's strenuous attempt to restore social harmony. By contrast, this kind of subtle undermining of the ideal which the work openly advocates is rare in religion-oriented epics, obviously because everything is ultimately under the control of an omniscient and omnipotent Providence. The divine machinery that keeps justice on a universal scale does not allow significant questioning of the legitimacy of the text's proposed ideal. In *Paradise Lost*, despite Satan's success in corrupting the first parents, the archenemy of God actually functions as a piece of His cosmological scheme, and the fall of the humankind is turned into *felix culpa* by Christ's intervention. All the frailty of mind and body is embodied by the central, human figures, such as Dante in the *Divine Comedy* and Adam and Eve in *Paradise Lost*, who are representative of the rest of their species. In this respect, a potential problem with the world–view of religious epic resides in the utterly irreconcilable difference between mortal and immortal as far as power is concerned, which centers on the free choice of human action. Without such freedom, and totally dependent on the Providential Will, human figures would look like "obedient servants" in Hegel's words. In fact, even this problem is not left untouched in religious epic. Milton's God, for instance, refutes the apparent lack of human free will by saying that He created them "just and right, / Sufficient to have stood [temptation], though free to fall," because, otherwise, they could not show any genuine evidence of "true allegiance, constant faith or love."[13] The divine will that keeps its creation under close surveillance for future recompense contrasts to the Homeric gods who, according to Adkins, "make isolated irruptions into human affairs."[14] The supernatural framework makes the religious type of epic overstretched, and yet the most stable in presenting its epic ideal.

Thus, although traditional epic appears stable within its own value system, it is actually interspersed with covert, yet perceptible self-doubt. In archaic epic, this self-consciousness might reflect the authorial viewpoint which, no matter how self-effacing the narrating voice might be, looks back at the ancient heroic values through a historical perspective.[15] The poet's contemporary concern is rather undisguisedly projected into imperial epic even if the subject matter is taken from a remote, obscure past. As a result, self-consciousness in an imperial epic means that the poet deliberately questions, however symbolically, what he himself writes about his contemporary issues. In religious epic, such questioning of its own value is almost completely precluded or suppressed in its cosmological machinery. This generic

heritage affects the direction of the later Western epic, for transitional epic attempts unsuccessfully to capture the stability of
the religious epic's value system. Consequently, insecurity manifests itself through the transitional epic's inbuilt doubt of its
own exalted ideal.

Japanese traditional epic, like its Western counterpart, subtly reveals the latent doubt of its own world–view. In *The Tale of
the Heike*, an obvious discrepancy exists between the work as it
is and what it promotes. As we have seen earlier, this work centers around two ideas: the transient nature of worldly matters
and the *samurai* ethical code. But if, as the entire story attempts
to illustrate, the world is impermanent and every mundane aspiration is futile in the face of ceaseless change, a long narrative
like the *Heike* should not have been written in the first place.
Whoever the initial author was, his great interest in social events
as well as his authorial ambition of creating a major literary
work contradicts what he overtly says in the highly figurative
opening lines about the sound of the Gion Shōja bells. Concerning the author's attitude toward his subject matter, Ishimoda
Shō notes:

> The author of *The Tale of the Heike* was deeply interested in
> many people who had struggled with, had escaped from,
> and had resisted against what, in retrospect, seems to be
> fate which had inevitably destroyed them. In other words, by
> narrating their struggle in a story, he fought with the idea
> that regards human activities as meaningless. Although
> seemingly contradictory to the author's intention and
> thought, that is objectively the case. Even though the
> author of the *Heike* appears to be swayed by a gloomy
> notion of destiny and *mujōkan*, he actually found the vari-
> ous ways of human lives in the civil war as well as their
> tragedies and comedies extremely interesting.[16]

At the same time, if all the warriors chose to pursue the ethical
code of suicidal death, a battle would be a huge disaster on both
sides, and there would be neither winners nor losers in the worst
outcome. The promotion of that ethical code actually presupposes the presence of a large number of soldiers who do not follow it, or who do not have to follow it. Thus, as a text, the *Heike*
depends on these two fundamental incoherencies. Because of
the sheer dynamics of the narration, however, the reader or the

audience usually does not notice such thematic incongruity.

In the case of *Gikeiki* and *Taiheiki*, such tension of incongruity between manifest value and underlying doubt appears in the titles. The title of *Gikeiki* (The chronicle of Yoshitsune) promises the biographical representation of the most illustrious Genji commander in the Genji-Heike warfare. But, as I have already noted, the work actually presents the relatively unknown, dark periods of Yoshitsune's life, completely leaving out his great achievements as a military leader. The description of his best days might be omitted because the *Heike* presents it comprehensively. In the latter half of the story, however, his importance as a protagonist is increasingly eclipsed by the feats of one of his faithful retainers, Benkei. Thus, *Gikeiki* as a whole inadvertently questions its expected premise of almost superhuman individuality. The textual tension that stems from the title is far more obvious in *Taiheiki* (The chronicle of great peace) which, after all, depicts nothing but decades of battles and deaths. The title might signify the historical path to peace eventually established by the Ashikaga shogunate. Even so, the irony of the title is conspicuous. This irony apparently casts doubt on the work's main theme, that is, the *samurai* ethics of heroism, loyalty, and ambition that kept the entire nation in turmoil for many years.

Such self-consciousness, which is covert in traditional Japanese epic, will manifest itself openly in Miyazawa's modern transitional epic as a result of his strong reaction to the warlike values that traditional epic represents.

The Fall of Hyperion and the Romantic Transitional Epic

John Keats began to write his epic *The Fall of Hyperion: A Dream* in July of 1819 (his *annus mirabilis*). By September of that year, he abandoned it and left the poem unfinished at the time of his death in 1821. This poem of more than five hundred lines was not Keats' first epic attempt. From the last months of 1818 to as late as April 1819, he had worked on an epic called *Hyperion: A Fragment.* As its subtitle indicates, this longer poem of almost nine hundred lines was also left incomplete. *The Fall of Hyperion* was a result of the poet's renewed effort to complete the earlier work in an altered framework. This situation raises the question of why Keats rewrote his poem after a break of a few months and why both poems were finally abandoned. A partial answer to the question is found in Keats' letter, dated 21 September 1819, to his friend John Hamilton Reynolds. In this letter, the poet says that he has abandoned the enterprise because he finds "too many Miltonic inversions in it."[17] Whether this remark refers to the entire Hyperion project or only to *The Fall of Hyperion, Hyperion* (the first version) is generally regarded as a rare instance of a traditional epic, in a late stage of that genre's development. There is no doubt about the literary influence of *Paradise Lost* on Keats' poem. Like Milton's poem, a great proportion of which treats the cosmological struggle among immortals, *Hyperion* depicts the aftermath of a large-scale battle between the rebelling, victorious Olympian gods and the defeated, yet undying giant race of the old hierarchy, whose king is old Saturn. The Titans, most of whom are now exiled from the heavens to the earth and are plotting a counter-rebellion against the new ruling deities, resemble Milton's fallen angels who conspire in their new dwelling place of Hell. In spite of new features, such as the materials of Greek mythology and the dominant statuesque stillness and silence,[18] the tone of the later poet's work obviously aims at the sublimity which the older poem possesses, through the combined effects of its motif, imagery, and style.[19] The last scene of *Hyperion* presents the deification of the infant Apollo, who is destined to supersede the powerful giant sun-god after whom the poem is named.

Although *The Fall of Hyperion* retains a number of almost unchanged lines and the same subject matter as *Hyperion*, the basic scheme of this later version is so greatly altered that it can claim its own autonomous aesthetic value. The style and the subject matter may still be called Miltonic,[20] but a conspicuous innovation of the new poem is its introduction of the poet-narrator "I." The whole poem is now told as the recollection of a vision which the poet-narrator experienced in a dream. In the dream, he meets Moneta (Mnemosyne in *Hyperion*), who is the goddess of memory and "[s]ole priestess of his [Saturn's] desolation" in the long-abandoned temple of the patriarch god.[21] With her guidance, he travels through time and space and witnesses the result of the war among the ancient Greek immortals, which is the topic of the earlier version of the poem. *The Fall of Hyperion* ends with the scene in which bad omens continuously disturb Hyperion's peace of mind.

On the narrative level, thus, the main difference between the two sister poems is that *Hyperion* models its narrative style on the Homeric tradition, including Milton, in which the poet does not assert himself; while *The Fall of Hyperion* follows the narrative mode of Dante's *Divine Comedy*, in which the entire work is related by a poet-narrator as his visionary experience. The contrast becomes even sharper because *Hyperion* lacks an invocation to the Muse, which gives a conventional epic poet an exceptional opportunity to proclaim the authorial presence and ideas in the first-person voice. This change of narrative mode suggests a possible reason for Keats' considerable revision of *Hyperion*. Not satisfied with his role as a mere, shadowy "voice" in the previous version, Keats in *The Fall of Hyperion* directly expresses his own view on his evolving creation as well as on his activities as poet.

Far removed from conventional, brief invocations, this extended, self-assertive display of an author's views in his work is a feature that was becoming common in the Romantic period. Such cases include William Wordsworth's *Prelude*, Lord Byron's *Don Juan*, and Percy Bysshe Shelley's *Prometheus Unbound*. These Romantic works are usually not considered epics because they are unconventional in presenting new values and new dimensions, while the standard epic ideals are often put in doubt. In a generational reaction against neoclassicism, the Romantics were all too ready to break with traditional literary conventions. I should like to suggest, however, that they do not dispense with the epic altogether but, rather, change its nature radically by restructuring its three thematic fundamentals.

For instance, the *Prelude*, Wordsworth's second longest poem, underwent an extensive, textual evolution (1799–1850) and resulted in two major versions (1805 and 1850). At the outset of both versions, the poem reveals an epic intention, including a few allusions to *Paradise Lost* and "[a] corresponding breeze" that inspires the poet with a longing to write "some work / Of glory . . . with some noble theme," whose characters will be "dwellers in the hearts of men / Now living, or to live in future years."[22] Other epic elements include lengthiness and the narrative mode, although Wordsworth's poem dispenses with conventional epic formulae such as military scenes. From the viewpoint of the three thematic fundamentals, the *Prelude* does not immediately seem an epic either. Instead of exhibiting a direct, communal dimension, the poem seems to be autobiographically personal, since the hero-narrator is always "I" or Wordsworth's spiritual self. As a result, its central theme is not so much how to deal with death and mutability, as how to bring forth what Wilkie calls "harmony, equipoise between self and environment."[23] The poet, in order to look into his own mind, seems to limit his external perspective to the events of his youth, which occurred in a small number of locales he knew personally, mainly in England and France.

A closer look at the poem, however, will show that the poet's intense gaze at his inner self does not limit, but broadens the communal horizon of the epic. The poem's concern with the process of the mind's maturation and with the reconciliation between mind and nature,[24] two entities which had been sharply separated in Western consciousness, extends far beyond the individual level. Wordsworth conceives of his experience in wonder-inspiring sympathy with nature and people as well as in bitter frustration with revolutionary zeal, not as a mere personal case but as "mainly an *exemplum*" for his extended community, that is, the human mind as a whole.[25] This is why the poem appeals to the minds of those who suffer from the isolation of the self in the socially, ideologically, and psychologically disturbing world. The dual external dimension of time and space, which weighs so heavily in traditional epic, is now replaced by the history and profundity of the mind. The introspection that absorbs spatial and temporal dimensions in the *Prelude* can be regarded as a further internalization of epic values, which gradually took place through the three types of traditional epic.

By contrast, *Don Juan*, which Byron began in 1819 and left unfinished five years later, contains many traditional epic conventions including two cantos devoted to "a little touch at warfare."[26] Moreover, like Wordsworth's *Prelude*, *Don Juan* conforms to the narrative mode and fills a large volume. But such conventions are certainly exploited and manipulated by a rebellious spirit. Throughout the poem, the narrator mockingly claims, directly and indirectly, that the work is an epic.[27] The Muse(s) are mentioned several times,[28] including a severely curtailed invocation: "Hail, Muse! *et cetera.*"[29] Such derisive use of conventions turns the poem into a conscious parody of the assumed genre. Furthermore, according to Wilkie, *Don Juan* is paradoxically consistent in the sense that it is "comprehensively aimless"; the poem reveals "an endless series of particular truths" that do "not add up to any Truth."[30] For these reasons, both Lukács and Bakhtin regard the piece as a good example of a novelized poem.[31]

Even so, Byron's repeated "epical pretensions to the laurel" hold a certain validity from the perspective of the three thematic fundamentals of the epic.[32] Instead of trying to achieve the reconciliation of mind and nature like Wordsworth, the poet in *Don Juan* keeps himself detached from his fellow creatures, thereby attempting to reveal every aspect of human nature in a satiric panorama. In this sense, although not directed toward some specific purpose, the work has a broad communal concern for the entire human race.[33] To bring about this effect, Byron uses two protagonists, that is, Juan, who is the central figure of the story, and the narrator, who appears to be a mouthpiece of the satirical poet. Through the young hero's wandering that exposes the evils and peculiarities of many societies, the poem reveals its geographical dimension. As in the *Prelude*, the time span of this work is shortened to the life of one person (Juan), because, in an open defiance of the *in medias res* technique,[34] the poem begins with his birth, proceeds chronologically with the events of his life, and is supposed to end with his untimely death. At the same time, the highly sarcastic comments that the narrator makes with his almost unstoppable digressions do not abide any spatial and temporal limitations. As for mortality or mutability, they are not prominent themes since the work is primarily concerned with showing the variety of human lives. Nevertheless, the poem essentially concerns men and women who appear on the stage of life only to fade away after a short while, for the narrator is aware that "nought was lasting, but now even / Change grows too changeable, without being new."[35]

Even more so than the *Prelude* and *Don Juan*, Shelley's *Prometheus Unbound* (1820) appears at first to be anything but an epic with regard to its form and figure. Subtitled *A Lyrical Drama in Four Acts*, Shelley's work is not written in the narrative mode, although it is apparently not intended for an actual presentation on the stage either. The unfragmented poem is relatively short. Moreover, inasmuch as all the principal characters are not people but "everliving Gods" or spirits,[36] the work might better be called a myth, which, as the poet acknowledges in the preface, was syncretized from Greek mythology with poetic license. Furthermore, the poem contains no show of violence except for the painful visions imposed on the fettered Titan by the Furies in act 1 and the sudden overthrow of Jupiter by Demogorgon in the first scene of act 3.

Nonetheless, the sheer magnitude of the work's conception as well as its concern with human sufferings intrinsically demands a term other than drama or myth, for the poem shows an indirect, yet significant communal concern. *Prometheus Unbound* is essentially a manifestation of the poet's unfulfilled political desire for an ideal world which is enacted by his unhindered, imaginative mythopoeia. He wants neither the reunion of mind and nature, nor a satiric overview of human nature. Instead, he wishes to reform the entire universe by expelling all authority that manipulates hate, power, and differentiation. At the end of act 4, the poetic drama creates a completely new reality, "a great democratic organism" as John Ower puts it,[37] in which every constituent of the universe, including even insentient elements, participates equally in an assembly of the cosmic "great Republic."[38] In this immense scheme, we can clearly perceive Shelley's interest in the welfare of the extended community, in which *unbinding* the human mind from a hatred-based domination comes foremost. In fact, the poem's most important turning point already takes place in act 1 when Prometheus renounces his old curse on Jupiter. This pity for his oppressor, which signifies a conceptual revolution, irrevocably subverts the *ancien régime* of the mind and ushers in the avalanche-like collapse of that system.

By way of comparison, *Paradise Lost* as a typical religious epic also has an extremely large scope of community in the creation of the world. Before the fall of man, everything is peaceful, and after the fall, everything shares the corruption of man. This does not mean, however, that nonhuman beings, animate or inanimate, are regarded as fellow creatures that constitute a significant part of one immense community. They are not equal with, but are subject to human beings, as Adam's naming of the animals symbolically illustrates (8.338–54). In a word, communally, the anthropocentrism in *Paradise Lost* marginalizes nonhuman creatures in contrast to their egalitarian inclusion in Shelley's work.

In *Prometheus Unbound*, along with the community, the other elements of epic grandeur are developed far beyond almost anything we find in literature. As the phrase "Heaven-oppressed mortality" indicates,[39] the gravest problem in human existence is not death itself but the acceptance of spiritual tyranny. The destructive force of mutability is annulled in the anarchically harmonious universe, which is the last phase of the world's evolution, and in which nothing perishes after "[t]he shadow of white Death has past" the lunar orbit.[40] Spatial immensity is evident in the mythical surroundings of the poem. In addition to the interspersed allusions to the theogonic genesis of the universe, a sense of history permeates the work that starts with the very last stage of Prometheus' sufferings of "[t]hree thousand years of sleep-unsheltered hours / And moments" and ends with the everlasting harmony of the last act.[41]

It is clear then that, in these examples from the Romantic period, one can still recognize the three thematic elements of traditional epic, although in a transformed configuration. The most noticeable transformation is that the problem of mortality is not so central to the Romantic works as it is to traditional epic. This shift in the epic's central concern seems largely due to Romantic idealism, in which the improvement of human life and the surrounding world through the exercise of poetic power is far more significant than any other set values such as religious faith or the sustenance of an empire. Such idealism is more fully revealed in the communal dimension. In Shelley's case, his ideal world in *Prometheus Unbound* does not abide any social or even physical differentiation in forms of existence. In the case of Wordsworth and Byron, although their works are very different from each other, they share an indirect, but profound interest in all of humanity. The paradox is that, in each case, the community is expanded via the intense gaze at the mind, directly with Wordsworth, generally with Byron, and symbolically with Shelley. The spatial dimension is either deeply internalized as in the *Prelude*, or far widened in the double exploration by the hero and the narrator as in *Don Juan*, and in the mythical and cosmic expansion of Shelley's poem. In *Prometheus Unbound*, the temporal expanse is cosmological, a sharp contrast to the short time spans in the other two poems. In these cases, the limited scope of time either overlaps an inner history of one's maturing self or deliberately defies an established, literary norm. In *Don Juan*, however, Byron also makes full use of the digressive freedom of an independent narrative voice to circumvent the temporal limitation of the main plot.

These Romantic works have another noticeable feature in common: the absence of a strong hero. The central figure in each poem cannot be called a typical epic hero of great might, either physical or spiritual. Wordsworth's entire poem depends on the presence of the narrator "I" who has nothing to do with martial or spectacular exploits. Thus, the poem's communal concern is expressed solely and indirectly through the poet's personal experiences. As Wilkie argues, his "heroic ideal does not consist in self-sacrifice, but in self-fulfillment."[42] Likewise, in Byron's poem, Juan does not possess a strong character despite his heroism in battle and elsewhere. The young man is naive at best. Often, the narrator occupies a more important role through his obtrusive nature that stimulates the digressive process of the work's development. In the case of *Prometheus Unbound*, there is no military extravagance, and Prometheus' hateful defiance of Jupiter does not solve anything. But heroism exists. Similar to the virtues advocated in religious epic, it is the heroism of patience, courage, and, above all, love. Significantly, this heroism is not centered on a single protagonist but is divided between equally significant male and female principles. We perceive heroic conduct not only in Prometheus' endurance and ultimate tolerance, but also in Asia's love of all creatures and her courage to explore the subterranean domain of Demogorgon. Forming the nucleus that revitalizes the world, the harmonious reunion of the two gender principles enhances the theme of universal egalitarianism.

As Bloom postulates, each poet makes laborious efforts to emulate his predecessors with established fame. In the case of these Romantic poets, the immediate target worthy of emulation turned out to be Milton, whose *Paradise Lost* had appeared as a religious epic of the grand scale during the last phase of the generic transformation of traditional epic. The Romantic poets tried to create works that matched or even surpassed the dimensions of Milton's poem while offering a specific, nonreligious, spiritual ideal. Consequently, they developed important elements from traditional epic. They inherit, especially from religious epic, the internalization of values, the deep concern for the whole of humanity, and the expanded view of the world without being particularly religious. These works, however, are not full-fledged epics of peace, but transitional ones, basically because they leave their ironic tendencies unresolved. Although the *Prelude* occasionally shows indignation at social injustice and inequality, it focuses not on the promotion of a peaceful mentality but on the growth of the mind. *Don Juan* still contains war motifs. *Prometheus Unbound* comes the closest to an epic of peace, but it still introduces a few violent moments, while its central figures are deities who, though humanized to some extent, do not have to face mortality.

The Romantic shift from the traditional to transitional epic exhibits the two tendencies also present in the gradual transformation of the traditional types of epic: the internalization of an advocated virtue and the magnification of the three elements of epic grandeur. Collectively, the Romantic poems take these two tendencies a step further than religious epic. In some way, they are all introspective. Wordsworth's poem is even more intense than a traditional, religious epic in exploring the potential power of the mind. Byron's work expands the role of the narrator (the poet's persona) as far as possible. Shelley represents the problem of the mind in mythic symbolism. At the same time, unlike religious epic with its set virtue of steadfast faith, the Romantic transitional epic has personalized the internalized value depending on each author's specific interest.

On the whole, the three elements of epic grandeur are magnified in these transitional epics. The community which the poet envisions tends to be no less than the totality of all human beings, or even broader with nonhuman beings. Although still significant, the problem of mortality and mutability turns secondary as the poet's concern with the community becomes foremost. Because of the personalized value system, one can notice disparity in the aggrandizement of the dual dimension of time and space. It is spiritually profound with Wordsworth, while both topically and geographically widened with Byron. In Shelley, both time and space are as extensive as they could be in any traditional type of epic. In this particular case, the poet's intention even defies the narrative mode, which shows that a transitional epic does not necessarily depend on this most basic of traditional epic convention.

At the same time, the Romantic poets' efforts at such an immense epic project often ended in frustration, perhaps caused by what Bloom calls the "anxiety of influence."[43] The fundamental problem lies in their attempts to create works as dimensionally grand as religious epic without relying on the structural stability that religious faith and its view of the universe provide. Consequently, two of the works result in some form of textual indeterminacy: either in fragmentariness with Byron or in double/multiple textuality with Wordsworth. In contrast, Shelley's poem barely keeps textual wholeness despite the unprecedented magnitude of its scope. Not depending on conventional, direct narration by the poet, most of *Prometheus Unbound*'s important parts are delivered in reports by the characters (i.e., indirect narration), in metaphysical dialogues, and, above all, in the sharing of dream visions (i.e., nonlingual communication). Without such modes of representation, *Prometheus Unbound* would either have lost its sublimity or have collapsed to pieces because of its own overlofty conception.

In general, the personalized ideal that should redeem the world and the magnified dimensions weigh too heavily on the central figure whose action is supposed to give organic coherence to the entire work. To bear such an impossible burden, the hero would have to be more than a mere mortal. Instead, the intense, schematic pressure of the two opposite directions, internalization and aggrandizement, has the effect of forging him into a hero of diluted capacity. In turn, the presence of such a weak hero at the center of the story further helps to make the literary text an unstable structure. The internalization of the epic ideal also reduces a martial motif of extrinsic virtue to a lesser theme which is either dispensable or unnecessary. In conclusion, the strain inherent in the grand schema of the epic, which has steadily grown through the generic development of the traditional types, is finally causing textual fractures and the further weakening of the hero. These two features characterize the self-consuming nature of the Romantic epic works in general. We shall see shortly that Keats' *Fall of Hyperion* perfectly fits this Romantic creative problem as well.

A Night on the Galaxy Railroad: Textual Background

A Night on the Galaxy Railroad, begun around 1924 and left unfinished by the author's death in 1933, is a short prose narrative. In the Japanese edition I have used here, the work has no more than seventy pages. The title sounds like that of a fantasy science fiction novel, and the story has elements of a children's tale. The central figure is Giovanni, a child who appears to be in an upper grade of an elementary school.[44] His father, who is a fisherman working on a distant, foreign northern sea, reportedly has been held in custody on the charge of poaching. With his father absent and his sick mother lying in bed at home, the burden of supporting the family falls on the small boy. Every morning before school, Giovanni delivers newspapers, and he also works as a part-time typesetter in a print shop after school. Always tired, he is often absent-minded at school. His close friend Campanella sympathizes with him, but some of his other classmates jeer at him, making him feel sad and miserable. One evening, during the Festival of the Galaxy (or the

Festival of the Centaur) celebrated by children with delight, Giovanni, humiliated once again by his classmates, does not feel like participating and instead goes alone to the top of a hill just outside the town. There he falls asleep and has a dream.

In this dream, he finds himself traveling with Campanella, who is inexplicably pale at first, on a small train which rides on a line called *Gingatetsudō* (the Galaxy Railroad) through stars and constellations from the north to the south of the firmament. The two boys wonder at the beautiful scenes passing by outside the train window, including fields, rivers, and forests, of the night sky. Getting off the train at the Station of the Swan, they make a short trip to the banks of a river, the *ama no gawa* (the river of the sky, the Milky Way).[45] They talk with a scholar who is conducting an excavation for his research on a bank called the Pliocene Coast. Back on the train, they see various kinds of passengers, such as a birdcatcher and a lighthouse keeper. When a conductor comes to check the passengers' tickets, Giovanni finds in his pocket a very special pass which enables him to travel not only through the strange space they are in now, but also anywhere he likes, even to heaven.

Soon, three new passengers—a girl about the boys' age, her small brother, and their young tutor—suddenly appear on the train and join the boys. The newcomers turn out to have sacrificed their lives to save other people in a sinking boat and are now on their way to "heaven." Their story makes the boys think about the nature of real happiness. Jealous of the girl who talks amiably with Campanella, Giovanni wishes, however, that the three newcomers would go away. They eventually disembark, with many other people, at the Southern Cross, which serves as the entrance to the Christian heaven. After the train leaves the station, Giovanni finds that Campanella, who had just promised to go with him to the end of the trip, suddenly disappears, apparently to be reunited with his mother. Left alone, Giovanni weeps bitterly.

Waking up, he finds himself lying on the grass of the hill. On his way home, he perceives many people gathered at the riverside. He hears the news that Campanella, after having saved a drowning friend, was himself drowned, and that his body has not been recovered yet. Hearing from Campanella's father that his own father will soon come back home from the northern sea, Giovanni hastens to his house with mixed feelings.

As it is clear from this brief summary, *Galaxy Railroad* is divided into three sections: before the dream, during the dream, and after the dream. But the textual history reveals much more complexity of plot elaboration. Due to the author's continuous revisions, at least four main manuscripts of *Galaxy Railroad* exist. Out of the four manuscripts, the last two are important textually because of their substantial bulk and relative completion of the plots, while the two earliest are short fragments. In the two early manuscripts, the first half of the story is missing and they begin abruptly in the middle of the dream. Following the critical practice in Japan, we will, therefore, call the third manuscript "the early version," the fourth "the later version," and refer to the first two fragmentary versions only when necessary.[46] The above account is a summary of the later version.

Apart from numerous small stylistic changes, the early version differs from the later version in three significant respects. First, the early version lacks the school, print shop, and home scenes that comprise the first three sections of the later version. Instead, it begins with Giovanni heading for a milk-shop to get undelivered milk for his sick mother on the evening of the star festival. In this beginning, he delivers a long, internal monologue about the ostracized self. In the later version, not only does this particular scene follow the three introductory scenes, but also Giovanni's introvert thinking prevalent in that scene is greatly reduced. With the added scenes providing us with the vivid details of the boy's situation in his town, Giovanni's initial sense of alienation is substantially objectified by this reduction.

Second, the early version has a different ending. When Giovanni cries because of Campanella's sudden disappearance from the train, instead of waking up immediately, he is consoled by another passenger who is "a pale-faced thin adult with a big black hat."[47] The stranger tells the boy the meaning of life, faith, and the universe by way of examples drawn from chemistry, history, and geography. His point is that human existence is no more than one changing phenomenon depending on the other changing phenomena of the universe. On the human level, one's personal happiness presupposes the happiness of all people. Giovanni determines to devote his life to this great cause. His dream ends at this point, and, on the hill, he is approached by a scientist named Dr. Bulcaniro. The scientist tells the boy that he has conducted, that night, an experiment of transmitting his thoughts to someone distant from him, and that Giovanni has been the subject of the experiment.[48] The stranger who consoled Giovanni on the train turns out to be a persona formed by Dr. Bulcaniro's transmitted ideas. The scientist gives the boy two gold coins for his unwitting participation in the experiment, and Giovanni runs back home full of new hope. No mention is made of either Campanella's drowning or the news of his father's expected return.

The third difference is related to this second point. In the early version, when Giovanni encounters many inexplicable phenomena during the train trip, he is often guided and given answers by a "gentle voice like a cello" coming from he knows not where.[49] This mysterious voice turns out to be that of the pale adult with a black hat. Giovanni, then, is under Dr. Bulcaniro's spiritual guidance not only at the end of his dream, but also throughout the dream journey. It is not clear whether the scientist fabricates the entire scheme of Giovanni's dream or remains an occasional guiding voice during the journey. In the later version, the mysterious guiding voice is completely erased, along with Dr. Bulcaniro and his "pale-faced" persona.

Besides its imaginative content and rigorous textual modification, *Galaxy Railroad* has several other interesting features. The work makes extensive use of scientific knowledge, especially astronomy.[50] Most names of the places in the sky are based on Western concepts of actual stars and constellations, such as the Swan, the Scorpion, and the Northern and the Southern Cross. Others, however, are purely fictional, including the Galaxy Station and the Pliocene Coast.[51] Miyazawa was also interested in botany,[52] chemistry, geology, meteorology, and mineralogy,[53] and he eagerly studied these subjects. Both his tales and his poetry are full of scientific terms and imagery. The use of scientific terms from such fields was not unique to Miyazawa, but no other Japanese author of his day employed them so abundantly.[54] Furthermore, Miyazawa's use of those terms is so effective as to make them an indispensable element of his style.

Apart from the supernatural sphere of Giovanni's dream, the geographical location of the story is not identified, or rather, it is intentionally blurred. Because of the curious mixture of Japanese, Western, and imaginary circumstances, not only the strange space of the night sky but also Giovanni's town ought to be considered purely fictional. In fact, this kind of mixture is found in many of Miyazawa's works.[55] The names of the two main figures, Giovanni and Campanella, are Italian,[56] while the names of the shipwrecked girl (Kaoru) and her brother (Tadashi) are Japanese.[57] Regardless of their nationality, the people on the train are all enraptured to hear Dvořák's *New World Symphony* sounding from the horizon of a cornfield when the train passes the plateau of the night sky. The landscape of the cornfield stretching all over to the horizon is native to North America. The story is clearly located where East and West meet and cultures become amalgamated.

Galaxy Railroad also has a complex religious dimension. Miyazawa was an enthusiastic believer in Buddhism; consequently, his Buddhist ideas appear in many of his other tales. Accordingly, Takao Hagiwara calls Miyazawa's works "at once ultra-scientific and ultra-primordial," and it is his "Buddho-animism, combined with Western modernism," which differentiates Miyazawa from Japanese authors of the mainstream, traditional culture.[58] In this particular story, however, no clear indication of his faith in Buddhism is apparent. Instead, we see Christian people being accepted into their heaven, which is clearly symbolized by the Southern Cross. I will further explain the religious aspect of *Galaxy Railroad* in the next chapter.

The misleadingly simple format of this work is fraught with problems, too. The use of a children's tale involves two consequences with Miyazawa's stories in general: vast potentiality and double marginality. On the one hand, for his mode of expression, Miyazawa presumably did not want to be trammeled by the mimetic representation of everyday reality that essentially characterizes the novel. Instead, Miyazawa chose the form of children's tale which strongly appeals to an adult's unconscious mind, in contrast to the novel which appeals more to the conscious field of this mind. In Miyazawa's advertisement to the first and only collection of his stories published during his lifetime, *Chūmon no ōi ryōriten* (A restaurant of many orders) (1924), he asserts that "anything is possible" in the literary world of children's tales, whereas, in implied contrast, this is not the case with the novel.[59] On the other hand, many of Miyazawa's stories, including *Galaxy Railroad*, are doubly marginalized. Their style as children's tales does not seem to be primarily intended for adults, while they are not easy for children to understand either, because of an extensive use of dialect as well as scientific imagery and religious terms.[60]

Finally, *Galaxy Railroad* possesses a sentimental quality. After all, it concerns a poor boy who suffers from his miserable situation at the outset and loses his closest friend at the end. This quality is a general feature of Miyazawa's works. His tales often treat creatures, including humans and nonhumans, who, being victimized, suffer from their weakness. For instance, in "Yodaka no hoshi" (The nighthawk star), the nighthawk, harmless despite his name, is threatened by a real hawk who demands that he renounce either his name or his life just because of his ugly appearance. When the nighthawk feeds on insects that evening as usual, he realizes that life demands the stronger preying upon the weaker, and that he is a part of the system. The bird then chooses to give up his existence on earth and ultimately becomes a star after attempting several desperate flights into the sky.[61] Although analogous to "The Ugly Duckling" by Hans Christian Andersen in terms of the motif of unsightliness turning into unexpected beauty, "The Nighthawk Star" is essentially dissimilar to Andersen's story in its approach to the problem of life and its solution involving death. In "Frandon Nōgakkō no buta" (A pig in the Frandon Agricultural School), using the same problematization of life in an altered situation, Miyazawa describes the psychology of a frightened pig. The animal is compelled to seal a document by which he agrees to die, before he is killed and becomes pork-chops.

The author's deep concern with the fundamental problem of life and existence sometimes turns his critical attention to social evils based on capitalistic greed and manipulation.[62] In "Obbel to zō" (Obbel and the elephant), an innocent, good-natured white elephant is exploited almost to death by the sly mill-owner Obbel before he is rescued by his fellow elephants. The same motif is utilized even more problematically in "Nametoko Yama no kuma" (The bears on the Nametoko Hill), which does not compromise the ending with an easy solution. The middle-aged hunter Kojūrō holds no hostility toward his animal neighbors, bears, who live peacefully on the nearby hills. He loves them, and they love him as well. But, urged by the necessity to maintain his family and exploited by a guileful merchant, he has to hunt bears more than his immediate need requires, and he is killed in the end by a bear who did not intend to harm him.

These are a few examples out of Miyazawa's many tales with a similar motif. The essential element in all these stories is the problem of life which is forced to give itself up in the cycle of the strong preying upon the weak, "the cosmic hecatomb" in Spariosu's words,[63] whether the problem is socially oriented or not. Another "fundamental characteristic" is that, as Kerstin Vidaeus argues, Miyazawa always "stands on the side of the weak."[64]

Whether the ending is tragic or not, he never abandons his feeble creatures but treats them with deep sympathy. Unlike most of Andersen's well-known tales, many of Miyazawa's sentimental works are not intended to induce cathartic, unadulterated sadness in the reader, because they somehow leave us with an unpurged sense that originates in the essentially unsolvable problem of our existence. *Galaxy Railroad* is no exception in this respect.

Because of their multiculturalism, their rich scientific and religious imagery, their communion with all creatures, especially weak ones, and their use of a children's tale form, Miyazawa's stories in general are unique in Japanese literature. In particular, *Galaxy Railroad*, which contains all of these characteristics, resists any easy generic categorization. The work is usually labeled for convenience's sake as a fantastic story for children. Mere "fantasy," however, is obviously not an exact term because of its unconventionality. For instance, Miyazawa's abundant use of terms from various fields, including science, religion, and music, gives the short piece a surprisingly wide, almost encyclopedic range of imagery. The work as a whole is often mentioned with all kinds of modifiers, such as, in Tsuzukihashi Tatsuo's words, "a vast fantasy stretching over the world of death."[65] According to Usami Eiji, the story even gives us "some mysterious fear."[66] Vidaeus expresses best the literary indefinability of *Galaxy Railroad* when she explains why she did not include it in her anthology of Miyazawa's works translated into Swedish, her native language: "I wondered whether I should include the work in my anthology . . . In many aspects, *A Night on the Galaxy Railroad* can be regarded as the most representative of the author's works. But I think that it should be treated elsewhere because it is too immense a work from a generic point of view as a children's tale."[67] Ōmi Masato concludes that the work is "an extremely futuristic, beautiful galactic epic."[68] All these critical remarks recognize a certain immensity or greatness in the work, which is unusual for a short prose piece, especially for a "fantastic" children's tale. In what follows, I shall show that *Galaxy Railroad*, no less than *The Fall of Hyperion*, typically illustrates transitional epic, which explains its mysterious generic nature despite its seemingly uncomplicated format.

5

The Epic Nature of
The Fall of Hyperion and
A Night on the Galaxy Railroad

The Fall of Hyperion and *Galaxy Railroad* can now be compared as examples of transitional epics, from the standpoint of the three elements of epic grandeur. For the time being, I shall assume that the works do not contradict themselves in presenting their respective world–views and that, in each case, the two textual versions complement each other. I shall therefore consider *The Fall of Hyperion* as a continuation of Keats' previous epic attempt, *Hyperion*, and shall treat the last two manuscript versions of Miyazawa's work as a whole.

The Communal Dimension

The communal element is thematically the most significant in both *The Fall of Hyperion* and *Galaxy Railroad*. On a first reading, Keats' perspective seems more personal than communal. The poet-narrator is singled out for favor by Moneta, the goddess of memory. Depending wholly on her guidance during their journey through the mythological world, he seems mainly concerned about his inferior existence as a poet. The self-concern and total reliance on divine favor on the part of the poet-narrator might appear contrary to the nature of the epic, in which the central figure should possess some kind of power and be concerned about the welfare of a group of people. In fact, the poet-narrator psychologically mirrors the author himself, to the extent that he seems to be a persona of the writing "poet." The situation is not peculiar to *The Fall of Hyperion*. In the *Divine Comedy*, to which Keats' poem owes much in terms of structural arrangement and narrative device, the narrator is supposed to be the poet Dante, and his dependence on his Providential guides during his supernatural journey is as extensive as that of the poet-narrator's in Keats' work. Keats' self-occupied, unlikely hero is so weak that the story can be told without him, just as Keats first did in *Hyperion*. As one might expect from the title of either version, the central figure in Keats' poem might be understood as either Hyperion, who remains the sungod, or Apollo, who will deprive the Titan of his position. In this sense, the poet-narrator is a peripheral character, no more than a "narrating" voice.

The poet-narrator, however, does occupy a central position in *The Fall of Hyperion* because, in the same sense as Dante's narrator, Keats' spokesman unifies the diverse components of the story through his perspective.[1] In spite of his total dependence on Moneta's guidance, his act of recording gives the work its coherent viewpoint. Moreover, he saturates the poem with self-assertion in *The Fall of Hyperion*. For instance, the monologue of Saturn grieving over his dethronement, which is one of the two passages taken from *Hyperion*, is quite shortened, less vehement and more pathetic, and accompanied by the poet-narrator's critical comments and long observations.

From another viewpoint, the communal dimension receives great emphasis in Keats' poem. There are two aspects to the dimension. On one level, the poem describes the battles between two mighty groups of immortals, the resurgent Titans whose king is Saturn and the triumphant Olympian gods. The poet-narrator is expected to witness the warfare, which took place in a remote past, and to report it to his contemporaries as well as to posterity in the form of his poem. The most important message to convey is found in the words which the deposed sea-god Oceanus utters in *Hyperion*. He is the wise old one of the Titan tribe and explains "all naked truths,"[2] including the cause of their defeat by the Olympians:

> As heaven and earth are fairer, fairer far
> Than chaos and blank darkness, though once chiefs;
> And as we show beyond that heaven and earth
> In form and shape compact and beautiful,
> In will, in action free, companionship,
> And thousand other signs of purer life;
> So on our heels a fresh perfection treads,
> A power more strong in beauty, born of us
> And fated to excel us, as we pass

> In glory that old darkness; . . .
>   For 'tis the eternal law
> That first in beauty should be first in might;[3]

When viewed from the victors' historiography, the same change could be rewritten in Nietzsche's terms: "out of the original Titanic divine order of terror, the Olympian divine order of joy gradually evolved through the Apollinian impulse toward beauty, just as roses burst from thorny bushes."[4] Although *The Fall of Hyperion* does not go as far as this scene, what is expressed here may have been the intended message in the later work, too. The poem presents a conflict between two huge communities as in the *Iliad* and *The Tale of the Heike*. But the passage distinguishes Keats' poem from the traditional epics in one respect. The poet proposes a governing principle for a world which, in the other epics, is essentially mutable and meaningless. Reminiscent of the first line of *Endymion* ("A thing of beauty is a joy for ever"),[5] Oceanus' words illustrate Keats' assertion that beauty determines the struggle for world order.

The other communal aspect in *The Fall of Hyperion* is related paradoxically to the poet-narrator's self-concern about being a poet. The idea, a vital element in the poem, appears in the newly created dialogue between Moneta and the poet-narrator. When Moneta tells him that nobody can come up to the altar at the temple of Saturn except "those to whom the miseries of the world / Are misery,"[6] she seems to be talking about humanitarians who, feeling people's sufferings, involve themselves directly in solving serious social problems. The lines succinctly summarize Keats' idea of how people should try to live. In the following passage, the poet-narrator asks the goddess about a great many people whom he should have met in that desolate, but sacred place:

> "Are there not thousands in the world," said I,
> Encouraged by the sooth voice of the shade,
> "Who love their fellows even to the death;
> Who feel the giant agony of the world;
> And more, like slaves to poor humanity,
> Labour for mortal good? I sure should see
> Other men here: but I am here alone."[7]

Disapproving of his implied vanity, Moneta reprimands the poet-narrator, saying that the people whom he talks about are "no

visionaries," since "[t]hey seek no wonder but the human face."⁸
He is counted as one of the "dreamers weak" and is advised to
"[t]hink of the earth."⁹ The goddess then distinguishes between
the poet and the dreamer by saying that "[t]he one pours out a
balm upon the world, / The other vexes it."¹⁰

While the distinction between poets, dreamers, and humanitarians is somewhat confused, Keats makes the communal
aspect clear. Such phrases as "the world," "their fellows," "poor
humanity," and "the earth" reveal that the ultimate community
which Keats envisions is the entire human society, regardless of
its diversity in race, ideology, or religion. A poet, not a "dreaming
thing," has the task of bringing relief and harmony to the suffering world. Two points ought to be made concerning this communal aspect. One is the huge totality of the community, which
comprises every member of the human race. The immensity of
the community resembles that of the traditional religious epic.
But the community of *The Fall of Hyperion* is more tolerantly
comprehensive, because the poem does not impose any sectarianism except that of poets who refuse to be mere dreamers. *The
Fall of Hyperion* thus has the immense communal dimension of
the religious epic without being a religious work.

The other point concerns the emphasis placed on a gifted
individual or individuals who can direct that huge community
toward a better end. In this case, the gifted are the poets, who
face human problems and attempt to solve them by means of
their poetic creations, unlike the humanitarians who do not need
any special talent except enthusiasm for their cause, or the
dreamers who escape from the pains of the world and remain in
the castles they build in the air. This curious balance of a belief
in powerful individualism with a concern for all of humanity is an
essential feature of Romanticism. In this world–view, a special
individual, particularly a poet, has the power to reform the cor-
rupted world. A glamorized personal power of imagination is here
combined with an enlarged communal concern in Romantic idealism. Only in a period when poets assumed the role of a god,
and poetry that of a religion, could this coalition take place.¹¹
Therefore, the communal dimension in *The Fall of Hyperion* has
the immense breadth of the religious epic with the Providential
Will replaced by the beauty principle and the poet's creative
power.

In spite of a radical difference in subject matter, *Galaxy
Railroad* shares with Keats' poem a broad communal concern

and a belief in an individual's power to transform the world. At first, before he has the dream, Giovanni, who is overwhelmed by his daily hard work as well as by loneliness, cannot think about anything other than himself and his distressing family situation. Like the poet-narrator in Keats' poem, he is initially full of self-concern. But the boy on the nighttime trip comes to think about the happiness of all people, and his scope of humanity is gradually, but unmistakably widened.

When he goes to work in the print shop, Giovanni thinks that people there "laughed at him coldly and voicelessly without turning toward him."[12] The boy is apparently quite paranoid about his miserable situation.[13] Similarly, in the early version, after he is mocked and isolated by his classmates, he says to himself, "I must look like a fox to everybody."[14] In turn, at the beginning of the train trip, Giovanni despises the poorly dressed birdcatcher. But, after a while, the boy feels sorry for having despised the kind and good-natured man who honestly performs his humble job every night. Giovanni now thinks that he will do anything for the happiness of the poor man. Thus, Giovanni's encounter with the birdcatcher generates his first realization of what his mission in life might be.[15] Furthermore, on hearing how the boat, after hitting an iceberg, sank, and how the young tutor chose to sacrifice his life with his two small protégés in order to make space for other people on a lifeboat, Giovanni, undoubtedly thinking of his father, says to himself: "Oh, isn't that big sea called the Pacific? At the northernmost sea where icebergs float, on a small boat, somebody is working very hard against the winds, freezing sea water, and awfully cold temperature. I feel really sorry for that person. What should and can I do for the sake of his happiness?"[16] These episodes mark Giovanni's inner, spiritual change which directs him away from self-concern to a consideration for other people. Toward the end of his dream in the early version, the change results in Giovanni's firm determination to "look for real, real happiness for myself, for my mother, for Campanella, and for all people."[17] Thus, the communal dimension is the thematic core of *Galaxy Railroad.*

Miyazawa's strong interest in two religions, Buddhism and Christianity, explains the immensity of the community in *Galaxy Railroad.* Of the two religions, Christianity's imprint is particularly apparent in the work. The two drowned Japanese children and their tutor are Christians. The night train which runs through the star-filled sky is the vehicle which carries the blessed dead from the world full of troubles to the long-desired Christian heaven. In addition, the two crosses in the night sky are unmistakable indications of Christianity. Sometime early in the trip, the small train passes by an island "radiating a pale halo" in the *ama no gawa*, and Giovanni and Campanella witness on the top of the island a white cross: "As if cast in the frozen cloud of the North Pole, with a transparent golden nimbus, it has been standing there quietly forever."[18] This is the Northern Cross. Standing up, all the passengers on the train say "hallelujah" and piously pray toward it. Spontaneously, the two boys also stand and find themselves full of "a new feeling resembling sadness."[19] The Christian element also appears in the description of the Southern Cross which is as mysteriously beautiful as the Northern Cross:

> They saw all the way down the invisible *ama no gawa* a cross, adorned with every kind of light like blue and orange and crowned with circling pale clouds like a halo, standing resplendent in the river as if it were a tree. The inside of the train became lively with small noises. All the people stood up straight and began praying as they had at that Northern Cross. All around, they heard only joyful voices, like that of a child at the sight of a melon, and inexpressible, deep, pious sighs. . . . "Hallelujah, hallelujah," echoed people's happy, bright voices, and they heard the voice of a crystal, ineffably delightful trumpet coming from the distant sky, from the cold sky far away.[20]

Evidently, Miyazawa holds great respect for the Christian religion. From this point of view, however, *Galaxy Railroad* treats a relatively small number of people in comparison to the size of the entire human community. The Southern Cross marks the entrance to heaven, which admits only blessed Christians. Thus, the work seems to be dogmatically circumscribed as in Western religious epic.

　　Yet one factor directs us away from Christianity and toward a different system of beliefs. This shift of focus occurs in the part of the train trip after the Southern Cross, especially with the early version that shows the Galaxy Railroad extending far beyond the special station. Just after passing the entrance to the Christian heaven, Giovanni and Campanella decide to go as far as they can, in order to look for happiness for all people. Then Campanella disappears, and Giovanni's solitary journey continues. This part of Giovanni's trip seems to suggest the existence of another dimension, another path to pursue beyond Christian faith. This path is Buddhism, even though Miyazawa makes no explicit Buddhist statements in his work, despite his being a devout member of a Buddhist sect.

The motif of selfless devotion for the sake of others is a key to the duality of the religious dimension. As we know from Giovanni's change, this motif is central to the work, and examples of the rigorous principle are perceived in several places. One of the most obvious instances is the scene of the sinking ship, which the young tutor narrates to other train passengers. Although he tried hard to reach a lifeboat and save the two children in his charge, he changed his mind when he saw many more small children and their parents in the way:

> But I thought that it would be really happier for these people [his two protégés] to go to God with three of us rather than I should save their lives mercilessly [at the expense of the others]. . . . Somebody said [Psalm] No. [about two spaces vacant]. Immediately, all the people [still aboard] sang it in many languages. At that moment, we suddenly heard a huge sound. I thought we got into the swirls of water, and, holding these people tightly, I lost my consciousness, and then I found myself here [on this train].[21]

The young Christian tutor, who remained voluntarily on the ship, manifests the virtue of self-sacrifice, and thus he is now on the train bound for the heaven of the Christian religion.

Later on the train trip, another instance of the same motif with a different religious implication occurs. It is the tale about a scorpion, which Kaoru tells Giovanni and Campanella when they see in the field of the sky "a big, crimson fire" flaming "more transparent with red than ruby and more beautiful than lithium."[22] The celestial flame stands for Antares, the chief red star of Scorpio. In the girl's story, the creature is metamorphosed into a red star because of its good, sincere desire, like that of the bird in "The Nighthawk Star." One day, a scorpion pursued by a weasel fell into a well. Almost drowned, the creature said to itself:

> Oh, I don't know how many lives I've taken, and this time when I was attacked by the weasel, I myself fled so hard. . . .

Why didn't I give my body to the weasel without hesitation? Then, the weasel, at least, would survive one more day. O God, please see my heart. Please use my body next time for the real happiness of all instead of throwing away my life uselessly like this.[23]

And, after a while, the scorpion found its body, now changed to a burning fire, shining in the darkness of the night. Although told by a Christian and sharing the same motif of self-sacrifice with the episode of the drowned passengers, the story within the story can also be regarded as a Buddhist allegory.[24] This kind of allegorical tale involving nonhuman creatures is common in Buddhism, because the transmigration of the soul from one form of life to another ("next time") as well as release from the endless life cycles constitutes a central belief of the religious system. In addition, although not identified with any real place, the word Bar(u)dora, which Kaoru mentions as the dwelling place of the scorpion at the beginning of her story, evokes India and Central Asia, with locations like Gandhara and the Pamir, where Buddhism was born and flourished. Miyazawa made use of the regions as the setting of many of his other stories.

In relation to the notion of psychic transmigration, self-sacrifice for the sake of others in Buddhism has a far different significance, not a different degree of importance, from that in Christianity. For instance, in a Buddhist traditional edifying story, Buddha gives one of his former lives to a starving tiger. The thematic resemblance to Miyazawa's tale about the scorpion is unmistakable. In "Tegami 1" (Letter 1), Miyazawa also wrote a story about a dragon who, restraining himself from harming other animals, is killed for the benefit of others in the end and is later reincarnated as Buddha. What is different here from Christianity is that the existence of human beings is not more important than that of other creatures, and that each creature, human or not, has the duty to help every other creature. In this respect, Buddhist fables, as well as Miyazawa's tales about nonhuman beings, are actually not allegories, because the nonhuman creatures maintain their own proper dignity and identity. This makes a radical difference from Christianity, in which humans are regarded as God's best creation, and all other creatures in this world, considered "inferior far beneath" people,[25] are by decree subject to human control. The contrast lies between Western humanism centered on *logos* and an Eastern world–view that comprehends marginalized beings.[26]

One word in the key phrase "for the real happiness of all" makes the notion of the Buddhist equality among all beings even clearer. The Japanese word for this "all" is *minna*. Although referring to people in its ordinary use, the word can refer to nonhuman beings as well, including flowers, trees, animals, frogs, and spirits, even insentient objects such as poles and rocks, all of which have a lively existence in the frequently animistic world of Miyazawa's stories. In "Kashiwa-bayashi no yoru" (An evening in the oak wood), for instance, forest trees dancing in the moonshine communicate with a human passerby. In "Hatake no heri" (The edge of the field), the world–view of frogs has the same validity as that of people. When human characters in *Galaxy Railroad* talk about the happiness of "all," we are inclined to think that the word refers to all the people in the world. But when the scorpion prays to God that his body should be used "for the real happiness of all,"[27] this "all" necessarily has to mean all living creatures, whether they are human or not. Giovanni's final determination to search for "real, real happiness for myself, for my mother, for Campanella, for all" must be considered in this context. One might say that the community of *Galaxy Railroad* is even greater than that of *The Fall of Hyperion*, which concerns only people, but less comprehensive than that of *Prometheus Unbound*, in which even inanimate things participate equally in the final cosmic assembly. When Miyazawa's entire literary creation is considered, however, his community rivals even the community of Shelley's piece because, in many of Miyazawa's tales, inanimate objects inspired with breath assert their distinctive ways of being. In this sense, one of the main themes throughout Miyazawa's works might be called the participation in "the festivity of existence."[28]

The idea of total self-devotion to such an immense community in *Galaxy Railroad* apparently derives from Miyazawa's belief in Buddhism. But Miyazawa's Buddhism is not the Pure Land sect. According to this sect, people should rely entirely on the benevolence of Amida Buddha, and admittance into heaven is guaranteed if people just pray to the god, as we saw in *The Tale of the Heike*. Obviously, such faith is not compatible with the rigor of self-sacrifice and Giovanni's quest of happiness for all. Instead, Miyazawa was an enthusiastic believer in *Myōhōrenge-kyō* or *Hokekyō* (the *Saddharma Pundarica Sutra* or the *Lotus Sutra*), and joined one sect of Mahayanist Buddhism called *Nichiren-shū*, for which the *Lotus Sutra* as the real word of Bud-

dha is considered the most important scripture.[29] Inevitable
mutability and endless metempsychosis are fundamental in the
scripture, too. Yet the world–view of the *Lotus Sutra* is not negative and pessimistic, but positive and dynamic. According to this
teaching, as Tamura Yoshirō explains, there is *myōhō* (*saddharma*, or ultimate and absolute truth) behind all the changes
in the universe, and "all things and laws are not fixed and independent of each other . . . but dependent on . . . and related to
each other in their perpetual transformation"; understanding
and believing the truth, which offers "a synthetic view of the universe and life," people are strongly expected to embody *myōhō* by
exercising self-sacrificial devotion to others, which is called
bosatsu-gyō (bodhisattva exercise).[30]

The title of the scripture and the phrases from it appear in
many of Miyazawa's works, and its teachings are essential to
his literature.[31] For example, in the prefatory poem to the anthology of his poetry, titled *Haru to Shura* (Spring and an Asura)
(1924), he explains the nature of his poems:

The phenomenon called I
Is one blue illumination
Of the hypothesized, organic, alternating electric light
(A complex of every transparent spirit)
With the scenery and everyone
Blinking quick and ceaseless
Steadily radiating
It is one blue illumination
Of the causal, alternating electric light
(With its light kept, its bulb lost)
· ·
(Everything that blinks with me
And that everyone feels at once)
Chains of shade and light
So far preserved as they are
These [his poems] are mental sketches
· ·
There is no doubt that these recorded scenes
Are the scenes just as they were recorded
If they are the void, the void is like this,
Which applies to everything to a certain degree
(Because, as everything is everyone within me,
[I am] everything within every single being)[32]

These lines are easier to understand in light of the Buddhist idea of causality and the theory of relativity in modern physics,[33] although no Buddhist terminology is found except the word *inga* (causal). Such is also the case with *Galaxy Railroad* in which Buddhist phrases are assiduously avoided. The *Lotus Sutra* strongly encourages individual self-sacrificial activities in this world rather than a desire to go to heaven. The teaching might account for the nonexistence of a Buddhist heaven in *Galaxy Railroad* as well as for Giovanni's lonely journey after the Southern Cross, in contrast to the Christian heaven into which many blessed people are accepted in a large group.[34]

In this light, the abysmal locus, which Giovanni witnesses in the night sky, might symbolize the Buddhist ideal of nirvana, or the absence of existence. Just after the train leaves the Southern Cross, Campanella points at a certain part of the sky, calling it "the Coalsack" and "the pit of the sky": "Giovanni started when he turned to that direction. At one place of the *ama no gawa*, there was a big, dark, deep hole. He tried hard in vain to see how deep it was or what was in the depth, and he had pains in the eyes soon."[35] Then, Giovanni declares that, unafraid of such a big darkness, he will search for the real happiness of all people. We might be tempted to call the dark spot in the midst of stars a black hole in today's terminology. If "the Coalsack" is intended to be a Buddhist symbol, Giovanni as an unaware novice of the discipline should be expected to overcome the fear of "the pit of the sky" as an ultimate, existential challenge in the course of his lifelong bodhisattva exercise. Ultimately, he would accept it as a desired end. Whether the identification of the dark celestial spot with nirvana is legitimate or not, the passage suggests that, totally apart from the Christian heaven, there exists beyond it a vast, unfathomable locus in Miyazawa's cosmography.

The two religions from East and West are thus curiously mixed in *Galaxy Railroad*. Christianity is manifest in the story, while Buddhism remains latent in its scheme. The coalescence might be partly due to the work's being written in the early twentieth century, when Japan was rapidly becoming westernized while nevertheless retaining many of its traditional values. No serious conflict occurs because of this intermingling in the work, however. This harmony is achieved because, despite Miyazawa's earnest faith in a particular Buddhist sect, one of his objectives here is to present the harmonious coexistence of multiple religions or the communal equality not only among creatures but also among religions. This sensitive issue is directly raised when Giovanni argues with Kaoru, who insists that she and other passengers should get off the train at the Southern Cross, whose God is the real one:

> "But we [Kaoru and others] have to get off here, because this is the passage to heaven," the girl said with a sad air.
> "You don't have to go to heaven, do you? My [Giovanni's] teacher said that we should make earth a far better place than heaven."
> "But my mother is there, and God says so."
> "Such a God is not a real one."
> "Your God is not a real one."
> "That's not true!"[36]

The passage shows that, in spite of his European name, Giovanni is not a Christian. Although Giovanni's proposition to "make the earth a far better place than heaven" sounds like a socialist motto, it more probably reflects Miyazawa's Buddhist ideal of bodhisattva exercise. Actually, it does not matter whether Giovanni is a Buddhist or not. What is important is the tutor's reconciliation of the two children, who are opposed to each other's religious views. The young mentor says that there exists only one real God (he does not specify which one), and prays that Giovanni and Campanella will soon meet those who now get off the train at the Southern Cross, including himself and his students, in front of that real God.

   With his words, the tutor probably means the Christian God. But, taken literally, his words identify one universal God for everybody regardless of differences in religious stance. The idea is more clearly revealed in a deleted passage of the early version. Toward the end of Giovanni's dream, the mysterious pale-faced adult with a large black hat, who must be Dr. Bulcaniro's persona, speaks to the boy comfortingly about how things operate in the world. He says that water is composed of oxygen and hydrogen, an example of evident truth revealed through science, and continues as follows: "Everybody says that his God is the real God. But we shed tears even about what people, who believe other gods, did. And we argue if our minds are good or evil. And we cannot decide which. But if you study so hard that you can distinguish a true idea from a false one with an experiment, if only the method of the experiment is decided, then faith will be like chemistry to you."[37] In this passage, Miyazawa is apparently suggesting that all people be united under one universal God who does not demand schismatic differentiation.

Two pieces of circumstantial evidence support this idea. One is the culturally transposed naming of the children. The Japanese children are Christian, whereas Giovanni, who has a European name, is apparently not, and they are all found on the same Galaxy Train. The other evidence is found in the previously cited scene of the sinking boat. The tutor reports that, in the face of extinction, the people who chose to stay aboard began to sing a Christian psalm all at once "in many languages." On the one hand, the phrase might just indicate the international acceptance of Christianity. On the other hand, the ship can be interpreted as the frequently used metaphor for a vehicle that forces its passengers of diverse interests to kneel before the same fate. As a metaphor for the global community, the boat was carrying people of all religious beliefs, and the passage is indicative of people's universal faith in Divinity, rather than of the multinationality of one particular religion. In fact, the possibility of harmony beyond ethnicity is accentuated three times during the train trip: when all the passengers pray to the Northern and the Southern Crosses with one accord, and when they are entranced to hear the *New World Symphony*. The passengers on the ship, suggestive of the Titanic, faced immediate death which they had chosen for the sake of others, and their souls spontaneously united and humbly turned to something merciful and profound beyond ordinary comprehension. On that occasion, their faith in Divinity was expressed in the form of a Christian psalm. It is the same case with the broader context of *Galaxy Railroad*: Christianity is foremost throughout Giovanni's dream, but, with Buddhist concepts implicit also, the work depicts Christianity as a representative of many other religious wills that converge in altruism. Thus, the cultural blending in Miyazawa's work reflects the author's idealism which cannot be pinned down to given specifics of time and place.

In *Galaxy Railroad*, then, Miyazawa maintains a broad sense of a community entailing the welfare of all humanity, as Keats does in *The Fall of Hyperion*. In both cases, the communal dimension is not restricted by religious dogmatism. Naturally, some differences exist between the two works here. *The Fall of Hyperion* does not have explicit references to any religion other than the ancient Greek one. Even Greek religion is treated not as a living faith on which people depend spiritually but as a long-dead mythology that simply provides materials for poetic consumption. Keats keeps a humanistically impartial stance by detaching himself from religion. *Galaxy Railroad* shows religious ideas, namely, those of Buddhism and Christianity. Behind the references to the two religions, however, there lies the notion of pan-religion rather than sectarianism.[38] *Galaxy Railroad* is a result of the author's efforts to harmonize various religions under one God toward one goal.

The community in Miyazawa's work, which includes non-human as well as human beings because of the Buddhist influence, encompasses a wider scope than in Keats' poem. Rigorous self-sacrifice that may even demand death comes from half-hidden religious ardor. Miyazawa, however, does not have confidence in one single person's power to work over the entire world. He chooses each individual's total self-devotion for others' sake, which, collectively, is supposed to relieve the world. Simply put, the people engaged in this activity might be Keats' humanitarians. In contrast, the belief in individual power is much stronger in Keats. A specially talented person, a poet whose concern should be the entire humanity, has the power to make the world better through the creations of his imagination.[39] Such differences notwithstanding, the two works resemble each other in terms of their immense communal dimension.

The Dimension of Mortality

In both Keats' and Miyazawa's work, the epic element of mortality contains two aspects: personal and communal. In *The Fall of Hyperion*, mortality at the personal level forms an unavoidable and almost insurmountable obstacle to attaining an immortal's view of the universe. On seeing the poet-narrator coming to the temple of Saturn, the goddess Moneta, who stands beside the altar at the top of the stairs, pronounces a "fierce threat" about treading on the inviolable stairs that drain life away:[40]

> If thou canst not ascend
> These steps, die on that marble where thou art. . . .
> The sands of thy short life are spent this hour,
> And no hand in the universe can turn

> Thy hourglass, if these gummed leaves be burnt
> Ere thou canst mount up these *immortal* steps.[41]

Here, "immortal" is used figuratively with the meaning "permanently enduring," but the word also suggests that the stairs are the path leading to immortality. When the poet-narrator tries to climb up the stairs, he literally experiences mortal agonies:

> suddenly a palsied chill
> Struck from the pavèd level up my limbs,
> And was ascending quick to put cold grasp
> Upon those streams that pulse beside the throat.
> I shrieked; and the sharp anguish of my shriek
> Stung my own ears. I strove hard to escape
> The numbness, strove to gain the lowest step.
> Slow, heavy, deadly was my pace; the cold
> Grew stifling, suffocating, at the heart;
> And when I clasped my hands I felt them not.[42]

"One minute before death,"[43] he manages to put his foot on the first step, and, reviving instantly, he runs up to join Moneta. The goddess explains to him the nature of his experience, saying briefly that "[t]hou hast felt / What 'tis to die and live again before / Thy fated hour."[44] In Charlotte Schrader Hooker's words, he thus "dies into life by suffering mortal anguish."[45]

Climbing up the "immortal" stairs, especially the first step, turns out to be the threshold into a new life of perception, and the physical elevation is translated into a metaphorical empowerment in the imagination. Having survived the simple, but critical rite of passage, the poet-narrator is now qualified for Moneta's guidance and protection and is ready to acquire further experience beyond his mortal share. He has risked his life to achieve an overview of a remote past, which should disclose an underlying principle of how the world evolves through its apparent flux and reflux. The goddess tells her new initiate that he shall "with these dull mortal eyes behold [scenes], / Free from all pain, if wonder pain thee not."[46] The episode constitutes the personal aspect of the mortality dimension in *The Fall of Hyperion.*

But mortality in the poem has a broader aspect as well. What the poet-narrator is privileged to witness about deities is far from heavenly peace. Moneta conducts the chosen man to the scenes of the defeated Titans. They have suddenly lost their sway over the universe, which they had held for innumerable ages, and now they suffer mortal miseries in spite of their immortality. The shock caused by this paradox is most remarkable in Saturn, the king of the giant tribe. He is shaken with new, unfamiliar emotions, such as sorrow and despair, when, suddenly deprived of the sovereignty which he had exercised from the sky, he finds himself, after a long stupor, grovelling powerless on the ground:

> Moan, Cybele, moan; for thy pernicious babes
> Have changed a god into an aching palsy.
> Moan, brethren, moan, for I have no strength left,
> Weak as the reed—weak—feeble as my voice—
> Oh, Oh, the pain, the pain of feebleness.[47]

His agony is expressed more dramatically in *Hyperion*, where his awareness of the new reality directly conflicts with his notion of what he used to be and ought to be:

>   I have left
> My strong identity, my real self,
> Somewhere between the throne and where I sit
> Here on this spot of earth. . . .
> Search, Thea, search! And tell me, if thou seest
> A certain shape or shadow, making way
> With wings or chariot fierce to repossess
> A heaven he lost erewhile: . . .
>   I will give command:
>
> Thea! Thea! Thea! Where is Saturn?[48]

This bitter agony, which should be peculiar to mortals, is now shared by the other members of the fallen tribe. Most of them remain prone in a huge, dark underground cave, which is called the "nest of woe."[49] Shattered by excessive physical and mental pains, they lie motionless without even giving a word or look to each other. At the miserable sight of his once mighty tribe, Saturn, who came to see them to discuss the possible recovery of their lost power, feels at once "all the frailty of grief, / Of rage, of fear, anxiety, revenge, / Remorse, spleen, hope, but most of all despair."[50] At this point, the reader perceives most clearly the nature of the change that has occurred in the Titan king and his followers: "Against these plagues [of emotions] he strove in vain;

for Fate / Had poured a *mortal* oil upon his head, / A disanointing poison."[51] The "mortal oil" has deprived Saturn not only of his kingship but also of his serenity as an immortal.[52] The Titans regret their defeat itself less than the fact that they must now taste mortality in their undying state.[53]

Even Hyperion, who still keeps his position as the sun-god in the sky, is not an exception to the general tendency of the Titan tribe, because he is unknowingly threatened by the rise of Apollo, who is destined to take over his divinely magnificent post. Thus, while he is performing his daily majestic duty of brightening the world, he sits in his burning vehicle "yet unsecure."[54] When he comes home and rests in his palace, he perceives unpropitious signs:

> For as among us mortals omens drear
> Fright and perplex, so also shuddered he— . . .
> But horrors portioned to a giant nerve
> Oft made Hyperion ache. . . .
>   while sometimes eagle's wings,
> Unseen before by gods or wondering men,
> Darkened the place, and neighing steeds were heard,
> Not heard before by gods or wondering men.
> Also, when he would taste the spicy wreaths
> Of incense, breathed aloft from sacred hills,
> Instead of sweets, his ample palate took
> Savour of poisonous brass and metal sick.[55]

His innocent immortality is now being tainted inwardly. Consequently, when the giant sun-god lies down "frenzied with new woes" outside his resplendent residence,[56] Coelus, who is the bodiless primordial sky-god and the parent of the Titans,[57] notices in Hyperion's countenance "fear, hope, and wrath; / Actions of rage and passion," which he usually finds "on the mortal world beneath, / In men who die."[58] And the meaning of mortal pains in immortals is unequivocally revealed when he says: "This is the grief, O son, / Sad sign of ruin, sudden dismay, and fall!"[59] Nevertheless, Coelus urges Hyperion to oppose his imminent fate, which would have shaped the core of the god's heroism if the poem had not been disrupted. Following his advice, the shining Hyperion flies down into the darkness of the night to join his dejected comrades and to organize a counter-rebellion against the victorious Olympian gods.

In Sherwin's words, "the Titans are being humanized."[60]
Their crippled divinity is acutely felt when their life is repeatedly likened and approximated to mortality. What the Titans
attempt to regain by challenging the new rulers is not only their
reign over the universe but, more significantly, a divinity devoid
of human sorrows and an innocence not infected with mortal
fears.[61] The struggle to escape from half-mortality is supposed to
fail in the work's larger scheme, in which whoever is most beautiful keeps hold of the world on the basis of principled mutability.
The paradoxical mixture of mortality within immortality, a kind of
death in life, is the seed from which the main plot of the Titanic
war is to develop. This paradox on the communal level makes an
interesting contrast to the personal mortality of the poet-narrator, which is temporarily purged and invested with immortality so
that he can be exposed to divine affairs.[62] The two paradoxes of
both personal and communal aspects constitute the topic of
mortality in Keats' two Hyperion poems.

Miyazawa's *Galaxy Railroad* also contains both personal
and communal aspects of mortality that weigh heavily in the
work's overall scheme. In the communal aspect, many people
choose to give up their lives in order to save others, as illustrated in the episode of the sinking boat. The Galaxy Railroad is
the single path that the dead, blessed people take in their passage from the world of human miseries to the heaven beyond
the starry sky.[63] Except for Giovanni, who somehow has a special
pass, and for the native inhabitants of the space which the railroad traverses, all the people aboard have died and are on their
way to their desired heaven.[64] Campanella, the Japanese brother
and sister, and their young tutor are just a few of those who
have died that day and happen to be on the same train.

In a way, the passengers on the night train resemble the
Titans in the Hyperion poems, because both groups occupy an
intermediary state of being between mortality and immortality.
They both aspire to a happy state of perfect pure immortality.
The difference, however, shows a dichotomic contrast. The intermediary condition in the train trip is, after all, a transitional
one, and the desired immortality in heaven is guaranteed for the
passengers, whereas the struggle of the Titans to regain
unstained immortality is destined to fail and, gradually absorbed
into the ground,[65] they have to abide the bitter mortal state inside
themselves forever. In other words, the symbolic vector of the
dead passengers is upward toward heaven and immortality, while

that of the undying Titans is downward toward earth and mortality. The passengers gain new life through death, in contrast to the Titans who continue to exist "deathwards progressing" with "an immortal sickness which kills not."[66] Although most of the characters in *Galaxy Railroad* and the Hyperion poems are "immortals," the communal dimensions of both works are thus inseparably related to the element of mortality.

At the personal level in *Galaxy Railroad*, mortality is not the immediate concern of the central figure, because Giovanni is too young to worry about such topics as his own eventual death and the nature of human existence. He does not really understand the situation of his fellow train passengers, including his close friend Campanella. Rather, Giovanni's main concern is directed toward communal welfare. In Keats' poem, because the poet-narrator can overcome his own mortality through the trial that Moneta imposes on the stairs of Saturn's temple, he is allowed to accompany her through the scenes of battles fought long ago. In *Galaxy Railroad*, however, Giovanni does not have to undergo any tribulation of that kind and does not make any conscious effort to board the vehicle. Instead, he finds himself somehow miraculously transported into the small train that is running past millions of stars. Asked by the conductor to show his ticket, the boy finds in his pocket a piece of folded green paper, which turns out to be a very rare pass. On seeing the pass, the conductor simply asks him if he has brought it from the "Three-Dimensional Space" and proceeds to the next passenger.[67]

The pass is described as follows: "He found on the pass only about ten strange-looking letters printed in a pattern like an arabesque, and when he watched it closely, he felt as if he would be taken into the paper."[68] Although somewhat inflated and humorous, the comment which the birdcatcher makes on the pass is of great importance: "Wow, this is something great. With this ticket, you can go even to the real heaven. Not only heaven. It is a pass with which you can go anywhere you like. I see, with this one, no wonder you can go as far as possible on the Galaxy Railroad of such an imperfect space like this Illusory Four-Dimensional one. You are marvelous."[69] Still alive, Giovanni is specially admitted into the space where only dead people heading for heaven are allowed to pass. In a sense, he finds himself in a life-in-death situation, but he does not have to experience the stings of death, because death in this space is not a curse but a blessing. The boy is admitted into the space intended for the dead presumably because of his potential to be useful to the happiness of all people, and because that desire coincides with the ideal of self-sacrifice which the passengers have illustrated with their own lives. In this respect, Giovanni resembles the poet-narrator in *The Fall of Hyperion*, who, because of his latent awareness of what a poet should do for the world, is also allowed to enter the sphere where no ordinary people live. Like the paradox of the poet-narrator who is temporarily endowed with immortality to witness mythical desolations in Keats' poem, the personal aspect of mortality in *Galaxy Railroad* centers on the paradox of Giovanni, who, although still living, unwittingly finds himself amidst the dead on the Galaxy Train.

The Dual Dimension of Time and Space

Examined in detail, the spatial and temporal aspects closely relate to each other in *The Fall of Hyperion* and *Galaxy Railroad*. In Keats' poem, the poet-narrator, guided by Moneta who is the only survivor of the Titan tribe and the companionless guardian of the temple of Saturn, witnesses the outcome of the war of gods which took place in a remote, mythological past. Moneta explains that the scenes which she intends to show him are kaleidoscopic in the sense that they are "[s]till swooning vivid through my globèd brain" and change with electric quickness.[70] Accordingly, a little later when the poet-narrator utters an eager assent to the divine favor, he asks her to reveal "[w]hat in thy brain so ferments to and fro."[71] All the scenes that he will perceive are the projection of past occurrences preserved in the never-fading memory of the goddess. Therefore, Moneta and her protégé do not have to travel by shifting their physical position in order to see one scene after another, however far away the actual locations of the scenes might have been from each other. The shift of their view is all within Moneta's power. For instance, as soon as the poet-narrator voices his request to show him her living memory of the dead past, he suddenly finds himself standing with his guiding deity at the bottom of the quiet, dark valley where the dethroned Saturn lies senseless:

> No sooner had this conjuration passed
> My devout lips than side by side we stood
> (Like a stunt bramble by a solemn pine),

> Deep in the shady sadness of a vale,
> Far sunken from the healthy breath of morn,
> Far from the fiery noon and eve's one star.
> Onward I looked beneath the gloomy boughs,
> And saw, what first I thought an image huge,
> Like to the image pedestalled so high
> In Saturn's temple.[72]

After the scene concludes with Thea's approach and Saturn's awakening, Moneta talks about the Titan sun-god who still keeps power. Then, with the words "[t]hither we tend,"[73] she expresses her intention to take the poet-narrator to Hyperion's sky palace, and he immediately finds himself and the goddess there:

> Now in clear light I stood,
> Relieved from the dusk vale. Mnemosyne
> Was sitting on a square-edged polished stone,
> That in its lucid depth reflected pure
> Her priestess-garments. My quick eyes ran on
> From stately nave to nave, from vault to vault,
> Through bowers of fragrant and enwreathèd light
> And diamond-pavèd lustrous long arcades.[74]

The sudden, spectacular change from darkness to light, from the depth of the earth to the height of the sky, from nature to artifice, is well calculated. It is as if the poet-narrator, although he is a creation of the early nineteenth century, were sitting comfortably on a seat and watching the panoramic shift of scenes on a large, cinematic screen.

The swift change of scenes without a shift in the observer's location is possible because of the divine power of Moneta. She projects her memory of the remote past into the poet-narrator's "dull mortal eyes,"[75] that is, his human consciousness.[76] Three points must be noted about this spatial dimension. First, this mode of travel suggests the immensity of space to be explored. In spite of his static position, the poet-narrator undertakes a journey beyond the possibility of human experience. Second, the scenes are simply shown to him—he cannot participate. Third, the scenes are nothing but the projection of what Moneta remembers, and so they are precisely "shades of memory," just like the goddess herself whom the poet-narrator calls by that name.[77] Although the scenes are exact reproductions of the past events, they are no more than unreal images.

Time in Keats' work is also far extended. On the one hand, time is cosmological, depicting the beginning of the world. In *Hyperion*, concerning the ancestry of his tribe, Oceanus explains the genesis of the universe as follows:

> From chaos and parental darkness came
> Light, the first fruits of that intestine broil,
> That sullen ferment, which for wondrous ends
> Was ripening in itself. The ripe hour came,
> And with it light, and light, engendering
> Upon its own producer, forthwith touched
> The whole enormous matter into life.
> Upon that very hour, our parentage,
> The heavens and the earth, were manifest;
> Then thou first-born, and we the giant race,
> Found ourselves ruling new and beauteous realms.[78]

This generic origin of the universe is apparently amalgamated from the Bible and Greek mythology. A corresponding reference to the end of the world, which could be expected of such a cosmogonic conception, is missing because of the early abandonment of Keats' mythopoeia.

On the other hand, as space expands beyond human sense at the will of the immortal goddess, so does time. All the events which Moneta shows to the poet-narrator actually happened in an ancient, almost timeless past, and the scenes recorded in her memory are now rehearsed for his sake. Time here is so proportioned to that of deities that its slow flow in these "immortal" scenes overwhelms human comprehension and racks man's endurance. Now invested by Moneta with "[a] power . . . of enormous ken / To see as a god sees,"[79] the observing poet-narrator finds himself barely able to sustain the temporal passage of one month which follows Thea's entrance, though it is supposed to be a mere span in divinities' terms:

> A long awful time
> I looked upon them: still they were the same;
> The frozen God [Saturn] still bending to the earth,
> And the sad Goddess [Thea] weeping at his feet,
> Moneta silent. Without stay or prop
> But my own weak mortality, I bore

> The load of this eternal quietude,
> The unchanging gloom, and the three fixèd shapes
> Ponderous upon my senses a whole moon.
> For by my burning brain I measured sure
> Her silver seasons shedded on the night,
> And ever day by day methought I grew
> More gaunt and ghostly. Oftentimes I prayed
> Intense, that death would take me from the vale
> And all its burthens. Gasping with despair
> Of change, hour after hour I cursed myself—[80]

The poet-narrator is only half-immortalized, because the metamorphosis affects his ability to perceive the external circumstances, but not his internal nature as a mortal. For a human being who is attuned to the world of ceaseless change, such a procession of time without a single motion is simply unbearable. In this situation, the enhanced cognitive power to "take the depth / Of things as nimbly as the outward eye / Can size and shape pervade" yields nothing but pains.[81] Comparable to the life-in-death suffering of Coleridge's ancient mariner, the man's senses are all but strangled with a corpse-like weight around his "weak mortality," that is, with the sheer pressure of a deathless, yet long dead sight.

The episode shows the Janus-faced nature of mortality in relation to time and change. Ever since Gilgamesh's bewailment and Achilles' tragic stance, the flow of time that entails death and mutability has been a great cause of human anxiety and, consequently, a significant element of the epic-producing impulse. Consciously or unconsciously, people wish their life long, even everlasting if possible, with their stable world unchanged. At the same time, however, as creatures of the changing world, they cannot do without change, a possible reason, as I have argued earlier, for Odysseus' longing to flee promised immortality on Calypso's island. This incompatibility of mortal nature with the immortal world is exactly what Moneta subtly warns Keats' poet-narrator of when she grants him temporary and partial immortality: he will witness the scenes of the long past without any pain "if wonder pain thee not."[82] In other words, the mutable nature of our existence, including death, is not rejected but accepted here as an essential element of our humanity.

Finally, the goddess Moneta relates the supernatural dimension of time to the equally supernatural dimension of space by

controlling time and space in her memory at will. In this respect,
The Fall of Hyperion is different from a traditional type of epic, in
which time and space are the two distinct aspects of physicality.

In the case of *Galaxy Railroad*, temporally, a gap occurs
between the two kinds of time, that is, time in the waking consciousness and time in the dreaming consciousness. The time
perceived in the mode of everyday life covers no more than a
small part of one specific night. When Giovanni wakes up, "the
position of the whole sky appeared not much changed" since he
fell asleep on the hill.[83] His dreaming time is more precisely specified at the end of the story. When the boy comes to Campanella's
father on the riverside, the man checks his watch with a scien-
tist-like precision and says, restraining his grief in a firm tone,
that it is now impossible to find his son alive because "forty-five
minutes" has passed since Campanella's disappearance into the
water.[84] His words suggest that Giovanni's dream probably lasted
for only about half an hour, considering the presence of Campanella, or rather of his soul, on the train from the beginning of
the trip and the time Giovanni spent descending from the hilltop.
In comparison, Keats' poem, which lacks the scene of the poet-
narrator's awaking, does not have this kind of temporal gap
between dream and reality.

Apart from our empirical understanding that the duration of
time in a dream is often felt to be longer than the measured
advance of waking hours, however, it is in the dream field that
time is greatly expanded in *Galaxy Railroad*. During Giovanni's
dream, there is a single, obvious reference to long ago. The
archaeologist, who is excavating fossils with three assistants at
the Pliocene Coast, briefly explains the nature of their work to the
two young visitors. He calls the 1.2-million-year-old walnuts,
which they often dig out there, "very new ones,"[85] and continues:
"This place is a wide, excellent stratum, and there are various
things to prove that the place was formed about one million and
two hundred thousand years ago. What I want to make sure is
whether the stratum really appears like such a stratum or looks
like nothing but winds, water, and empty sky to beings different
from us."[86] The age of the place named after a geological period is
considered *as short as* one million years or so because of the
evidence of celestial archeology. The history in *Galaxy Railroad*
thus proves to be that of the cosmos, viewed half-scientifically
and half-imaginatively. The scientific stance in Miyazawa's work
makes an interesting contrast to the mythological orientation of

The Fall of Hyperion. Moreover, unlike Keats' poem, Miyazawa's work does not explain how the universe began. Still, the two works do share the awareness of a tremendous temporal scope.

Excluding the cosmological time which the fossils suggest, *Galaxy Railroad* does not provide a clear scope of history. Another sense of temporal dimension becomes possible, however, when the structural nature of the train trip is considered in relation to many details about the movement of the train. At the very beginning of his dream, Giovanni, in his still-vague consciousness, hears "the Galaxy Station" repeatedly called,[87] just as we hear an announcement when a train approaches a station. Campanella, who appears to have come on board before Giovanni, has somehow obtained, at the Galaxy Station, a beautiful black map made of obsidian. On that map of the nocturnal firmament, with each sign inlaid with a beautiful light, Giovanni sees "one railroad stretching south along the left shore of the white *ama no gawa.*"[88] The map also includes the schedule of the train. Thus, the boys know that the vehicle will arrive at the Station of the Swan "at eleven sharp."[89] At that station, under a clock which points exactly to eleven o'clock, they read the words "Twenty-Minute Stop,"[90] and so they decide to make the short trip to the riverside. At another time, Campanella realizes, by identifying small triangular signs outside with those on the map, that they are about to reach the Station of the Eagle. The whole metaphor of the train trip intimates that, by nature, the journey on the Galaxy Railroad, which runs on a time schedule just like a train on the earth, takes place every night. It is the trip which the souls of dead people make on the night of their death as they move toward their believed heaven, and it is repeated night after night, generation after generation, century after century, as long as people inhabit the surface of the earth.

The endlessly repeated journey through time and space is made possible by a train.[91] By integrating the double dimension into one meaning, the mechanical vehicle functions in the same way that Moneta does in *The Fall of Hyperion.* Although the train functions as an inanimate means of transportation in contrast to the goddess who chooses to conduct the poet-narrator through the space of a remote past, the constant movement of the train has a significance almost equivalent to the will of the goddess. This is all the more apparent in the early version of Miyazawa's work, in which Giovanni is under the spiritual guidance of Dr. Bulcaniro's transmitted thought during the entire train trip.

With regard to the spatial dimension of *Galaxy Railroad*, its extent is typically suggested when Giovanni and Campanella are recognized on the train as having come "from far."[92] The Galaxy Railroad ranges from the earth to the world of stars and constellations. But the spatial dimension in the work is not merely immense; it consists of several spaces, such as our world, the special space called Illusory Four-Dimensional, the heaven(s), and the pit of the sky. In fact, the term "the Illusory Four-Dimensional (Space)" suggests that there are many other spaces in addition to the ones manifest in the work.[93]

Interestingly, quite analogous to the situation of the poet-narrator who observes one scene after another in Keats' poem like someone watching a movie, Giovanni enjoys panoramic views from the comfort of the train. Together with his companion Campanella, the boy delightedly watches splendid scenes pass by one after another among the stars and constellations, scenes such as the *ama no gawa*, the Northern and Southern Crosses, many stations, fields, forests, and migrating birds and dolphins. Not surprisingly, the space in *Galaxy Railroad* has the three features that have already been noted in our discussion of space in *The Fall of Hyperion*. For instance, Giovanni can experience the vast and dynamic expanse of the night sky without taking one single step as long as he stays on the train. It is not the boy but the train, the mysterious vehicle that connects the earth to the heaven, that keeps on moving forward. Giovanni is similar to the poet-narrator who, thanks to Moneta's divine power, travels through a vast expanse of space without moving a finger.

Moreover, as long as he stays inside the advancing train, Giovanni cannot participate in what exists and takes place outside. Even when the train makes a stop and he has a chance to get off for a short trip, the relation of the boy to the external world remains basically unchanged. On their way back from the Pliocene Coast to the Station of the Swan, Giovanni and Campanella, in a hurry not to miss the train, find themselves endowed with a strange running power:

> They could run really like a wind. They never became out of breath, nor did their knees become hot.
> Giovanni thought that he could run like this all over the world.
> The two passed that riverbed previously seen. The electric light of the ticket gate emerged bigger and bigger, and,

soon, the two were sitting on the seat of their car and watching from the window the direction from which they had just come back.[94]

In this passage, the places being passed seem to come to the boys more than the boys advancing toward them. The running boys see the places pass by with the same kind of comfort they enjoy when they watch the outside world from within the moving train. Their transportational ease, probably a qualitative extension of the train ride itself, suggests that, even when they are not on the train, the boys have little power to interfere with the external world. In fact, away from the Station of the Swan, Giovanni and Campanella scarcely affect and interact with the environment. All they do at the Pliocene Coast is to trifle with what they find there such as the sand, the stream, and fossilized walnuts and briefly talk with the archaeologist who would rather not be distracted from his excavation by the boys' questions. The key verb, not only in this episode but also throughout the work, is to "see" or "view." The similarity to Keats' poet-narrator's situation, in which the same verb holds equal importance, is obvious. Giovanni and the poet-narrator are both stationary observers.[95]

Finally, the space through which Giovanni travels appears unreal. From what the birdcatcher says about Giovanni's special pass, we learn that it is called "the Illusory Four-Dimensional [Space]."[96] This appellation makes the substance of the special space uncertain in the system of multiple space. Thus, both *Galaxy Railroad* and Keats' poem share the unreality of space. In each case, the unusual space where the main story takes place maintains its imaginary, "shadowy" existence somewhere independent of other spaces. Furthermore, the special space of each piece is neither exploited for a specific, mundane purpose as in Western imperial epic, nor is the ordinary world subjugated to the special space as in religious epic. Admittedly, there are differences between the two works, such as whether the agent of locational change is a deity or a machine, whether the central figure can leave the agent, and whether the space is a reproduction of the past or not. Nevertheless, the basic similarities centering on spatial dimension are remarkable.

In addition to this manifest spatial dimension of *Galaxy Railroad*, one must explore Miyazawa's cosmography further, because his work contains a certain holistic view of the universe that still needs to be explained. In the case of *The Fall of Hyper-*

ion, such a detour is unnecessary, because, unlike Miyazawa's piece, the mode of shifting the scenes fully benefits from the omnipotent authorial viewpoint that takes the form of instantaneous mnemonic flight. The special significance of Miyazawa's organic universe centers on the symbolism of the celestial, streaming water called the *ama no gawa*, and this symbolism involves not only the spatial dimension but all the other thematic elements of the epic as well.

The literal translation of the *ama no gawa* is "the stream of heaven" or "the river of the sky." This study preserves the Japanese expression untranslated for Miyazawa's aerial river.[97] On the one hand, its English counterparts, "the Milky Way" and the "galaxy," are somewhat incompatible with Miyazawa's image of the ethereal stream, because the latter term remotely suggests milk in its etymology (*gala* = "milk" in Greek) while the former expression directly points to it. The Japanese word *ginga*, on the other hand, literally means "the silver river," and it should be taken as an equivalent of the English "galaxy" in its denotation. Compared with the folkloric *ama no gawa* and the mythic Milky Way, the two words are used as scientific terms in their respective languages. For this reason, I have translated the title *Gingatetsudō no Yoru* as *A Night on the Galaxy Railroad*.

But "the Milky Way" is not a totally unsuitable translation either, for the *ama no gawa* does have some relation to milk in *Galaxy Railroad*. In fact, milk is one of the central images, and it is associated with the galaxy at the very beginning of the story.[98] The English "Milky Way" would just make the intended symbolism, which is deliberately subtle in the original Japanese, too obvious. The initial association of the *ama no gawa* with milk is made twice by Giovanni's teacher during a science class. He first refers to the Greek etymology indirectly ("this vague, white thing which was sometimes considered a river and sometimes a trace of spilt milk"), and then he likens the galaxy to "a large stream of milk," in which stars and planets float just like "tiny balls of fat."[99] Moreover, in a sense, it is milk which occasions and closes Giovanni's visionary trip. He leaves home early in the evening to bring the undelivered milk for his bed-ridden mother. At the end of the story, he hurries home with it for the waiting patient who is expected to recuperate thanks to the liquid nourishment. In this sense, the *ama no gawa* stands, in Kuwahara Hiroyoshi's words, for "the stream of life" which cures illness,[100] on top of its indirect linkage to the expression "Milky Way" and its direct association with the galaxy in the science lecture. The water of the *ama no gawa* is the milk of the universe which Giovanni brings back to his mother.[101] In an extended metaphor, the water is what Giovanni has sought on his personal mission. Archetypally, water is often the fundamental source of life, physically and spiritually.[102] Giovanni's journey away from home allegorizes his quest for the archetypal water with which he should relieve the spiritual drought within himself and the world.

In fact, the river of the sky implies not only life but also death. The following passage, which describes the scene of the search for the submerged Campanella shortly after Giovanni's awakening, suggests the mysterious double nature of the *ama no gawa*:

> Everybody else was watching the river, too. Nobody was saying a word. Giovanni felt his legs trembling a lot. Many acetylene torches used in fishing were busily passing around here and there, and one could see the dark water of the river flowing with small, flickering waves.
>
> In the downstream, the galaxy was reflected full and large on the river, and it looked just like the sky without water.
>
> Giovanni keenly felt Campanella could now be found only at the end of that galaxy.[103]

The celestial river, which is visually linked to the actual one, makes a stream of immense dimension stretching from heaven to earth, or, in Hagiwara's terms, "a huge circle" that "symbolizes the unity and the order of the entire universe."[104] Giovanni stands back in life on this side of the river with a portion of its bottled water, while his friend is drowned in the water only to find himself in afterlife on the other side. The cosmic river flows on the border between life and death.

The river barely visible with diffused reflection recalls the ethereal water of the *ama no gawa* in which Giovanni and Campanella dip their hands earlier in the story. From Giovanni's point of view at least, the two boys are the closest to each other at this moment during their night journey, because Giovanni feels that he fully and exclusively enjoys Campanella's company and friendship. The scene takes place before they are joined by the other train passengers, especially Kaoru, who disturbs Giovanni's mind with jealousy. The two boys are also symbolically closest to each other at the river, because dipping their hands signifies a purifying, baptismal rite of passage for both of them. The water induces the oblivion of the past events like the Lethean stream and demarcates the final border between life and death. At the initial stage of their trip, the two boys keep the memory of their life on earth, such as the names of their classmates. But soon after they come back aboard from the *ama no gawa*, they can "by no means remember any more" where they are from.[105] Giovanni cannot even specify that "somebody" working "[a]t the northernmost sea where icebergs float, on a small boat,"[106] although the unnamed man must contextually be his father. The forgetfulness is not meant to be a perfect one. But after the boys' excursion to the river shore, there is only one direct reference to people and events of their ordinary world when Giovanni argues with Kaoru about whose God is the real one and mentions his teacher.

In contrast, the Japanese girl and her company still clearly remember what has happened in this world, including the last moments of their lives, the sobriquet and music of Dvořák's Ninth Symphony, and a few tales they learned about twin stars, a comet, and the scorpion. This is because they are not exposed to the water of the river yet. At the Southern Cross, Giovanni and Campanella witness the Christians, who have disembarked from the train, "kneeling humbly in a line on the shore of the *ama no gawa* in front of that Cross" when "one godly person in white" comes toward them across the river with arms extended.[107] The two boys do not see them go across the stream because the train leaves the station when the "silvery fog" covers the scene.[108] But the passage of the group to the other shore is undoubtedly anticipated. Cleansed of the painful memory of their past, the Christian people are supposed to remain there happily ever after.

It follows that the *ama no gawa* flows through the night sky between life (memory) and death (loss of memory), and its water has the effect of purification. The inviolability of the demarcation is indicated by the fact that the train line always runs on "the left shore" of the *ama no gawa*.[109] The train that carries people who retain the memory of earthly life never goes across the river. Crossing the river means a crucial rite of passage, and touching its water, a baptismal ritual. By performing the same action on the Pliocene Coast, however, each of the two boys undergoes a ritual of a different nature. For Campanella, it signals his rebirth to an eternal life through death. For Giovanni,

the mystic water stands for what he has been searching to revitalize life, relieve the world of its woes, and gain a new self. Before
they play with the stream, the difference between them appears
almost nonexistent. After all, they are both souls of errant consciousness, because the two boys have left their bodies behind in
some way or other. At the very moment they feel as one at the
shore, however, a symbolical, irreversible cleavage begins to distance them. In this sense, the dream section of the story can be
divided into two parts: the pre-ritual stage when the two boys are
not disturbed by other passengers and feel close to each other,
and the post-ritual stage when they mingle with several train
passengers and increasingly feel within themselves the difference between the dead and the living.

Two totally different kinds of ritual can be performed with
the same water, because the *ama no gawa* is the stream of existence that comprehends life and death. In the space through
which Giovanni travels, the dichotomy of existence (life versus
death, form versus nonform, organic versus inorganic) means
very little, because the stream is the flow of pure energy before
matter and everything that has form originates in it.[110] The flow
runs through the aerial space and affects its entire nature with
almost transparent radiation. For instance, the descending birds
(form) turn to sand (virtual nonform) on the river shore:

> But there were more birds which, uncaught, alighted safely
> on the sand of the *ama no gawa* than the ones caught [by
> the birdcatcher]. They [Giovanni and Campanella] saw those
> birds shrunk and flattened like melting snow as soon as
> their feet touched the sand. Soon, the birds spread on the
> sand and the pebbles like liquefied copper out of a blast-fur-
> nace. The shape of birds was kept on the sand for a while,
> but it took the color of the surroundings after its light went
> on and off a few times.[111]

As long as the birdcatcher gets hold of the birds before they land
on the sand, he can sell them as his "goods" because, once
secured in his bags, the birds transmute themselves to sweets
without losing their shape.[112] The ease with which the birds are
transformed into sand, as if it were the way they rest and sleep,
makes us imagine how smoothly the sand might retake the
shape of birds later to continue their flight away from the riverside. Indeed, they are a tiny fraction of the "migrating birds,"

including swans, cranes, white herons, and wild geese, which fly over a crossing of the river in "tens of thousands."[113] And the birdcatcher, who is an expert on the winged creatures, tells the boys that "all the herons emerge by themselves out of the congealed sand of the *ama no gawa* and they always come back to the river."[114] The basic premise of life or death, form or formlessness, is irrelevant to these creatures.

The Galaxy Railroad that runs in the same direction with the river forms a parallel line to the flow of cosmic power. This explains why the dead find themselves traveling along the stream on that train. They have to get through a state in which the binary form of existence is reduced to original monism, before they go across the river to be accepted into their heaven. The train ride is a symbolic ritual for the transition. And because the space where the stream and the railroad run side by side stands almost beyond the division of life and death, Giovanni, who is still alive, can temporarily be there, too. It is not the world of the dead as it might appear at first. The dead pass through the space as a necessary process for their heavenly rebirth and abide there no more than Giovanni the living does.

As the cosmic river, the *ama no gawa* derives its power from its source in the north on which Miyazawa placed great significance. The hill, at the top of which Giovanni falls asleep, is situated to the north of the town. To get there, the boy walks through the dark wood toward "the Great Bear in the north" on a "small, white stretch of a starlit trail."[115] At the center of the open, plain hilltop stands a pole called *tenkirin no hashira* (literally, "the pole of the weather ring"). The model, structure, and nature of this pole have been interpreted in widely divergent ways.[116] Whatever it might be, it is certain that the pole has something to do with Giovanni's dream journey, because he sleeps at the foot of the pole, probably to the south of it. Just before falling asleep, in his growingly dim consciousness, he sees "the blue star of the Lyre [probably Vega] split in a few twinkling pieces," which "alternately extended and drew back a leg several times and finally grew the leg like a mushroom,"[117] apparently toward the pole. This vision marks the opening of the passage from the hill to the world above, through which Giovanni's dreaming self is transported. The pole of the weather ring functions as one end of the ladder for the transmigratory soul.[118]

While Giovanni is watching it, the pole metamorphoses into a triangular sign standing straight "in the dark, steely blue field of the sky," and he suddenly finds himself riding on a small train that has just left behind the voice announcing "Galaxy Station."[119] The field outside is filled with similar triangular signs which, "shining phosphorescent, stood beautifully here and there,"[120] often in groups, with a variety of colors, degrees of brightness, and configurations such as triangle, square, lightning, and chain. Obviously, the triangular signs stand for stars in the night sky, and their various group arrangements for constellations. A curious element should be noted here. In spite of abundant references to the names of stars and constellations, the North Star is never mentioned throughout the story. The lack of reference to such a significant star is all the more conspicuous at the beginning of Giovanni's visionary journey, because his aerial passage from the pole of the weather ring to the Galaxy Station is closely associated with the Great Bear and the Lyre, both constellations of the northern sky. Another northern attribute around the Galaxy Station is the "steely" quality of the dark blue sky, a quality shared by the Northern Cross which appears "as if cast in the frozen cloud of the North Pole."[121] This is not the case with the Southern Cross, whose multicolored body looks "as if it were a tree."[122] Apparently, the mention of the North Star is carefully avoided.

This does not mean that the North Star is insignificant in Miyazawa's cosmography. The star around which all the sky turns is popularly considered to be the axis of the universe. Because of its centrality in the night sky, the astrological worship of the North Star is found in many parts of the world, including a sect of esoteric Buddhism in Japan. As we have seen, Buddhism is another referent without reference in *Galaxy Railroad*. Although, or perhaps because, Buddhist ideas are so essential to the theme of the story, the author has carefully shunned any explicit references to them. The North Star must have as much significance as Buddhism.

Taking all these factors into account, one must assume that the Galaxy Station, the starting terminal of the railroad, is located close to the North Star. Apart from the actual Milky Way, Miyazawa's stream of existence springs out of the pivot of the universe, eternally runs through the night sky, and flows toward the antipole in the south, which also remains unseen, as the reflected image of the cosmic river suggests at the close of the story.[123] With religious piety as well as artistic humility, Miyazawa must have felt it sacrilegious and hardly possible to touch upon the source of existence itself. Instead, he created the Galaxy Station as the materialized double of Polaris. The architecture as a shadow of the original substance supposedly stands close to the North Star. The Platonic correspondence is underscored later in an extended metaphor in which the visually materialized Galaxy Railroad always runs along the ethereal, hardly expressible *ama no gawa*. Both the station and the railroad have the word "galaxy" in their names, not simply because they are situated amidst an intense concentration of stars, but because they are related to the existence of the universe by symbolic parallelism. Still, with a profound awe of the mystery called existence, Miyazawa does not even show us the material version of the North Star. Dazed with pervasive brightness, Giovanni on the starting train only hears "a strange voice" announce the name of the station twice.[124]

With regard to the pole of the weather ring, behind the Japanese text, a word play in English is possibly intended between this *pole* and the implied *polar* star, because *tenkirin no hashira* can also be rendered as "the pole of the atmosphere of heaven" or "the pole of the heavenly essence." In the symbolism of geological movement, the North Pole of the sky corresponds to the North Pole of the earth. It follows that the pole of the weather ring, which stands at the very top of the hill to the north of the town, stands for the northern surface point of the axis around which the globe rotates. Although "traditionally known as the indicator of the North Star," the Great Bear is located with denotative stress "in the north," which "probably suggests the extreme northern position of the hill."[125] Some of Miyazawa's tales and poems, such as "Hyōga-nezumi no kegawa" (The fur of glacier mice), his preface to *A Restaurant of Many Orders*, "Hanayasai" (Flowery vegetables), and "Fuyu to Ginga Station" (Winter and the Galaxy Station), reveal the author's unfailing interest in the north. In real life, too, Miyazawa showed a strong fascination with the same direction by making a few major, northbound trips to Hokkaido and Sakhalin. One of those trips was a journey of requiem for his dear sister Toshiko, in which his undiminished grief resulting from her death was sublimated into his poetry. Ikegami Yūzō argues that Miyazawa's trip to the north met his wish "to go upward, that is, to reach heaven" because of the geographical directions in a map, where the north is located at the top.[126] It is also conceivable that Miyazawa expected the effect of spiritual purification in the less fertile, northern climate.

Miyazawa's special attraction to the north offers another reason why sad, ostracized Giovanni heads for the hill in the north and his dreaming consciousness is transported from the earthly North Pole to the heavenly counterpart. Miyazawa wished for an existence devoid of guilt and trouble, which he found neither in the south teeming with life and thus entailing more strife for survival, nor in the east, where the vast ocean suddenly brings disastrous tidal waves as happened by strange coincidence in the years of his birth and death,[127] nor in the west where Japan waged wars. His praying imagination was turned toward the only direction where the problem of existence could be resolved by the influence of the unmentioned North Star.

The benign influence of the North Star, or of the *ama no gawa* as its extension, over the earth constitutes the central myth of the communal celebration which is sometimes called "the Festival of the Galaxy" and sometimes "the Festival of the Centaur."[128] That evening, the town's children shout, "Centaur, let the dews fall," while they play with "the blue fireworks of magnesium."[129] Here, the three important elements are the water of the heaven, the Centaur, and the stellar sparkles. The dews the children innocently crave are the same drops from the *ama no gawa* that Giovanni seeks. Without knowing the ritualistic significance of their words, the children wish to be purified with those dews from the original sin of existing. Children are the participants of the festival because, as representative of the community, they are relatively taintless.[130] Then, the annual joyful event invests its myths and rituals with cosmic implications, and it becomes a festival of existence that purifies the world community.[131]

As the children's brisk prayer indicates, the Centaur presides over the festival. The importance of the mythic, constellated figure on the festive occasion is also hinted by an artifact that Giovanni happens to observe. Just before Giovanni hears the other children make the ritualized cry on his way to the milkshop, he stops for a while in front of a timepiece (jewelry) store. He is fascinated to see a few items on display for the special evening, including an owl of stone with red, turning eyes, a small telescope on a tripod, and a large picture of the figured constellations. In the midst is a thick, glass disk on which many kinds of jewels and "a copper *jimba*" (man-horse = the Centaur) turn slowly.[132] The disk "of the sea-like color" has "a round, black planisphere" at its center.[133] The oblong opening of the rotatable planisphere can be adjusted by days and hours, and it now shows the map of the current night sky with the galaxy across the microcosm "like a vague, smoky band."[134] Many symbols are recognizable here. The entire scene foreshadows Giovanni's night trip and is a liminal inducement to it. The repeated turning imagery stands for the perpetual, universal rotation that hinges on the North Star. The fact that the whole display is in a timepiece store is related to the precise, gradual movement of the macrocosm. The small telescope stands beside the rotating disk as an optic bridge between microcosm and macrocosm. The apparatus prefigures the tripodic star that, "split in a few twinkling pieces," will extend its mushroom-like leg toward Giovanni to transport his dreaming consciousness from the hilltop to the world above.[135]

In the symbol-fraught context, the Centaur, whose figure solely and commandingly appears on the gem-studded turning disk, bears special significance among the stars and the other constellations at the time of the festivity. As Hagiwara argues, the "supernatural creature" might be made from the liminal coalescence of conscious (people) and unconscious (beasts), hence "symbolic of the synthesis of ordinary time and un-ordinary time," upon which a dream is formed.[136] This view places equal significance on the creature's beastly nature as well as his human nature. But the centaur commemorated in the night sky cannot be one of the licentious wedding guests who, inebriated, violently ruin the reception and are killed by Hercules. Far from exhibiting such untamed crudity, it is more likely Chiron, who instructed both young Achilles the brave, and Asclepius, the god of medicine and healing, just as Aristotle did the boy Alexander. The image of a good, beneficial teacher is appropriate for the festive rite in which children participate for their spiritual growth. The Centaur is selected from among the constellated figures to have the authority of letting fall the water of existence as the supernatural, wise man of heaven.

Along with the lights of *karasuuri* (snake gourds) which the children let flow on the river on the eve of the festival, the blue sparkles of magnesium fireworks have their own mythic relevance. The fires are variations of the drops from the *ama no gawa*, which is the heatless, yet fire-like stream in the dark blue sky.[137] What is intended here is the unity of opposites, or, in Hagiwara's terms, "*coincidentia oppositorum*," between fire and water.[138] In fact, as Hagiwara points out, such unity of opposites is found in the very chemical composition of water that is formed by the oxidation (slow burning) of hydrogen.[139] Again, in such a coalescence, binary conflict is dissolved into monistic harmony. It follows that the children symbolically involve themselves in the unification of existential opposites by burning the magnesium fireworks. Probably modeled on the summer Buddhist festival in which people send off their ancestral souls on small, paper-made, floating lanterns, the act of letting the snake gourd lights flow down the stream ritualizes the rebirth that casts off the old self of contradictory existence.

The blue firework sparks at the beginning of the story antic-ipatively correspond to the celestial signal fire which consistently appears at the end of Giovanni's dream in the first three manuscripts. In the early (third) version, the mysterious adult with a large hat ends his comforting lecture on the system of the universe, which touches on the atomic formation of water as an instance of truth, with the following words:

> "Look, over there, it's the Plesios. You have to resolve the chain of that Plesios."
>
> At that moment, a signal fire was shot up from beyond the dark horizon, and its whitish blue light, bright as a day, illuminated the inside of the train. And that signal fire kept on shining suspended high in the sky.[140]

Although not precisely identifiable, the Plesios presumably refers to the Pleiades. Apparently, Miyazawa imagined the luminous cluster of stars as having the shape of a chain. Thus, some of the triangular signs in the field of the sky are arranged in the shape of chains.[141] As Mita Munesuke and Hara Shirō argue, the chain in heaven might also have derived from a passage in the Book of Job (38:31) as "a symbol of what people cannot solve."[142] In this sense, the celestial chain symbolizes the original sin of exis-tence, in which opposites never mingle and the stronger feed on the weaker.[143] The symbol of such a fundamental problem of existence should not be forcibly destroyed (*kowasu*) as Alexander cut (*kiru*) the Gordian knot with a sword, nor can it be simply removed (*hazusu*) like the chains binding Shelley's hero for three thousand years in *Prometheus Unbound*. The problem will not disappear and cannot be eliminated, and somehow the chain has to be resolved (*toku*). In other words, as Hagiwara suggests, Giovanni has to "understand" the nature of happiness for all before he "achieves" it.[144]

Without making any reference to the Plesios chain, Giovanni is greatly moved at the sight of the blue signal fire, which
he calls "the nebula of Magellan,"[145] and he finally declares his
determination to work for the happiness of all. In reality, the
Magellanic clouds are situated about twenty degrees away from
the South Pole of heaven, and they cannot be perceived by the
people who live in the Northern Hemisphere. Giovanni's sighting
of the nebula suggests that he is now close to his destination. His
journey stretches along the *ama no gawa* from the unmentioned
source of existence at the North Pole toward the unseen southern
point that the grand flow of existence reaches in the end. In the
form of baptism with the water of that stream, he has undergone
the rite of passage to obtain a new life in this world, and he
finally acquires self-confidence and belief in his mission. The
ascendant signal fire is elementally identical with the water of the
ama no gawa. It signals Giovanni's fully realized inner transformation. In this light, the blue sparks of the magnesium fireworks which the children hold in the Festival of the Galaxy are
meant to be the metonyms of the bluish Magellanic clouds, with
which they wishfully ritualize their own spiritual growth to the
benefit of the rest of the world. Meanwhile, the chain of the Plesios remains suspended in the night sky as a visual reminder of
the problem Giovanni is expected to solve back on earth.

Thus, the symbolism of the *ama no gawa* reveals the organic
immensity of Miyazawa's universe that involves all the three thematic elements of the epic. It follows that those fundamental
epic elements—the hero's attitude toward his mortality, his relation to the community, and the dimension of time and space—
contribute to the epic nature of both *The Fall of Hyperion* and
Galaxy Railroad. In comparison with traditional epic, the communal dimension, as well as the dual dimension of time and
space, is tremendously magnified, almost to the limit of the imagination. The two works achieve the dimensional immensity of
religious Western epic without being primarily religious. With
regard to the attitude toward mortality, however, a conversion of
values occurs, for the question is how to make one's life and
death meaningful for others, rather than how to face and overcome death and mutability. The altruistic principle has ever been
present in the communal dimension and has been gradually
enhanced through the development of the three types of traditional Western epic. But what underlies the principle is some

kind of transcendental value that should annul the anxiety of existence. By contrast in Keats' and Miyazawa's work, the ontological concern with mortality, although still important, does not weigh so much as the welfare of humanity.

The epic impulse of *The Fall of Hyperion* and *Galaxy Railroad* originates in each author's individual concern. In the making of his imaginary, mythological world, Keats attempted to assimilate his early belief that "a thing of beauty" should be "a joy for ever" to the world of change as its governing principle of order. This personal belief in the beauty principle replaces what the *Faerie Queene* posited as an answer to the problem of the mutable world: the law of orderliness inherent in the very cyclical process of change. In Miyazawa's case, Kojūrō in "The Bears on the Nametoko Hill" had to perish in the reality fettered with the problem of life feeding on others, including commercial exploitation. The ugly-looking bird in "The Nighthawk Star" could release himself from the problem of existence by self-annihilating flight into the night sky. But this is the salvation of just one soul. In the immense dream-formation replete with his religious enthusiasm, Miyazawa opted for a universal solution in the direction of the vast space that opens up above reality.

One can also perceive similarities with regard to the central figures. In each case, the central figure is too weak to be called "an epic hero" in the ordinary sense of the word. He lacks not only physical strength, but also spiritual might, especially self-confidence. Giovanni is always worried about his social stigmatization as the son of an alleged poacher. Likewise, Keats' poet-narrator is unsure about his *raison d'être*. The two heroes are special only because each of them is somehow allowed to enter an unusual space to which ordinary people are denied access. Their journeys are spiritual ones in the sense that they overcome their initial weakness in the process. Giovanni learns to live for the sake of others, while the poet-narrator realizes his importance as a poet who is expected to relieve the world of its pains. Their earnest commitment to communal welfare is comparable to the Aenean devotion to the imperial cause which, however, is supplanted and surpassed by the widened scope of community.

Such characterization of the central figures recalls the *Divine Comedy*, for Dante the poet-narrator undergoes a similar spiritual growth. The Italian figure is depicted at first as an ordinary, morally feeble man full of troubles and doubts in the midst of his life. Through his providentially granted journey in the three spheres of afterlife, however, he obtains a total view of the universe and regains confidence in his life, faith, and the world. Dante is also a visionary who virtually does not interfere with the given construct of images. He simply observes and goes on. The parallelism between Dante and the two characters of the later works yields one more analogy in the relation of the weak central figure to the extended community. As in Dante's case, Giovanni and Keats' poet-narrator, typically weak, troubled beings, bear the symbolic representation of all humanity upon their single selves. But with a conspicuous difference: with his mission simply given, Dante the traveler is unaware of his representation; specially guided as they are, the other two take the initiative in realizing their particular position as the signifiers of the symbolism toward the signified world.

This new concept of the epic hero, which the poet-narrator and Giovanni posit in their characterization, foregrounds the absence of martial action. It is true that, in the conventional *in medias res* manner, *Hyperion* begins with a tranquil scene following the untold insurrection of Zeus and his cohort. Had they not been left unfinished, both Hyperion poems would have depicted the counter-rebellion by the subdued Titans. The fact remains, however, that the Hyperion poems are devoid of military scenes. This absence of battle can therefore be equally ascribed to the poet's artistic dilemma between two unlikely alternatives. In presenting the expected battle scenes, he would have had to force himself to expose either the obsoleteness of ancient, Homeric warfare in the age of Napoleonic strategy, or the inadequacy of introducing into a mythical context the blatantly anachronistic weaponry such as the artillery of "deep throated engines" in the wake of Milton.[146] In relation to the oscillation, another reason for the double textuality is conceivable. Keats recast the narrative in preference of his articulating double to the defiant Hyperion as the hero of the poem, because the centrality of the latter insinuated a reversion to the Achillean value system with its relentless heroic stance. Such atavism would preclude any political compromise required to dismantle the antagonism between the two parties whose existence is imperishable by definition. Some distancing from the archaic type of hero was therefore needed. In short, Keats was reluctant to present any violent battle scene against the prevailing tendency, inherent in other Romantic poetry as well as in his poems, to replace military valor with more peaceful, spiritual virtues.

Miyazawa's work is likewise totally devoid of militarism. His religious pacifism partly accounts for this feature. At the same time, his reaction to the traditional norms in Japanese literature ought to be considered. As has been pointed out earlier, his adoption of the narrative style of a children's tale is probably meant as a stance against the novel that is the prevailing, mimetic mode of representing the world. In fact, his literary creation as a whole disregards continuity with the established norms of literature in its unique approach to the overflowing potentiality in life. His disavowal of the literary canons fundamentally comes from his marginalized activities away from the locales of established cultural gravity, especially from the nation's capital. What he rejects includes traditional aesthetics as well as the novelistic mode of representation. In a significant portion of his poetry, he does have recourse to the traditionally sanctified formulae such as *tanka*. Even then, however, he makes innovative experiments with form and rhythm, and he does not follow the aesthetics handed down from classical Japanese literature.

One possible exception to Miyazawa's distancing himself from the mainstream tradition is his sympathetic attitude toward the vulnerable. As we have discussed earlier, a poetics based on lyricism, from Heian court literature onwards, fostered the national predilection for the weak and even had a great part in shaping the warrior ethical code. Similarly, sympathy with the weak characterizes Miyazawa's tales that are fraught with lyricism. It is quite likely that the traditional sympathy with the weak might have somewhat affected his perception of the world. But, even in this case, his topical commitment to the motif is so marked by idiosyncrasy in style and outlook on life that the affinity between individual and cultural mainstream appears more coincidental than indicative of causality. In the context of such a clear dislocation of the tradition, the lack of martial motif in *Galaxy Railroad*, as well as in Miyazawa's works in general, is not just symptomatic of his intrinsic pacifism. Probably, it also implies his opposition to the prevailing culture that has the *gunkimono* tradition, including *The Tale of the Heike*, as part of its important literary legacy. In the intentionally simple guise of a children's story, Miyazawa created an entirely new kind of work which is non-agonistic and is of such an unprecedented scale in Japan that it is comparable to Keats' epic pieces in every dimension. In this sense, I suggest that *Galaxy Railroad* be called an epic of peace, or at least an attempt at one, even though it does not have any of the conventional generic trappings.

The enormous scope of Keats' *Fall of Hyperion* creates a generic continuum from traditional Western epic in the shape of a dimensional magnification and an internalization of values. The three types of traditional epic, including the archaic, the imperial, and the religious ones, have all affected the making of Keats' poem as hereditary forces. At the same time, the Hyperion poems share the same features with other Romantic works, such as a weakened central hero and a nonreligious ideal, in addition to the two major tendencies inherent in the generic development. In comparison, Miyazawa's work displays the same kind of enormous dimensionality as Keats' poem by both resisting the defining force of tradition and tacitly upholding a nondogmatic religious vision. In each case, an independent, creative impulse burning with idealism creates a literary work of an epic nature. For all their manifest differences, *The Fall of Hyperion* and *Galaxy Railroad* thus prove intrinsically similar in their ambitious attempt to present the wholeness of their individual belief in people and the world.

6

The Self-Consciousness
of Transitional Epic

Our analysis of *The Fall of Hyperion* and *A Night on the Galaxy Railroad* has revealed significant similarities and differences between the two works in terms of the three epic elements of communal concern, attitude toward mortality, and the dimension in time and space. While retaining the fundamental generic elements, both the Japanese and the English work show certain departures from the traditional epic modes. Apart from the three thematic elements, a significant premise so far has been that the epic should be constructive, that is, exhibit an epic ideal that can serve as an elevated moral and spiritual norm. When the proposed ideal is extremely high and apparently impracticable, however, some doubt about its feasibility creeps in and undermines the work's noble aspirations. I have already pointed out the subtle manifestation of such a self-contradictory tendency in the traditional epic. This tendency is symptomatic of recent epic works as well, rendering them essentially unstable. In the case of *The Fall of Hyperion* and *Galaxy Railroad*, the instability intrinsic to what they openly encourage appears threefold: double textuality, fragmentation, and dream visions. In our previous discussion, the two versions of each work (the last two major manuscript drafts in the case of Miyazawa's work) were treated constructively as if the two versions supplemented each other and constituted a whole. From now on, we will reverse our stance to point out what discordant differences exist between the first and the second versions and to suggest why the works were rewritten and finally given up.

The Epic Ideal in Transitional Epic

Before going on to examine the elements of self-contestation, let us briefly recapitulate what epic ideals are advocated and therefore exposed to unacknowledged doubt in the two works. *Galaxy Railroad* exalts individual self-sacrifice for the sake of other people. This ideal of selflessness is most clearly expressed in the ending of the early version, after Campanella's sudden disappearance. At this point, Dr. Bulcaniro, who has been Giovanni's mentor as a guiding voice during the boy's spiritual journey, appears and speaks to Giovanni, first as the stranger with a large black hat in the dream and then directly as the scientist after Giovanni's awakening. When the boy complains about Campanella's broken promise that they could travel farther together, the mysterious adult answers as follows: "Yes, that's true. Everybody thinks so. But you cannot go together. And everybody is Campanella. Everybody you meet ate an apple and took the train many times with you. So, as you thought a little while ago, you should search for the best happiness for everyone and go there soon with everybody. Only there, you can really go with Campanella forever."[1]

The repetition of "everybody" makes clear the importance of the broad communal dimension as one essential element of the work. According to the exhortation, Campanella stands for all the people whom Giovanni has met or is going to meet in his life. When Giovanni makes his fresh determination, the stranger continues to encourage the boy: "Listen, hold your ticket firmly. You have to stride straight through the flames and the violent waves of the real world instead of the railroad in your dream. You should never lose the only real ticket in the *ama no gawa*."[2] By the ticket, he means the boy's determination to search for "the real, real happiness for everybody's sake."[3] Giovanni wakes up from his dream, and the scientist, who now appears in person, further encourages the boy. He gives Giovanni a small piece of folded green paper, explaining that it is the ticket which he dreamed about. Thus, the early version is indispensable to understanding what Miyazawa wishes to emphasize most in *Galaxy Railroad.*

In the case of *The Fall of Hyperion*, although the poem is similarly concerned about the communal dimension, the epic ideal is inseparably related to aesthetics. The poem categorizes those who significantly affect the world into three groups, that is, poets, dreamers, and humanitarians. One of the poem's main problems appears to be how to evaluate the poets' creation in a world of suffering. When the poet-narrator overcomes the challenge of climbing up the deathly stairs of Saturn's temple and stands at the altar before Moneta, the goddess at first distinguishes between humanitarians and "visionaries."[4] The former devote themselves to working on behalf of the afflicted humanity. By contrast, the visionaries are severely condemned by Moneta, who identifies her novice as such:

> And thou art here, for thou art less than they.
> What benefit canst thou do, or all thy tribe,
> To the great world? Thou art a dreaming thing,
> A fever of thyself. . . .
> Only the dreamer venoms all his days,
> Bearing more woe than all his sins deserve.[5]

The attitude of dreamers toward fellow creatures is basically the same as that of humanitarians, since both of them, "to whom the miseries of the world / Are misery,"[6] are eager to redress the various kinds of misfortune that befall people. On account of their concern for others, visionaries and humanitarians are equally entitled to come to the altar and share the history preserved in Moneta's memory. Humanitarians, however, who "seek no wonder but the human face,"[7] engage themselves in directly improving their world and have no "dream" of acquiring knowledge of the long forgotten past. That knowledge is granted as a favor to the dreamer who, in spite of his "good will,"[8] does nothing but fashion impractical ideas from intellectual labors and thus spoils life, making more trouble than necessary. Dreamers are obviously ranked below humanitarians in terms of the service they can perform for the world.

The distinction between dreamers and humanitarians is not difficult to understand. But the same demarcation becomes dubious when the poem differentiates poets from dreamers. The essential difference lies again in what they can do for their fellow creatures. The poet is defined as someone who soothes people's suffering and makes society bearable to live in, whereas the dreamer disturbs people's thought. The poet-narrator is consistently regarded by Moneta as one of the dreamers who disturb people. The question is what the poet's position is in relation to the dreamer's and the humanitarian's. As a visionary who creates an imaginary world with language, the poet seems to be inferior to the humanitarian. At the same time, the poet is declared to be "[d]iverse, sheer opposite, antipode[s]" of the dreamer.[9] The poet's creation (poetry) exerts a healing power ("a balm") upon the world of pain in contrast with the dreamer's activity that not only does not bring about any solution to problems but even aggravates them.[10] Thus, the poet possesses a much higher function than the dreamer. Is it not, then, that the poet is as useful to the world as the humanitarian? In fact, the poet's creative power sounds more far-reaching than the humanitarian's individual efforts.

Another point that blurs the differentiation is that dreamers are also a kind of poets, including "mock lyrists, large self-worshippers / And careless hectorers in proud bad verse."[11] Although contemptuous of the dreaming poets, the poet-narrator does not mind being counted as one of them now that he is given the special favor of Moneta's company. He wishes that Apollo's "misty pestilence" would exterminate all these worthless poets.[12] Here, we can perceive two contrasting aspects of the Greek god of poetry. On the one hand, the healing power as a god of medicine is attributed to "real" poets. On the other hand, the god, who mercilessly sends a plague upon the Greeks at the beginning of the *Iliad*, is now conjured for the same purpose against bad poets.[13] By the sharply divided use of the two kinds of poetic effects, Keats might be suggesting the disintegrating power of contemporary poetry, in comparison with ancient poetry which, symbolized by Apollo, integrally possessed both aspects. With that god "[f]aded" and "far-flown,"[14] poetry can be either therapeutic or pathogenic now. The good poets who produce the former effect should rightly be held in respect, while the bad, dreaming poets deserve to be destroyed by the very effect they bring about.

In any case, despite the obscure relation between the poet and the humanitarian, the classification above indicates that the dreamer is an inferior poet to whom the other two kinds of people are superior. Apparently, the selected dreamer (i.e., the poet-narrator) is expected to aspire dialectically to what combines the *virtutes* of the poet and the humanitarian. Although contrasted as "antipodes," the poet and the dreamer are not irreversibly opposed to each other because they both write poetry. The condemnation of the dreamer for not being like the humanitarian suggests that the dreaming poet, like the humanitarian, might somehow be useful to the world by means of his poetry. What *The Fall of Hyperion* proposes is the poet's self-awareness of the need for artistic improvement in order to revitalize the world with literary creation. The acceptance of the poet-narrator by

Moneta seems to assure the feasibility of the grand objective, and the imaginative journey which he makes with the goddess should indicate the process through which he would become a true poet.

The Uncertainty of Space

Let us now examine the elements that underlie and threaten to disrupt the schemes overtly asserted in *Galaxy Railroad* and *The Fall of Hyperion.* In each work, the most conspicuous deconstructive undertone appears on the uncertain basis of the space from which the protagonists draw their special experience. In the Japanese work, for instance, when the two boys dip their hands in the *ama no gawa*, they find its water much different from the streams they know on earth: "But that strange water of the galaxy was much more transparent than hydrogen. Still, they could see it flowing, because their wrists immersed in the water looked a little mercuric and floating. Besides, the waves made against their wrists radiated beautiful phosphorescence and appeared to be flaming feebly."[15] All the sands on the riverside turn out to be crystal in which a small fire is burning. If the birds are out of the birdcatcher's reach, they alight on the ground and turn to such sands. When one peels "the big apples beautifully colored with gold and scarlet" which the lighthouse keeper offers to the other passengers, the rind of the fruit "evaporated shining gray without making a noise" before it reaches the floor.[16] That the space is full of examples of this kind shows the unsubstantiality of its matter and produces a sense of unearthly beauty.

The ethereal unreality of that region is also seen in how people move there *un*-physically. The inhabitants of that sphere take it for granted that they can shift from one place to another without moving their bodies at all. The birdcatcher provides a good example when he suddenly disappears from the moving train to catch some birds flying down on the field outside. When he returns in the same manner, he says to Giovanni that "he came back because he wanted to" and finds it strange that the boys wonder at such an ordinary fact of life.[17] I have already mentioned the similar, unearthly sprightliness of the boys on their way back from the riverside to the train station. No matter how fast and weightlessly the boys can go, however, they still have to exert physical energy in the form of running, in contrast to the native inhabitants who change their location just as a matter of will. Because Giovanni and Campanella are strangers "from far,"[18] they are not yet completely assimilated to their new environments, especially before their baptismal rituals at the river. But when Campanella says that he can perceive his mother, who has presumably been dead for years, outside the train shortly after the vehicle leaves the Southern Cross, he vanishes from the moving train in the same manner as did the birdcatcher.[19] He is probably reunited with her because he just wished to be. Giovanni, who cannot see her, is left alone on the train. What makes the difference is death. Campanella is now a soul ready to cross the threshold into the realm of the dead, whereas Giovanni has his living body waiting on the hill while his dreaming consciousness strays into that strange space.

The extraordinary beauty of the dreamed sphere, as well as its motions devoid of physical energy, might be indicative of the ideal state of existence. In fact, several passages intimate that some providential power is working there to keep the region free from earthly problems. As Giovanni and Campanella notice at the beginning of their journey, the train itself does not need coal for its fuel, as the trains of Miyazawa's days did. In the early version, the cello-like voice tells the boys that the train is not fueled by steam or electricity. Instead, the vehicle moves "just because it is predetermined to do so."[20] Similar to people's change in location, production with labor is little more than a matter of will. As the birdcatcher says, people work there "just enough for health" and get as much harvest as they want.[21] According to the lighthouse keeper who also lives in that sphere, plants, once sown, grow by themselves and produce husk-free grains which are "ten times as big as" those around the Pacific and "smell better."[22] Concerning the toilfree life of that place, Nakamura Minoru asserts that the world through which the Galaxy Railroad runs stands for "the ultimate state of the utopia which he [Miyazawa] dreamed of."[23]

Repeated references to the "real heaven" for which the Galaxy Train presumably heads, however, indicate that the land it traverses is not an ideal world. For example, although agricultural labor is so easy in the sky field that it is almost entertaining, in sharp contrast to the exhausting labor on earth,[24] people still have to take trouble to produce food. Most typically, an old passenger who is apparently a resident of that space says that "even corn does not grow unless you make holes two feet deep with a stick and plant the seeds" on the plateau.[25] In spite of the similarity to the primitive way of agricultural production which Miyazawa associates with playfulness and dancing somewhere else,[26] the words are intended to evoke the pains and troubles of field labor. Moreover, the lighthouse keeper, who also belongs to the unusual space of the Galaxy Railroad, says that "there is no more agriculture" in the place where most of the passengers are going, probably meaning heaven.[27] Twice, then, the space of the Galaxy Railroad is indirectly denied its ultimate ideality by its own inhabitants.

Hagiwara argues that Miyazawa's "other space" is "truer, better, more beautiful, more complete" than this world and is "a place of primordial innocence" from whence "people are expelled forever as all the mythologies in the world attest."[28] If the other world Miyazawa envisioned is so perfect, we have to identify it as the destination of most of the train passengers in an undisclosed locus termed heaven. There in heaven, the food consumption based on killing life as well as food production is not the law of survival. In fact, because food is not needed any more for the sustenance of the body, the exploitation of life for another life is totally annulled. According to the lighthouse keeper, foods there such as "apples and sweets leave no dregs and vanish into the air through the pores in a slight, fine odor which smells different depending on each person."[29] Food, therefore, is taken for the nourishment of the spirit, not the body, which reminds us of what Miyazawa says in his preface to the collection of his tales, *A Restaurant of Many Orders*. He wishes that his children's stories, which he conceived "all from a rainbow and the moonlight in a wood or a wild field, or on a railroad," will be the reader's "transparent, real foods" pure like "the cleanly transparent wind" and "the pink, beautiful morning sunshine."[30] Apples and sweets symbolize purity and innocence devoid of struggle for life in Miyazawa's literary world. In *Galaxy Railroad*, the halo of the Southern Cross is compared to "apple flesh,"[31] and the two boys smell apples and wild roses, instead of decomposing bodies, just before the young tutor and his two students suddenly appear on the train.

In Miyazawa's presumed heaven, food is taken for the joy of the spirit, and the vegetarian imagery replaces the imagery of slaughtered animal life.[32] In a marked contrast to this vegetarianism, the food on the train is directly related to the death of creatures. Although breaking like chocolate and tasting much better, what the birdcatcher kindly offers the boys turns out to be a limb of a congealed wild goose he has caught. When he opens his luggage, the boys discover "about ten bodies of herons" a little flattened and shining pure white "like that Northern Cross."[33] The good-natured man is known only by his occupation, which suggests that his livelihood constitutes his innate self. The birds that descend from the sky do not make any resistance when he simply grabs them with his hands. In depriving such harmless creatures of their freedom for his livelihood, the birdcatcher stands for all lives trammeled in the problem of existence. Interestingly, the man "abruptly raised both hands like a shot soldier at the moment of his death" just after he finishes his catch outside and before he comes back inside the train.[34] Instead of the birds, he the hunter appears to be shot to death. The birdcatcher thus undergoes a symbolic death every time he infringes on other lives. In this light, the strong pity Giovanni feels for him arises not only from his regret for not having treated him more kindly but also from his sudden intuition into the man's hard, inescapable fate representative of all life forms. It follows that, although the dichotomy between life and death means little in the space of the Galaxy Railroad, that space is not entirely innocent of the original sin of existence. Characterized as a laborer who is poor, hard-working, and simple-minded, the birdcatcher will never think of quitting his work, and he will never cease to be a part of the unusual space. By his mere presence, the space inherently loses its ideal status.

The rejection of this space as ideal becomes irretrievable when the same birdcatcher calls it "the Illusory Four-Dimensional (Space)" in reference to Giovanni's special pass.[35] To make his meaning clearer, he further describes the sphere as "so imperfect."[36] With these words, the birdcatcher explicitly acknowledges his own dwelling space as something which does not really exist. In concert with the birdcatcher's remark, the archaeologist conducts an excavation on the riverside in order to ascertain whether the stratum there "really appears like such a stratum or looks like nothing but winds, water, and empty sky to beings" who do not live in that sphere.[37] The scholar thereby admits the possibility of the vacuity of his space from a scientific viewpoint, and his ongoing research has proven nothing to the contrary.[38] All these casual remarks point to the unsubstantial nature of the space these people inhabit, unintentionally threatening its very basis. Giovanni's unreal space cannot be the ultimate, ideal locus that brings about "a state of innocence filled with joy" as Hagiwara puts it.[39]

The space is illusory because it constitutes the setting of Giovanni's dream, a fact that undercuts the high objective of *Galaxy Railroad.* Generally speaking, in traditional dream-vision stories, the unreality of the dream space is frequently employed as a meaningful device to show its liminal, ambivalent status between this world and the other world, and consequently both its fictionality and its higher truth. Miyazawa's unreal space is not exceptional, but it is presented with a particularly negative connotation. Thus, when Giovanni wakes up from his sleep after Campanella's disappearance and finds himself still alone on the hill, the scenes he has traveled through on the train turn out to be no more than phantasmagoria of his dreaming mind. The lessons and experience acquired through the journey come to mean very little, because the space across which the Galaxy Railroad runs is an illusion after all. In fact, Giovanni does not reflect upon the meaning of his dream. The story goes on until he reaches the place of Campanella's drowning, but this last episode does not have much relevance to the dream except that it explains why Campanella was on the train. The later version of the work is discernibly uncertain in asserting its message, which is merely hinted at in separate episodes.

The situation is different in the early version, where the main theme is Giovanni's realization through Dr. Bulcaniro's guidance that he should devote his life to the welfare of other people. Self-sacrificing humanitarianism, which is identified as the most important but somewhat vague ideal in *The Fall of Hyperion,* appears in Miyazawa's early version to be upheld unquestionably as the utmost objective of one's life. One of Dr. Bulcaniro's last statements to Giovanni establishes the high argument as the central theme: "You have to stride straight through the flames and the violent waves of the real world instead of the railroad in your dream."[40] Ironically, the scientist's very words invalidate what the text strenuously maintains. The phrase "instead of the railroad in your dream" dismisses Giovanni's dream experience externally as a mere vanished illusion,[41] while the term "the Illusory Four-Dimensional (Space)" rejects it internally. The metaphorical expression "through the flames and the violent waves" also betrays an ill-concealed suspicion. The phrase is probably applied to suggest the infeasibility of complete self-sacrifice in this world. When the dream is repeatedly exposed as illusory and vaporous, the question has to be asked whether Giovanni's newly obtained knowledge of supposedly higher truth, with its naive belief in humanity, is valid and transferable directly from the dream sphere to the reality of waking consciousness without causing frictions. Thus, unlike the later version that forces Giovanni to confront the reality of Campanella's death, the early version does not show Giovanni any more after the hopeful boy disappears into the night's darkness that envelops its ending.

The author himself provides an example of a failure in realizing his nobly motivated commitment to a small community that surrounded him.[42] Probably this is why he deleted, from the later version, Dr. Bulcaniro as Giovanni's guiding voice during the train journey, as well as the dialogue between the scientist (or his persona) and the boy.[43] Revising the early version on his deathbed, Miyazawa must have keenly felt the unrealizable nature of his noble argument, which is most directly expressed through Dr. Bulcaniro's triple roles.[44] Miyazawa could not find "the method of the experiment" through which faith could be "like chemistry."[45] Suggestive of his growing hesitancy, Giovanni's conversation with the scientist "does not contain any single word that denotes the theme of self-sacrifice despite the repeated emphasis on 'the best happiness for all people.'"[46] Thus, with the space of the train self-negated, and its doubts about selfless devotion not entirely suppressed, the early version also seems uneasy about asserting its ideal.

Although the deletion of Dr. Bulcaniro resulted in a more straightforward later version, the omission deprived this version of much of the work's spiritual significance. But the later version still keeps the episodes that show the motif of self-sacrifice in isolated instances, such as the shipwreck and the star of the Scorpion. In the process of revision, we can perceive Miyazawa's struggle between his contradictory belief and disbelief in the ideal. Miyazawa could not solve the conflict until his death, and we are left with the two versions either of which cannot claim the finality of completion in their mutual strife for textual independence as well as in their hermeneutic interdependency. Miyazawa's doubt about his own ideal thus underlies the story of Giovanni's quest for the meaning of his life.

A similar latent disbelief in its noble aim, implicit through the rejection of the traveled space, is found in *The Fall of Hyperion*. In this case, the key words indicative of the undermining ten-

dency are "shade" and "hollow," which imply the immediate transience of the experienced vision, like Miyazawa's more direct
"illusion." The space to be explored is first explained by Moneta
as "scenes / Still swooning vivid through my globèd brain."[47] The
image comes from the weakening of something alive confined in
a hollow vessel. Therefore, the poet-narrator eagerly wishes to see
"what things the hollow brain / Behind enwombed; what high
tragedy / In the dark secret chambers of her skull / Was acting."[48] He implores the goddess to show him the knowledge that
disturbs her mind by saying: "Let me behold, according as thou
said'st, / What in thy brain so ferments to and fro."[49] The scenes
that took place in the mythological past have been preserved
clear and lively in Moneta's memory. Through the divine power of
Moneta, the scenes are projected externally so that the poet-
narrator can witness them. Since the space to be traversed
changes at her will, the scenes, not the two figures themselves,
shift throughout their journey.

   Although she possesses such a supernatural power, Moneta
is little more than a mere receptacle of unknown history. In fact,
the two passages quoted above give us the impression of an
empty cell filled with airy, sprightly objects. The image of Moneta
as a vase is subtly elaborated in the poem. When the goddess
lifts her veil in response to the poet-narrator's request, he finds a
most unearthly face there:

>   Then saw I a wan face,
> Not pined by human sorrows, but bright-blanched
> By an immortal sickness which kills not.
> It works a constant change, which happy death
> Can put no end to; deathwards progressing
> To no death was that visage; it had passed
> The lily and the snow;[50]

The lines capture the paradox of immortality suffering mortal
agonies, a second nature forced upon all her tribe after Saturn's
dethronement. As a member of her fallen family, "Moneta is trag-
ically caught in a web of process-as-mutability from which she
will never escape."[51] The "constant change" on her face stands not
only for an irrepressible externalization of her memory stirring in
the mind but also for her mortal nature subject to the transience
"which happy death / Can put no end to." The passage reifies the
absolute inaccessibility of human sensations to this embodied

paradox, and the excessive whiteness of her countenance works as an impenetrable barrier to emotion-fraught human communication.

The pale lifelessness, which denies any possibility of human contact, resembles the "[c]old pastoral" in "Ode on a Grecian Urn" (1819).[52] The ancient container appears at first to invite a beholder into the beautiful world depicted on its surface. With the potter long dead, however, the time of the urn is frozen, and the seemingly warm vitality of the "leaf-fringed legend" turns out to be a deception of art.[53] The urn may not exactly be "deathwards progressing," but the causality of its eventual destruction is innate with the fragility of the artifact "still unravished."[54] What probably awaits it is a permanent pseudo-life which never comes to fulfillment. Although the ceramic preserves some ancient sights, due to the loss of their society and the meaning of its rituals, the overlaid pictures only elicit a series of unanswered *whats*, *whos*, and *whys* from the viewer. Thus, no matter how beautiful and friendly it looks, the urn, which keeps its silence, does "tease us out of thought / As doth eternity" and rejects any human approach with its inorganic indifference as well as its self-contained principle of beauty as truth.[55] Contrary to the explicit message of *Endymion*, in both the urn and the goddess of memory, beauty remains forever aloof without yielding unalloyed joy, because beauty is intermingled with the shadow of death.

In addition to her image as a hollow vessel, Moneta thus has a strong affinity with the ancient vase. Similar to the ornate urn, Moneta's case shows the paradox of death in life, for a human form manifests inorganic inaccessibility. The paradox in a familiar human shape brings about not mere disillusionment, but an irrepressible fear. On looking at Moneta's pale countenance, the poet-narrator instinctively almost "fled away,"[56] just as the poet's day-dreaming consciousness in "Ode to a Nightingale" (1819) shrinks back on the threshold to "fairy lands" that are "forlorn" and are devoid of life.[57] The fear is similar to what Giovanni feels when he sees "the pit of the sky."[58] Giovanni's fear arises not from a death-imbued complexion but from unfathomable, absolute nothingness, and the nihilism is used to occasion the boy's determination, which should not falter even in face of such an ultimate incomprehensibility. In *The Fall of Hyperion*, only the goddess' somewhat humane eyes "with a benignant light" keep the poet-narrator from running away from another incomprehensibility of materialized death in life.[59] Even the eyes, however, which "saw me not" and do not care about "[w]hat eyes are upward cast,"[60] are "impersonal, impartial . . . albeit benign."[61] Infected with human emotions inside, she nevertheless cannot express them through the disinterested mien that defines her immortal nature.

Despite her awe-inspiring divinity, Moneta serves as little more than a fragile reservoir of history, almost an anthropomorphized ceramic artifice in the deserted temple of Saturn. Her role is adumbrated earlier by the objects which the poet-narrator finds lying "[a]ll in a mingled heap confused" in the temple:[62]

> Upon the marble at my feet there lay
> Store of strange vessels and large draperies,
> Which needs had been of dyed asbestos wove,
> Or in that place the moth could not corrupt,
> So white the linen; so, in some, distinct
> Ran imageries from a sombre loom.[63]

The passage presents a few symbols of Moneta as an incorruptible mnenonic holder of images with an exceedingly pale face "veiled in drooping white . . . linens."[64] This symbolism essentially reduces her importance to the level of indestructible objects. Considering her power "still a curse," the goddess preserves the memory of her annihilated race "[w]ith an electral changing misery" against her will.[65] Ironically, the curse is a condition for her existence. The memory may be perpetually weakening, but it will never fade away, just as her divine body decays to no decay. The imperishable painful memory in the undecayed frame is her essence, pointing to what immortality plagued with mortality means for her. If someone does not look into the preserved history, she is virtually equivalent to an empty vessel. At the same time, the memory of the mythological past, which the goddess conveys through eons, would perish without her existence. In this respect, Moneta and her memory are as fragile and unreal as the Illusory Four-Dimensional Space in *Galaxy Railroad.*

The unreality of Moneta's existence is repeatedly described with such words as "shade" and "shadow" by the narrating poet from his awakened viewpoint. The metaphorical expressions compare Moneta standing faintly in the smoke beside the "lofty sacrificial fire" to the dark nonexistence that always accompanies a lighted object.[66] At the same time, the words metonymically suggest the nature of her perishable, unsubstantial existence.

The figurative speech might be ascribed to the fact that the entire scene takes place in a fleeting dream, and the poet might not be certain about Moneta's appearance after his awakening. But the metonymic connotation becomes irrefutable when the poet-narrator *in his dream* directly addresses the goddess with such apostrophes as "Majestic shadow" and, most importantly, "Shade of Memory."[67] Unaware, he hits upon her essence as a fragile receptacle of history. Like "the Illusory Four-Dimensional (Space)" in *Galaxy Railroad*, his utterances are self-referential because the dreaming poet directs the tropes toward the goddess who presides in his dream. And the phrases similarly question and undermine the validity of Moneta's existence and her memory. Together, his addresses to the goddess self-negate the overall scheme of the dream, which is underscored by Moneta's acquiescence to the appellations.

A fundamental problem that unsettles the poem's grand motivation of offering a better world lies in the uncertain memory which, contained in a self-negated vessel, offers the spatial basis of the protagonist's enterprise. Through Moneta's power, the poet-narrator is allowed to witness the rise and fall of divinities in the forgotten past, and what he reports in the form of poetry is supposed to have a soothing effect upon the world of agonies. This task is a requisite for the poet-narrator to elevate himself from "a dreaming thing" to a true poet.[68] But if what he witnesses is a mere projected image of frail memory preserved in such an invalidated vase, we must question the authenticity of his experience and the wisdom he gains in the journey, as we have done with *Galaxy Railroad*. The scenes, which the goddess reveals to the poet-narrator as a favor, have no reality except in her existence which is equated to a hollow vessel close to shadowy nonexistence. When the projected and explored space has such an unstable basis, what is asserted as truth by way of the experience in that space loses its solid foundation.

In fact, just like Giovanni's humanitarianism, the message the poet-narrator is expected to deliver as "a balm upon the world" is doubtful as to its feasibility.[69] The poem's intended message is the aesthetic evolutionism found in the words of Oceanus in *Hyperion*. As we have seen, the deposed sea-god tries to persuade the Titans to accept their defeat by the Olympians by saying that it is "the eternal law / That first in beauty should be first in might."[70] The centrality of beauty makes the precept sound propitious to the peace and harmony of transition. Evidently, however, the idea is far removed from the actual world. A look into the aesthetic principle of power succession discloses a serious problem. If a new species is destined to replace an old, less beautiful one, there must be a sense of continuity that culminates in a generic perfection currently possible. Keats' cosmology is largely a revision of Hesiod's *Theogony* and other Greek sources.[71] First, "chaos and blank darkness" were deprived of supremacy by "heaven and earth," which came from the two primordial substances through the leaven of light.[72] Then, "heaven and earth" were supplanted by the Titans, who are their children. Successively, the Titans have been driven out of power by the Olympians, who were "born of us."[73] It necessarily follows that the Olympian gods who now hold hegemony will and should be set aside in the future by a new, more beautiful generation to be born from them. On the one hand, no existing group of divinities can succeed the Olympians in terms of lineage and aesthetic progressionism. On the other hand, it would be an artistic suicide and historical absurdity for Keats to create an entirely new generation of gods purely out of his imagination. This indeterminacy means the poet's tacit acknowledgement of a disruption in his mythopoeic historiography. The uneasy anticipation of the unrealized, unrealizable species is one reason why *Hyperion* was left unfinished.

Furthermore, the change of power configuration involves force. The Olympian gods will succumb through strife to a generation coming after them, just as the Titans were overthrown by them. That new generation will then have to be forcibly taken over by another generation. Keatsian evolutionism implies no end to conflicts between generations. The grim outlook is also the case even if the planned ending of *Hyperion* was the reconciliation between the Titans and the Olympians through some intervention, accompanied by the restoration of peace in the war-stricken world.[74] The principle of aesthetic progress remains potential, inciting further strife for name and power that are explicit in beauty. With the future line of divinity unwarranted, only the perspective of continued struggle remains. The dismal outlook also accounts for the incompleteness of *Hyperion*. More significantly, it subverts the promised "balm upon the world" of *The Fall of Hyperion*, unless, like Oceanus, Keats intends for the humankind resignation to its fate and sufferings. Thus, the later poem also remains fragmental and its message, undelivered.

In this respect, the ending of *Hyperion* contains a self-contradiction. The poem breaks off at the very moment when Apollo is deified on a secluded island. Through the infusion of untold history from Mnemosyne, the "youth" takes the first step to overthrowing the Titan Hyperion.[75] In one of his letters to his friend Benjamin Robert Haydon, Keats talks about Apollo's function as follows:

> [T]he nature of *Hyperion* will lead me to treat it in a more naked and grecian Manner—and the march of passion and endeavour will be undeviating—and one great contrast between them will be—that the Hero of the written tale [*Endymion*] being mortal is led on, like Buonaparte, by circumstance; whereas the Apollo in Hyperion being a foreseeing God will shape his actions like one.[76]

Apollo stands for unstoppable progress here. But if Apollo weaves his own future at his fingertips, how can he be subject to the eventual loss of his divine power, as suggested by the struggle for power that centers on beauty? Hyperion cannot foil his impending expulsion from the seat of power, because Apollo's predecessor is a god of the sun, but not of prescience. On the other hand, Saturn was almost omniscient and "fate seemed strangled" in his hands.[77] But "[o]ne avenue was shaded" even from his knowledge, and this one blind spot was the cause of his downfall.[78] Therefore, the dethroned king speaks to the prostrate congregation of his tribe:

> Not in the legends of the first of days,
> Studied from that old spirit-leavèd book
> Which starry Uranus with finger bright
> Saved from the shores of darkness, when the waves
> Low-ebbèd still hid it up in shallow gloom— . . .
> Wherefrom I take strange lore and read it deep,
> Can I find reason why ye should be thus.[79]

The same fate cannot befall Apollo, who is clearly defined as "a fore-seeing God."

An undisguised incoherence lies here between being and becoming, future perfect and progressive, the lineality of Apollo's advancement and what affects him in the tidal cyclicity of generational change. The "[k]nowledge enormous" which Apollo inherits from Mnemosyne makes him aware of such changes and sufferings as "dire events, rebellions, . . . agonies, / Creations and destroyings."[80] A "fore-seeing God" secure with the knowledge of changes, including his own, is an oxymoron.[81] The contradiction leaves Apollo's deification aposiopetic with his cries of unmitigated pains from "[dying] into life,"[82] a process which can be only half-finished in his immortal perfection.

Concerning the poem's message that is supposed to alleviate the sufferings of the world, a similar inconsistency is found at the beginning of *The Fall of Hyperion*. Before the poet-narrator meets the goddess of memory at the foot of a huge statue, he finds himself in the precincts of "an old sanctuary with roof august, / Builded so high it seemed that filmèd clouds / Might spread beneath, as o'er the stars of heaven."[83] The enormous structure is Saturn's temple with "the silent massy range / Of columns north and south, ending in mist / Of nothing" and "black gates . . . shut against the sunrise evermore."[84] Here, the age of the long-abandoned building as well as its size is emphasized:

> So old the place was, I remembered none
> The like upon the earth: what I had seen
> Of grey cathedrals, buttressed walls, rent towers,
> The superannuations of sunk realms,
> Or nature's rocks toiled hard in waves and winds,
> Seemed but the faulture of decrepit things
> To that eternal domèd monument.[85]

Even before the poet-narrator stands before the statue of Saturn, the building symbolizes the patriarchal god in the sense that it is huge and majestic while immemorially old and desolate. These early lines already suggest that the theme of the renewed poem is not the optimistic progress of beauty as in *Hyperion* but the fluctuation insidiously inherent in the tenet. What is intended is the adjustment to the world of change so that the power struggle can be encompassed *a priori*.

The place, including the statue of Saturn, is important as both the starting and returning points of the poet-narrator's journey. During the journey with Moneta, he observes events, which might include a reconciliation between the two generations of the ancient deities. But once the journey to the past is over and the poet-narrator is back in the present, he still finds Saturn unrestored and his holy sanctuary long deserted. All he finds there is "a dream which is a repetition of reality," and he has to realize that "the past already contains the problems of the present."[86] In fact, even before the journey, he is fully aware that Moneta is, in his own words, "[t]he pale omega of a withered race."[87] When he calls Hyperion's successor "far-flown Apollo,"[88] he admits that there is no happy progress or hope in the world of change. His utterance at the altar destroys the whole optimistic scheme of the poem, divulging the unwritten but irrefutable fact that the next generation of gods after the Titans, of which Apollo is a member, have also been out of power and have been long gone from the stage of history. In the face of this unquestionable desolation, the poet-narrator has no message or poetry to soothe the suffering world with, and he loses his unique opportunity to become a true poet. His spiritual journey turns out to be fruitless.[89] Thus, the conception of *The Fall of Hyperion* carries a genetic element that grows to the point of hindering and interrupting the expected unfolding of the textual matrix.

The poem's self-repudiating stance from the very outset reflects the poet's indecision about how to handle belief that is dissonant with knowledge and experience. Nakedly announcing the inevitable downfall of the Titan sun-god, the poem's title itself contains the duality irreconcilable in the poem. *The Fall of Hyperion* identifies transience as the driving force of the universe, in contrast to *Hyperion* that stresses optimistic progress based on the principle of beauty. Instead of dissipating the poet's uncertainty, the revision only aggravated his self-doubt about what he was articulating in writing. Keats' faltering conviction in asserting his role as a world reformer is manifest in his relatively modest words about what poetic power can actually accomplish.[90] He merely says that a poet at his best can neutralize human pains ("pours out a balm upon the world") with his art. This view of the poet's social function makes a noticeable contrast, for instance, to Shelley's more confident statement that defines poets as "the unacknowledged legislators of the World."[91]

Biographically, one might be tempted to infer that the shift of emphasis between the two versions was brought about partly by the death of Keats' brother Tom, whom the poet nursed to the end. We know from his letters that Keats composed *Hyperion* as a kind of escape from seeing his brother fatally suffering and daily weakening from tuberculosis.[92] Aesthetic progressionism might have been Keats' psychological self-defense in the form of literary creation against the vivid agonies at hand. But however hard he asserted his optimism, his brother died. It is no wonder that *The Fall of Hyperion*, which was written after Tom's death, incorporates the poet's tragic experience. The poem rejects the optimistic belief in beauty and poetry, although the belief constituted the thematic core of such early poems as "Sleep and Poetry" (1816) and *Endymion*. In the poet's taxonomy, *The Fall of Hyperion* was born of the "burden of the Mystery" that "on all sides" leads "to dark passages," and not of "the Chamber of Maiden-Thought" that is full of "light" and "pleasant wonders."[93]

In any case, because of its internal incongruity, *The Fall of Hyperion* can neither uphold the explicit message of *Hyperion* nor illustrate its own high objective of reconstructing the world through poetic power. Here, we can perceive an attempt similar to Miyazawa's in revising *Galaxy Railroad*. In each case, the rewriting might have been due to the author's bafflement in his personal life. But the attempt was aborted in suspension between two versions. Equally significant, the two versions extrinsically vie for textual legitimacy and artistic superiority, while their fractures in idea and form intrinsically call for plenitude through mutual supplementation. The ultimate rupture comes from the author's irrepressible doubt in self-articulation. Similar to "the Illusory Four-Dimensional (Space)" in Miyazawa's work, such tropes as "Shade of Memory" and "far-flown Apollo" in Keats' poem are indicative of the growing hiatus through which the author's repressed disbelief in his own belief reveals itself.

The uncertain basis of the space where most of the story takes place might suggest the field of potentiality that allows the needed change for the protagonist. When the overall implications are considered, however, spatial instability indicates a covert, yet significant manifestation of the two authors' hesitancy in art and life. In each case, the author could not directly expose his central figure to the law of the agonistic world where the frail figure would not succeed. Instead, he created a special, probational sphere so that the transposed figure could undergo the expected self-transformation. In the process, the author connived at a creature that redefines itself not by jostling against others but by simply observing what is offered. What is essentially at stake is belief in artistic expression, for a self that effects inner change without direct interaction with the external world is what art aims at through its influence. The author's guilty awareness of the improbable character and his waning confidence in the power of artistic creation made space an unreal, uncertain place where nothing really decisive happens.

The Collapse of the Dream Vision

Another deconstructive aspect of the two works concerns the dream structure as a narratological device, because each work presents the most important part of its story in a dream vision. In Miyazawa's narrative, Giovanni's journey on the Galaxy Railroad, which occasions his spiritual growth, takes place in the boy's dream on a lonely hill outside his town. Similarly, Keats' poem is told as a recollection of the dream which opens a prospect for the poet-narrator to become a genuine poet.[94] From medieval stories like *Piers Plowman* through *Alice in Wonderland* in Western literature, as well as in various literary pieces around the world, the dream vision has often been employed as a meaningful device to give credibility to a story which otherwise would sound unbelievable. Such credibility applies to both *Galaxy Railroad* and *The Fall of Hyperion*. If it were not for the dream framework, the two works would sound like mere fantasy stories that do not invite serious reading.

From another point of view, however, the credibility attached to dream visions is necessarily strained. As long as a dream vision is used to adjust the story to the acceptable range of common sense, the very presence of the dream vision can suggest that the story is a ridiculous one after all. In conventional dream-vision stories, this ambiguity is often exploited to veil the intended satire with a pretense of innocence and to evade political persecution. Unless a dream vision is aimed at such a practically intelligible effect, its use entails no small danger of presenting the work, although unwittingly, as absurd and insignificant. Both Keats and Miyazawa were very sensitive to the two-edged nature of a dream vision. Their serious concerns are manifest ironically in the identical device of a dream within a dream.

In *The Fall of Hyperion*, such a double dream structure is perceived very distinctively, and what the first, transitional dream stage stands for is closely related to the absence of a conventional epic invocation. Apart from Moneta's classification between poet and dreamer, Keats' preoccupation with the dream framework is obvious in the poem's subtitle (*A Dream*) in contrast to the subtitle of the previous version (*A Fragment*). Considering that the later version is also a fragment, we can see how much significance Keats places on the dream structure in *The Fall of Hyperion*. It is not surprising then that the poem begins with an argument about dreams, and the argument serves as a sort of preface.[95] The first eighteen lines say that everyone "whose soul is not a clod / Hath visions,"[96] including religious fanatics and uncivilized people. If someone expresses a dream vision "well nurtured in his mother tongue" which he loves,[97] he is a poet. The poem declares itself a dream and makes a self-referential remark about its future, saying that "[w]hether the dream now purposed to rehearse / Be poet's or fanatic's will be known / When this warm scribe my hand is in the grave."[98] Taking into account the later distinction between humanitarian and two kinds of visionaries (poet and dreamer), a poet should be someone who can communicate a dream with good use of his or her native language, and whose creation (poetry) has a healing effect upon the suffering world. At the same time, we notice another distinction between poets and fanatics. According to the lines, religious fanatics are a kind of dreamers, for "[f]anatics have their dreams" by which they also create literary sanctuaries of their own.[99] The distinction, which does not occur again in the poem, is relevant to the first dream stage that immediately follows the first lines.

The narration of the dream begins with the phrase: "Methought I stood where trees of every clime, . . . made a screen."[100] This introduction is allusive of the well-known initial lines in the *Divine Comedy*. In spite of similar perplexity with the troubles of life, however, the poet-narrator in Keats' poem does not find himself in Dante's dark forest. Provided with the "mixed forest," fountains, odors, and an arbor, the place described in Keats' poem as the dream's starting-point is a pleasant one, a typical *locus amoenus*, one of the favorite motifs in European poetry.[101] The description easily reminds us of Eden in *Paradise Lost*, the "delicious Paradise" where "[a]ll trees of noblest kind for sight, smell, taste" grow.[102] The association with Milton's poem becomes direct when the poet-narrator finds on the ground many fruits which "seemed refuse of a meal / By angel tasted, or our Mother Eve."[103] He eats some of the leftovers. The reference to Eve might suggest that the garden is Eden itself,[104] and that the poet who eats the fruit of knowledge is taking up the epic tradition left by Milton.

The identification, however, does not have to be so specific, because the allusion can just imply the poet's intention to participate in the making of a great poetic heritage.[105] It is more important to notice that Keats' direct and indirect references to both Dante and Milton, the two authoritative poets in the religious epic, can be read as an ambitious poet's intention to create a new kind of epic.[106] The perspective of his poem is communally broader than that of the religious "[f]anatics" who "weave / A paradise for a sect."[107] The poet-narrator swears not by any god, as is customary in oaths, but by "all the mortals of the world, / And all the dead whose names are in our lips" before he drinks from "a cool vessel of transparent juice" to ease his growing thirst after having eaten his fill of the deserted, plentiful left-overs.[108] The liquid drunk by the poet-narrator may be compared to the water of "Hippocrene," which the poet craves for poetic inspiration in "Ode to a Nightingale,"[109] because he openly confesses that "[t]hat full draught is parent of my theme."[110] Now that he passes through the garden of poetry and drinks the water that inspires poetic imagination, the poet-narrator should be ready for his innovative undertaking.

Yet, to come into the main part of the poem, the poet-narrator somehow has to cross the threshold of another dream. The liquid he has tasted is so strong as to be compared with legendary narcotics or fatal medicines:

> No Asian poppy, nor elixir fine
> Of the soon-fading jealous Caliphat;
> No poison gendered in close monkish cell,
> To thin the scarlet conclave of old men,
> Could so have rapt unwilling life away.
> Among the fragrant husks and berries crushed,
> Upon the grass I struggled hard against
> The domineering potion; but in vain—[111]

The poisons intended for the assassination of prelates are evoked as a continued negative image of religious sectarianism. Although decolorized, unlike the "blushful," vinic liquid in association with the "Provençal . . . warm South" in "Ode to a Nightingale,"[112] the "transparent juice" brings about anesthetic inebriation, and the poetic inspiration symbolized by the draft proves much more powerful than the drugs in the wrong hands. The water almost instantly deprives the poet-narrator of his consciousness. The loss of consciousness here resembles death. Together with the deadly trial he later experiences on the steps of the altar, the poet-narrator undergoes symbolic death twice in the poem. But the first symbolic death is more like falling into a dream, a "cloudy swoon."[113] In fact, after an unspecified time, he wakes up and finds himself in the completely different surroundings of the temple of Saturn.

The question here is twofold. Why does the poet-narrator quaff the liquid instead of beseeching the Muse to fill him with divine breath? And why does he have to cross a threshold to another dream stage in the form of a symbolic death? The absence of an epic invocation is highly awkward, given the unabashed use of the other epic conventions, such as lofty style, long similes, a long list of characters, and a military motif, in the overall scheme of the Hyperion poems. Even formulaic phrases are employed as a pure convention just to reassure us that we are reading an epic.

But Keats does mention the Muse twice in the earlier poem. The first instance occurs when the narrating voice shifts its topic from a list of the dejected, prostrate Titans in the dark, almost subterranean "nest of woe" to the approaching pair of Thea and her consort Saturn:[114]

> For when the Muse's wings are air-ward spread,
> Who shall delay her flight? And she must chant
> Of Saturn and his guide, who now had climbed
> With damp and slippery footing from a depth
> More horrid still.[115]

Situated far after the introduction of book 2, the passage is obviously not an invocation to Calliope, the Muse of epic poetry. Instead, it is intended to be a cunning figure of speech. The second instance sounds much more like a conventional invocation to the goddess:

> Oh, leave them [the Titans], Muse! Oh, leave them to their woes;
> For thou art weak to sing such tumults dire;
> A solitary sorrow best befits
> Thy lips, and antheming lonely grief.
> Leave them, O Muse! for thou anon wilt find
> Many a fallen old Divinity
> Wandering in vain about bewildered shores.
> Meantime touch piously the Delphic harp,
> And not a wind of heaven but will breathe
> In aid soft warble from the Dorian flute;[116]

Indeed, the passage could be considered an invocation in a few respects. It is found at the beginning of a new book, the poet is addressing the Muse directly, and there is a reference to the breath of "a wind" which will come "[i]n aid." Upon closer scrutiny, however, the ten lines form something other than an authentic invocation. The poet is not appealing to the Muse for inspirational assistance. Rather, he is giving the goddess a direction about what topic she should choose next. Moreover, not the poet but the Muse needs a breath of wind as help for creative energy. This Muse is a meek, lonely, feeble ("thou art weak") power rather than a traditionally held deity who possesses the poet with her divine breath to dictate the verse. She is no more than a figurative manifestation of the poet's mind, whose voice would admittedly suit the softer modes of poetry ("[a] solitary sorrow"), such as odes, better than the self-imposed lofty strain of the epic.

It follows that there is no real invocation to the Muse in the Hyperion poems. What we have instead is the draft of the "transparent juice" in *The Fall of Hyperion*. The liquid, which induces the main dream part of the story, works as a source of poetic inspiration, a function usually attributed to the wind as a divine breath. By this substitution, the poet symbolically declares his determination not to rely simply on the given tradition, thus paralleling his covert defiance of sectarianism in religious epic. He might make use of some epic conventions for the sake of conventionality, but in pursuit of literary innovations his pride as a poet forbids him to imitate what has been achieved by other poets. What he should strive for is emulation, and his ambition is implied again by the oath he makes before he tastes the water. Certainly, his swearing by "all the mortals of the world, / And all the dead whose names are in our lips" sounds too solemn for just drinking a beverage without anybody's permission. Moreover, if a guilty conscience were involved in acting so, he should have made the "pledging" before he began to eat "a feast of summer fruits . . . deliciously."[117] His serious oath is indicative of his refusal to cling to the tradition and his willingness to partake of the dynamism of poetic creation.

For all his firm stance, however, Keats' ambition already wavers in face of the barely undertaken project. An able poet keenly knows what can be achieved with his or her imaginative power. Therefore, the Romantic idealism, which places so much importance on the creative power of the poet's mind, necessarily entails its own self-consciousness that results in the so-called Romantic irony. In Keats' case, the poet's lack of self-confidence is manifest in his choice of a narcotic drink, rather than a conventional breeze or breath, as a means to bring forth poetic inspiration. While he willingly renounces the help of tradition, he has to drug his artistic self into a creative trance by some artificial means. On the one hand, with the crucial choice of the watery element over the airy one, he asserts the independence of his creative mind from the fetters of the tradition. On the other hand, the same choice betrays a sense of uncertainty and trepidation about breaking into an untrodden field of creation all by himself. Wishing to keep himself from imitating the past masters such as Dante and Milton by having recourse solely to his imagination, Keats falls into the Romantic trap of unstable self-apotheosis.

The precarious confidence in the form of water is symbolically manifest not only in *The Fall of Hyperion* but also in *Hyperion*, although far less intelligibly. Notably lacking a traditional supplication to the epic Muse, the first several lines of the earlier poem describe the intense quietness of the valley where the Titan king lies "nerveless, listless, dead, / Unsceptred" with "his realmless eyes . . . closed."[118] The stillness there is even deadly, because the passage stresses Saturn's new, half-mortal nature by persistently using such words as "the dead leaf," "deadened," and "dead."[119] In this scene, the four elements are arranged in the traditional order of weight from light to heavy. First, the place is described as "[f]ar from the fiery noon, and eve's one star."[120] Then come references to the elements of air and water:

> No stir of air was there,
> Not so much life as on a summer's day
> Robs not one light seed from the feathered grass,
> But where the dead leaf fell, there did it rest.
> A stream went voiceless by, still deadened more
> By reason of his fallen divinity
> Spreading a shade; the naiad 'mid her reeds
> Pressed her cold finger closer to her lips.[121]

And finally, we find Saturn's "old right hand" lying paralyzed "[u]pon the sodden ground."[122] Along with stifling silence, what is emphasized in the initial passage is the complete nonexistence of the elemental activities of air and fire as well as the solid presence of the two heavier elements. Most importantly, the only element that makes the static scene *alive* with motion is the running water, also personified by the water nymph naiad.

In place of an invocation to the Muse, without even the slightest breeze blowing, the rivulet functions as the source of inspiration for the poem, supposedly flowing out of the spring on Mount Helicon, that is, Hippocrene sacred to the Muses. Although more traditionally molded than its later twin poem, *Hyperion* contains only one implicit allusion to the Muse at the outset, and a few other references to the goddess are dispersed throughout the rest of the poem as we have seen above. Already inclined not to rely on the conventional mode of poetic imagination, Keats began his first epic attempt without a formal invocation. But the opening scene is so quiet that the only motion there forbids itself utterance. The total absence of articulation suggests not only the sad state of Saturn deprived of godly power and speech, but also the perplexity of the poet who forces himself to originate a poem without having recourse to a traditionally available expression. That perplexity centering on a liquid element for poetic inspiration is later to reemerge, with the advent of the poet-narrator, in the more direct form of the water he drinks at his first dream stage in *The Fall of Hyperion*.

In this light, the answer to the second question, why Keats needed a dream vision within the framework of another dream in the later poem, is self-evident. The beautiful, but deserted, garden with the "transparent juice" at the initial dream stage might be just a substitute for the more conventional device of an invocation to the Muse for poetic inspiration. Irene H. Chayes points out that, in dream-vision stories, there is often "a further distinction between the initial dream and the particular 'vision' the dreamer is allowed to see or participate in once he has entered his new state."[123] Still, a dream within a dream is an unusual structure. Perhaps, the double dream vision implies that the main topic to follow is beyond our ordinary understanding or experience, more surprising than suggested by a conventional single dream structure. More likely, however, Keats' double dream structure is indicative of his great anxiety about the magnitude of what he is going to attempt for the first time in literature. Thus, the poet-narrator's symbolic death into life has to be a hesitant one, not thorough because it is done anesthetically. In this respect, the central figure is similar to the prospective hero Apollo, who is trapped in his transformation between mortality and immortality at the abrupt ending of *Hyperion*.

In *Galaxy Railroad*, no such double dream structure occurs when Giovanni falls asleep. While watching the night sky on the hill, the boy's consciousness simply merges into the world of millions of stars without his noticing that he is now dreaming.[124] On the other hand, Giovanni's dream suddenly breaks off when he is deserted by his friend Campanella on the small train. Then, the boy finds himself back on the hill of the actual world and returns home. In the later version of the work, Giovanni's train journey is treated consistently as a special event within a single dream. When, however, the two versions of the work are considered together, there are three stages of awakening.

The first stage is the last part of Giovanni's dream in the early version, in which the boy is consoled by an adult with a large black hat after Campanella's disappearance. This section is different from the preceding part of the dream, because his conversation with the mysterious adult reveals to Giovanni the meaning of his spiritual journey, which is a kind of awakening to the truth, although Giovanni is still dreaming. The next stage is the actual awakening scene, in which Dr. Bulcaniro tells the boy about his experiment. Giovanni understands that he was the subject of that experiment in which the scientist transmitted his thoughts to the dreaming boy. Thus, the reason why such an unusual dream occurred is explained at this stage. The early version ends with Giovanni running down the hill, and there is no scene of Campanella drowned in the river. With Campanella's presence on the train left unexplained, the lack of this last stage, which provides another awakening to more truth, gives the work an awkward ending. Campanella, who "looked a little pale and suffering somewhere" in "a really black jacket as if drenched" at the beginning of the trip,[125] somehow happens to be on the train. With a coherent ending added in the later version, Giovanni's dream can finally achieve its full meaning.

Obviously, the first and last stages are not exactly scenes of awakening from a dream. They are not like the two distinctive thresholds of falling into a dream in *The Fall of Hyperion*. But Giovanni's awakening from his dream, which requires a coherent meaning, can be completed only through the three stages. On the one hand, Miyazawa indicates the unusual significance and occurrences of the story by distancing the main story from us through the threefold awakening. On the other hand, the same complex device ironically suggests that the author himself feels some uneasiness about the unusual content and about the high ideal he advocates. In this respect, the awakening scenes in *Galaxy Railroad* resemble the double dream structure at the beginning of Keats' poem.

The three stages of awakening are mutilated, because the first two stages are found only in the early version, while the third stage is added to the later version with the first two deleted. In fact, in some of the early publications of *Galaxy Railroad*, it was an editorial practice to provide a mixed ending out of the manuscripts that were posthumously found and were not well organized before strenuous examination distinguished the four major steps of textual development. In that case, the awakened Giovanni converses with Dr. Bulcaniro on the hill as in the early version, and then he wakes up again to go down the hill all alone as in the later version. The composite ending, a result of textual confusion, offers a double dream structure exactly like that at the beginning of Keats' poem. This textual grafting was obviously designed to avoid a plot incoherence concerning Campanella's death. But recent editions of *Galaxy Railroad* no longer adopt this composite ending, because it duplicates Giovanni's awakening scene, leaving the work's ending even more conspicuously incoherent.

The early and later versions are incompatible with each other in terms of how to treat the professed ideal. For, as we saw, Miyazawa found in the early version that he could convey his ideal only via the persona of the man with a large black hat, who himself is a persona of Dr. Bulcaniro. To straighten the entangled narrative method and make the work sound less didactic, in the later version Miyazawa deleted all the passages in which Dr. Bulcaniro and his persona appear. But the deletions deprived the piece of its explicit spiritual significance and made it look more like an imaginary, strange adventure tale. Although Miyazawa was shaping the later version out of the early version until his death, there is no indication that he considered the last manuscript satisfactory enough to stop his rigorous modification. We thus do not have a finally completed version of the story, and Giovanni's divided awakening reflects the author's indecisiveness.

The Fragmentation of the Narrative Structure

Finally, a different kind of dead end can be perceived at the close of *The Fall of Hyperion*. If a work is a fragment, the fact usually allows two possible interpretations. The negative connotation is that the work is unfinished and is not perfect. The positive interpretation is that the fragmentariness offers an open ending to the poem, and thus a large potential for development. Because of its peculiar narrative structure in which the narrator talks about the dreams he has had, the fragmentariness in Keats' poem has special significance. In this way of narration, the ending must be the point where the story originally begins. That is to say, when the poet-narrator ends his dream and wakes up, he faces the enormous task of relating it by means of poetry. Furthermore, while writing the poem, the poet again experiences the dream, in which he is assigned the job of writing a poem about the dream after awakening. The ending that never ends in its centripetal circularity is obviously modeled on the *Divine Comedy* in which, too, the narrator is assigned the task of recording his entire vision. In the case of *The Fall of Hyperion*, however, the implied spiral nonending is broken by its fragmentary textual condition. The poem thereby loses the symbolically structured organicity of what the entire schematization of the dream vision promises.

In relation to the fragmentariness of *The Fall of Hyperion*, the narrating voice shows a sign of disintegration in the second canto of only sixty-one lines with which the poem discontinues. Moneta, who is describing Hyperion as insecure in his sky palace, turns into the narrating voice of the poem and takes over the poet-narrator's role for about fifty lines. Her sudden function as the narrator of the poem is actually not so unexpected, because it comes from her essence as memory to be related. The narration is then resumed by the poet-narrator until the end which comes shortly after. He simply observes the sun-god and his palace without offering subjective comment. Almost all of the lines in the new, short canto are taken unchanged from *Hyperion*. Unlike the early version, however, the narration of the scene is fractured into two voices. The narration overtaken by Moneta, which partly originates in her uncertain existence, suggests that, after having revealed the personal significance of the poem, the poet-narrator is now losing his *raison d'être* with his first-person perspective. Because the assertive voice of the poet-narrator frames *The Fall of Hyperion* and distinguishes it from its earlier twin piece, the blurring of the narrative point imperils the self-identity not only of the central figure but also of the poem itself.

In the later version of *Galaxy Railroad*, there is no such disintegration of the narrative mode. But the work, too, contains a disruptive element concerning the end of the dream. We have seen that the temporal extent of the work is structurally expanded by the metaphor of the train trip that suggests the endless, nightly recurrence of the operation. When the train reaches the zenith of the firmament, the old man, who talks about the corn growing around that area, calls the place a "terrible plateau" several thousand feet above the *ama no gawa*.[126] A little later, when the train runs along an extremely high cliff, the same man says as follows: "Yes, we have a downslope from here. It's not an easy thing because we have to go down at a stretch to the water level this time. Because we have the declivity, the train never comes from over there to this side. You see, it's already getting faster and faster."[127] The train trip, which is a one-way service, directly refutes the metaphorically promised, nightly perpetuity and destroys the structural continuity of temporal expanse.[128] Perhaps another train of an identical model runs on the same time table the following night. All the same, after the Christians get off at the Southern Cross and the train becomes "more than half empty,"[129] we are not informed where the small train, which never returns, heads for as it advances through the uncertain space with a handful of passengers including the companionless Giovanni. The uncertainty about the train destination reflects the author's own uncertainty about his creation and what he proposes in it. Consequently, regardless of whether the boy has learned wisdom or not, Giovanni has to leave the dream sphere in the midst of nowhere, without ever reaching the structurally implied terminal South Pole that lies further ahead. Giovanni's abrupt return to the hilltop ruptures the ongoing realization of the immense circular organicity of Miyazawa's universe that only the streaming *ama no gawa* and its reflected image remotely suggest at the closing scene. In this case, too, the broken circularity threatens the text's symbolic integrity.

In *The Fall of Hyperion* and *Galaxy Railroad*, both Keats and Miyazawa lack a definite viewpoint about the meaning of life. Their hesitation is inevitable since their self-imposed ideals require such a huge task for such an immense community. Their irresolution, which they do not openly acknowledge, manifests itself in the elements that undermine the professed statements of the two works. Thus, *The Fall of Hyperion* and *Galaxy Railroad* reveal a certain tendency toward self-disintegration while still conveying a sense of greatness about humankind and the world that encompasses it. A fundamental similarity resides in the two authors' unsuccessful attempts to create what has never been achieved before in the history of world literature: an integral work that affirms the dignity of life, sustaining peace and harmony with an unfragmented world–view, on a grand scale. In this sense, the two works can be considered typical transitional epics.

Although we can find a number of examples of transitional epic, the epic of peace, the concept of which I have proposed in this study, has not yet been fully actualized. But epic development is a long process. Many of the epics that still enjoy wide acceptance have as a rule appeared centuries apart in response to historical moments of social and spiritual crises. I believe that we have reached such a critical moment, in fact, an unprecedented one. The two relatively recent works I have examined reflect, implicitly yet sensitively, a sense of growing insecurity in modern times: Keats witnessed the collapse of the French Revolution, and Miyazawa died just before World War II. In their call for harmonizing principles and selfless commitment, one can detect efforts to resist the desolation of the spirit. Therefore, by their transitional nature, *The Fall of Hyperion* and *Galaxy Railroad* express the unspoken desideratum for an epic of peace which, if ever realized and popularly accepted, would herald a new era in human society.

NOTES

Preface

1. When, based on what I had written in my Ph.D. dissertation, I was further speculating on the changing nature of the epic, I came across the expression, "an epic of peace," in a multicultural motion picture titled *Wings of Desire*. In a scene of this film, an old poet wanders a hinterland of West Berlin, saying in monologue that nobody has written an epic of peace yet. Wim Wenders, dir., *Wings of Desire*, prod. Antole Dauman and Wim Wenders, 130 min. (Paris: Argos Films; Berlin: Road Movies; Köln: Westdeutscher Rundfunk, 1987), videocassette.

1. Theories of the Epic

1. Based on linguistic, historical, and archaeological evidence, scholars theorize that the *Iliad* and the *Odyssey* were created by two different poets, either on one of the Aegean Islands or somewhere on the coast of Asia Minor, probably with the latter poem produced one or two generations after the former piece, sometime around 700 BCE. Accordingly, although I use the term "Homeric" to refer to these poems, I do not presume the historical presence of one poet called Homer as the single author of the two poems. See M. I. Finley, *The World of Odysseus* (New York: Viking, 1954), 4; Jasper Griffin, *Homer* (New York: Hill and Wang, 1980), 5–6. All references to Finley's work are to this edition. See also Giambattista Vico, *The New Science of Giambattista Vico*, trans. Thomas Goddard Bergin and Max Harold Fisch (Ithaca: Cornell University Press, 1948), 789, 804, 863, 873, 875, 878, 880, 881. All references to Vico's work are to this edition.

2. C. S. Lewis, *A Preface to "Paradise Lost"* (London: Oxford University Press, 1942), 12.

3. In philosophical debate, it is an important point of contention whether the dialogue in Plato's works, composed in the dramatic mode with Socrates as the protagonist, conveys Plato's original ideas or just reports Socrates' words. But because this question is not essential to my argument, I shall simply refer to Plato as a major source of philosophical reflections on the epic.

4. Plato, *Phaedrus*, in Walter Hamilton, trans., *"Phaedrus" and the "Seventh and Eighth Letters"* (Harmondsworth, U.K.: Penguin, 1973), 274–75.

5. Plato, *The Republic*, trans. Desmond Lee, 2nd ed. (Harmondsworth, U.K.: Penguin, 1974), 597e, 602c. All references to this work are to this edition. Unless otherwise indicated, further documentation in the text is to this work.

6. See Mihai I. Spariosu, *God of Many Names: Play, Poetry, and Power in Hellenic Thought from Homer to Aristotle* (Durham, N.C.: Duke University Press, 1991), 173–74.

7. Concerning Plato's objection to the archaic, heroic mentality, see further Spariosu, 147–48, 177.

8. Plato, *The Laws*, trans. Trevor J. Saunders (Harmondsworth, U.K.: Penguin, 1970), 803.

9. See Spariosu, 190–91.

10. Aristotle, *The Poetics*, in S. H. Butcher, trans., *Aristotle's Theory of Poetry and Fine Art*, 4th ed. (New York: Dover, 1951), 24.9. All references to this work are to this edition.

11. Aristotle, 25.17.

12. Ibid., 25.17, 24.10.

13. Sir Philip Sidney, *"An Apology for Poetry" or "The Defence of Poetry,"* ed. Geoffrey Shepherd (London: Nelson, 1965), 124. All references to this work are to this edition.

14. Sidney, 110.

15. Ibid., 119.

16. Torquato Tasso, *Discourses on the Heroic Poem*, trans. Mariella Cavalchini and Irene Samuel (London: Oxford University Press, Clarendon Press, 1973), 28. All references to this work are to this edition.

17. Tasso, *Discourses*, 6, 17, 5.

18. Aristotle, 9.2.

19. Ibid., 9.3.

20. Sidney, 107.

21. Tasso, *Discourses*, 40.

22. Ibid., 43.

23. Nicolas Boileau-Despréaux, *The Art of Poetry*, in Ernest Dilworth, trans., *Boileau: Selected Criticism* (Indianapolis: Bobbs-Merrill, 1965), 30. All references to this work are to this edition.

24. G. W. F. Hegel, *Aesthetics: Lectures on Fine Art*, trans. T. M. Knox, 2 vols. (Oxford: Oxford University Press, Clarendon Press, 1975), 2:1059. All references to this work are to this edition.

25. Hegel, 2:1057–58.

26. Vico, 639. Unless otherwise indicated, further documentation in the text is to Vico's *New Science*.

27. Friedrich von Schiller, *Naive and Sentimental Poetry*, in *"Naive and Sentimental Poetry" and "On the Sublime": Two Essays*, trans. Julius A. Elias (New York: Frederick Ungar, 1966), 143, 111. All references to this work are to this edition. Unless otherwise indicated, further documentation in the text is to this work.

28. Friedrich Nietzsche, *The Birth of Tragedy or: Hellenism and Pessimism*, in *"The Birth of Tragedy" and "The Case of Wagner,"* trans. Walter Kaufmann (New York: Random House, Vintage, 1967), 43. All references to this work are to this edition. Unless otherwise indicated, further documentation in the text is to this work.

29. Georg Lukács, *The Theory of the Novel: A Historico-Philosophical Essay on the Forms of Great Epic Literature*, trans. Anna Bostock (Cambridge, Mass.: MIT Press, 1971), 41. All references to this work are to this edition. Unless otherwise indicated, further documentation in the text is to this work.

30. Nietzsche, *The Birth of Tragedy*, 23.

31. Aristotle, 1.8. Unless otherwise indicated, further documentation in the text is to Aristotle's *Poetics*.

32. Longinus, *Longinus on the Sublime*, trans. W. Rhys Roberts (Cambridge: Cambridge University Press, 1899), 9.1. All references to this work are to this edition.

33. Longinus, 9.11, 9.13.

34. Ibid., 33.2.

35. Julius Caesar Scaliger, *Select Translations from Scaliger's "Poetics,"* trans. Frederick Morgan Padelford (New York: Henry Holt, 1905), 17. In accord with Sidney and Tasso, Scaliger believes "the sovereignty of the epic," stating that epic poetry is "one perfect orginal to which all the rest [of poetry] can be referred as their norm and standard" (54).

36. Sidney, 103.

37. Lodovico Castelvetro, *Castelvetro on the Art of Poetry: An Abridged Translation of Lodovico Castelvetro's "'Poetica' d'Aristotele Vulgarizzata et Sposta,"* trans. Andrew Bongiorno (Binghamton, N.Y.: Center for Medieval & Early Renaissance Studies, State University of New York at Binghamton, 1984), 95. All references to this work are to this edition.

38. Castelvetro, 97, 96.

39. Ibid., 90, 221.

40. Boileau, 12.

41. Ibid., 28.

42. Ibid., 32.

43. Ibid., 30.

44. Ibid., 28.

45. Ibid., 31.

46. Ibid., 28.

47. Henry Fielding, preface to *Joseph Andrews,* ed. Martin C. Battestin (Middletown: Wesleyan University Press, 1967), 10. All references to this work are to this edition. Unless otherwise indicated, further documentation in the text is to this work.

48. Johann Wolfgang von Goethe, "On Epic and Dramatic Poetry," in *Essays on Art and Literature,* trans. Ellen von Nardroff and Ernest H. von Nardroff, ed. John Gearey, vol. 3 of *Goethe's Collected Works* (New York: Suhrkamp, 1986), 193. All references to this work are to this edition. Unless otherwise indicated, further documentation in the text is to this work.

49. Hegel, 2:1046. Unless otherwise indicated, further documentation in the text is to Hegel's *Aesthetics.*

50. M. M. Bakhtin, *The Dialogic Imagination: Four Essays,* trans. Caryl Emerson and Michael Holquist, ed. Michael Holquist (Austin: University of Texas Press, 1981), 11. All references to this work are to this edition. Unless otherwise indicated, further documentation in the text is to this work.

51. Schiller, 126n.

52. Brian Wilkie, *Romantic Poets and Epic Tradition* (Madison: University of Wisconsin Press, 1965), 4.

53. William Calin, *A Muse for Heroes: Nine Centuries of the Epic in France* (Toronto: University of Toronto Press, 1983), 9–10.

54. Paul Merchant, *The Epic* (London: Methuen, 1971), 1.

55. Merchant, 44.

56. Ibid.

57. Calin, 5.

2. Epic Grandeur

1. Wilkie calls the same epic quality "greatness" (5–7). According to him, the criterion of greatness suggests that "the epic is not simply a literary genre" (7). Concerning differences between epic and drama, Lukács says that "[t]here is such a thing as great epic literature, but drama never requires the attribute of greatness and must always resist it" (49).

2. Northrop Frye, *Anatomy of Criticism: Four Essays* (Princeton: Princeton University Press, 1957), 33–34, 366.

3. Ibid., 33.

4. Ibid.

5. Ibid.

6. Friedrich Nietzsche, *Twilight of the Idols or, How One Philosophizes with a Hammer*, in *The Portable Nietzsche*, trans. Walter Kaufmann (Harmondsworth, U.K.: Penguin, 1954), 494.

7. Discussing the number of the central figures in an epic, Thomas Greene argues that "[t]he act which induces heroic awe must be performed by a single individual or at most by a very small group of individuals." Thomas Greene, *The Descent from Heaven: A Study in Epic Continuity* (New Haven: Yale University Press, 1963), 15.

8. Concerning this point, Lukács says: "[T]he completeness, the roundness of the value system which determines the epic cosmos creates a whole which is too organic for any part of it to become so enclosed within itself, so dependent upon itself, as to find itself as an interiority" (66).

9. Vico, concerning his methodology, argues that, along "poetic metaphysics, . . . poetic wisdom branches off into physics and thence into cosmography and thus into astronomy, whose fruits are chronology and geography" (687).

10. Wilkie, 13.

11. Frye classifies the epic under the large entity of "encyclopaedic forms" (315–26). But the epic is not always intended to be particularly encyclopedic, as pieces like *Gilgamesh* and *Beowulf* testify.

12. Blaise Pascal, *Pascal's "Pensées,"* trans. H. F. Stewart (New York: Pantheon, 1950), 83.

13. Friedrich Nietzsche, "Attempt at a Self-Criticism" before *The Birth of Tragedy*, 18, 21.

14. Finley, 15.

15. About the progress of the human comprehension of the world, Finley goes on to say: "Homer occupies the first stage in the history of Greek control over its myths; his poems are often pre-Greek, as it were, in their treatment of myth, but they also have flashes of something else, of a genius for ordering the world, for bringing man and nature, men and the gods, into harmony in a way that succeeding centuries were to expand and elevate to the glory of Hellenism" (15–16).

16. Concerning the hero "whose basic virtue is natural nobility in body and soul," Ernst Robert Curtius says: "The hero is distinguished by a superabundance of intellectual will and by its concentration against the instincts. It is this which constitutes his greatness of character. The specific virtue of the hero is self-control. But the hero's will does not rest here, it presses on into power, responsibility, daring." Thus, to gain the status of an epic hero, a figure must overcome emotions, desires, and, often, interest of survival. See Ernst Robert Curtius, *European Literature and the Latin Middle Ages*, trans. Willard R. Trask (Princeton: Princeton University Press, 1973), 167.

17. *The Epic of Gilgamesh*, trans. N. K. Sandars (Harmondsworth, U.K.: Penguin, 1960), 61. All references to this work are to this edition.

18. *The Epic of Gilgamesh*, 95, 97.

19. Tasso argues that the epic and "heroic poems called romances" belong to "one and the same poetic genre" because they represent the same actions in the identical manner and means (*Discourses*, 68, 70). But his identification of romance with the epic is apparently motivated by his willingness to fend off the criticism of Italian Renaissance poems, including his own *Jerusalem Delivered*, concerning their topical fancifulness and incredibility.

20. Vico points out that, throughout the *Iliad*, neither does Achilles show "the faintest indication of amorous passion at being deprived of" Briseis nor Menelaus gives "the slightest sign of amorous distress or jeal-

ousy of Paris" (708). With this statement, Vico contrasts the epic indifference to love with the "gallant heroism" of the "growing effeminacy of later times" (708), thereby intending a generic dividing line between epic and romance. Fully aware of this kind of argument against romance, Tasso attempts to broaden the meaning of love by categorizing friendship, such as the one between Achilles and Patroclus, as love. What he has in mind, however, is "chivalric love," and love and friendship, which he claims as "subjects entirely suitable for the heroic poem," often do not extend much beyond private affairs (*Discourses*, 47, 48).

21. Greene, 15.

22. For this view of Milton's Satan, see, for example, Shelley's preface to his *Prometheus Unbound*.

3. The Transformation of Traditional Epic

1. See Greene, 1–3.

2. See Wilkie, 10–15; Joan Malory Webber, *Milton and His Epic Tradition* (Seattle: University of Washington Press, 1979), 5; Merchant, passim; and C. M. Bowra, *From Virgil to Milton* (London: Macmillan, 1945), passim. More generally, in his discussion of sentimental poetry, Schiller argues that "no single type of composition has ever remained entirely what it was among the ancients, and that often very new types have been executed under the old names" (147n).

3. Harold Bloom, *The Anxiety of Influence: A Theory of Poetry* (London: Oxford University Press, 1973), 5.

4. The transformative nature of the epic stands against what Bakhtin formulates about the genre. He also notes, however, that "the growth of literature is not merely development and change within the fixed boundaries of any given definition; the boundaries themselves are constantly changing" (33). If we replace literature with the epic, this remark applies to the kind of change I propose about the epic elements as well.

5. Lewis, 12, 30.

6. Homer, *The Iliad*, trans. Robert Fitzgerald (Garden City, N.Y.: Doubleday, 1974), 585.

7. Arthur W. H. Adkins, *Merit and Responsibility: A Study in Greek Values* (London: Oxford University Press, Clarendon Press, 1960), 18.

8. Spariosu, 31. Spariosu further defines the *oikos* as an "archaic, rural" community "based on strictly hierarchical, aristocratic power

configurations" (31). Finley explains *oikos* as "all the people of the household and its goods," and "'economics' (from the Latinized form, *oecus*)" as "the art of managing an *oikos*," meaning "running a farm, not managing to keep peace in the family" (54).

9. Finley argues that there is this kind of strong "[f]amily attachment" in the Homeric world because "one's kin were indistinguishable from oneself" (125). The idea points to the problem of self-identity, a sense of which Odysseus tries to regain by coming home.

10. Spariosu considers "[m]oral scruples" about "ethical responsibility toward fellow humans at large" to be "irrelevant in a heroic society, where intentions count less than performance, and where performance is judged largely in terms of success and failure" (6).

11. Vico, 712, 715.

12. Finley points out that this change of heroic values started early in Greek history, for "the community could grow only by taming the hero and blunting the free exercise of his prowess, and a domesticated hero was a contradiction in terms" (125). See also his argument on the relation of heroism with the growth of the *polis* (129); Bowra, 9–14; Curtius, 173; Spariosu, 30–31.

13. Virgil, *The Aeneid*, trans. Robert Fitzgerald (New York: Random House, Vintage, 1983), 6.1014–20. All references to this work are to this edition.

14. *The Aeneid*, 1.375.

15. Luis Vaz de Camoens, *The Lusiads*, trans. William C. Atkinson (Harmondsworth, U.K.: Penguin, 1952), 39.

16. Curtius, 174.

17. Vico, 727.

18. John Milton, *Paradise Lost*, ed. Alastair Fowler (London: Longman, 1968), 10.692–93. All references to this work are to this edition.

19. Paul Sherwin, "Dying into Life: Keats's Struggle with Milton in *Hyperion*," *PMLA* 93.3 (1978): 387.

20. Concerning the importance of these spaces in the *Divine Comedy*, Lukács says that "[t]he immanence of the meaning of life is present and existent in Dante's world, but only in the beyond: it is the perfect immanence of the transcendent" (59).

21. W. P. Ker, *The Dark Ages* (Edinburgh: William Blackwood and Sons, 1904), 58. See also Lewis, 30–31.

22. While he says that "Beowulf has nothing else to do" beside killing the monsters (252), Ker elsewhere says as follows:

> What is distinctly Northern in the myth of the Twilight of the Gods is the strength of its theory of life. It is this intensity of courage that distinguishes the Northern mythology (and Icelandic literature generally) from all others. . . . It is the assertion of the individual freedom against all the terrors and temptations of the world. It is absolute resistance, perfect because without hope. . . . [T]he gods, who are defeated, think that defeat is not refutation. The latest mythology of the North is an allegory of the Teutonic self-will, carried to its noblest terms, deified by the men for whom all religion was coming to be meaningless except "trust in one's own might and main." (57–58)

This observation is easily applicable not only to the mythology but to the heroic poetry of the same culture.

23. Edmund Spenser, *The Faerie Qveene*, ed. A. C. Hamilton (London: Longman, 1977), 7.7.56.2–3. All references to this work are to this edition.

24. *The Faerie Qveene*, 7.7.58.4–9.

25. Nietzsche, *The Birth of Tragedy*, 35.

26. Certain Chinese characters were used as phonetic symbols to record the Japanese poems in *Man'yōshū* in the absence of the native writing systems (*hiragana* and *katakana*) that were later developed. Those Chinese characters are called *man'yōgana*. In addition to *tanka* poems, *Man'yōshū* contains a number of *chōka* poems which are basically extended versions of a *tanka* poem.

27. Ki no Tsurayuki, "Kanajo: The Japanese Preface," in *Kokinshū: A Collection of Poems Ancient and Modern*, trans. Laurel Rasplica Rodd and Mary Catherine Henkenius (Princeton: Princeton University Press, 1984), 35.

28. William Wordsworth, "Preface to *Lyrical Ballads, with Pastoral and Other Poems*" (1802), in *William Wordsworth*, ed. Stephen Gill (Oxford: Oxford University Press, 1984), 598.

29. Concerning this point, as well as Horace's contribution to Western poetics, see Earl Miner, *Comparative Poetics: An Intercultural Essay on Theories of Literature* (Princeton: Princeton University Press, 1990), 8–9, 24–31. I owe a part of my book's subtitle to Miner's work.

30. Concerning this historic tendency in Japan, see Ivan Morris, *The Nobility of Failure: Tragic Heroes in the History of Japan* (New York: Holt, Rinehart and Winston, 1975).

31. Miner, 9. Miner calls "lyric-based poetics" such as Tsurayuki's "affective-expressive," against which the Western poetics based on Aristotle and Horace should be termed not simply mimetic but "mimetic-affective" (9).

32. The first version of the *Heike* was apparently created in the early thirteenth century, a few decades after the historical fall of the Heike clan. The identity of the original author is not established, although it is well known that Yoshida Kenkō in section 226 of his *Tsurezuregusa* (Essays in idleness) (around 1330) ascribes the initial *Heike* story to Shinano Zenji Yukinaga (Yukinaga, the former governor of Shinano). See Helen Craig McCullough, introduction to *The Tale of the Heike*, trans. Helen Craig McCullough (Stanford: Stanford University Press, 1988), 6–7.

33. Kenneth Dean Butler, "The Textual Evolution of the *Heike Monogatari*," *Harvard Journal of Asiatic Studies* 26 (1966): 5.

34. See Butler, "Textual Evolution," 5; McCullough, 6.

35. The *Heike* has a long and complicated textual evolution. The numerous variations of the text can be divided into two groups: one for singing and the other for reading. McCullough's translation of *Heike monogatari*, which I use in this book, is based on the Kakuichi text (1371), which has been accepted as the standard reading text. Concerning the textual evolution of the *Heike*, see Atsumi Kaoru, *"Heike monogatari" no kisoteki kenkyū* (Basic research on *The Tale of the Heike*) (Kasama Shoin, 1978), 54–318; Butler, "Textual Evolution," 5–51; McCullough, introduction to *The Tale of the Heike*, 6–8. All the writings, the titles of which are listed in romanized Japanese, are published in Tokyo.

36. Ryusaku Tsunoda, William Theodore de Bary, and Donald Keene, comps., *Sources of Japanese Tradition* (New York: Columbia University Press, 1958), 191–92.

37. *The Tale of the Heike*, trans. Helen Craig McCullough (Stanford: Stanford University Press, 1988), 23. All references to this work are to this edition.

38. Although there is another word, *bushi*, for the same meaning, I employ *samurai* to refer to the Japanese warrior class or individuals, partly because it is widely accepted in the English vocabulary, but mainly because the *Heike* often uses it.

39. In this sense, many of the *samurai* figures, who are called "retainers" in McCullough's translation, are comparable to certain members of the *oikos*. Finley says that the "retainers (*therapontes*)" of the *oikos* offered their service in exchange for "a proper place in the basic social unit, the household," and the exchange "gave them both material

security and the psychological values and satisfactions that went with belonging" (54). The way the *samurai* figures fight in the battlefield is also quite similar to the way Homeric warriors do. According to Spariosu, a Homeric hero first "wanders around the field in search of a worthy match," and "[o]nce he spots his man," instead of beginning to fight at once, he "pauses to find out his identity and fighting record" by engaging in "a sort of verbal contest" that takes the form of "a vow or boast (*euchè*)" (9). It is also crucial for a *samurai* figure to declare proudly his name, lineage, feudal affiliation, native place, past exploits, and so on, before he actually starts a physical fight. By exchanging self-identification, he makes sure of the worthiness of his opponent and assures the opponent that he is a worthy adversary to engage. There are also some differences, however. Spariosu points out that the Homeric heroes occasionally "decide not to fight, but rather to exchange courtesies and gifts, as in the case of Diomedes and Glaucus" (9); on other occasions, the encounter in a Homeric battle might end not "with the death (or ransom) of the defeated" but "with additional parting words from both sides" (10). Spariosu continues to point out that, otherwise, "[t]he slaying of the vanquished" is "followed by the victor's no less ritualized despoiling of the corpse, over which renewed fighting may break out" (10). By contrast, a peaceful parting in the midst of a battle is not within the *samurai* martial code. Moreover, the encounter ends with the decapitation of the defeated in Japan, because, instead of the armor or the entire corpse, the severed head serves as the trophy of the fight.

40. *The Tale of the Heike*, 365.

41. On the *samurai* code idealized in the Japanese work, see Kenneth Dean Butler, "The *Heike Monogatari* and the Japanese Warrior Ethic," *Harvard Journal of Asiatic Studies* 29 (1969): 93–108.

42. *The Aeneid*, 3.477.

43. Spariosu, 27.

44. *The Tale of the Heike*, 259.

45. In her introduction to her translation, McCullough asserts:

It would be wrong to claim direct influence from *Heike monogatari* for all of the hundreds of literary and artistic productions inspired by the Genpei [Genji and Heike] campaigns. . . . But we can probably say that no single Japanese literary work has influenced so many writers in so many genres for so long a time as the *Heike*, and that no era in the Japanese past can today match the romantic appeal of the late twelfth century. (9)

Thus, Butler calls the *Heike* "the national epic of Japan" ("Textual Evolution," 5).

46. McCullough, introduction to *The Tale of the Heike*, 9.

47. *Yoshitsune: A Fifteenth-Century Japanese Chronicle*, trans. Helen Craig McCullough (Stanford: Stanford University Press, 1966), 123.

48. Lukács, 61; Vico, 667.

4. The Cultural Background of *The Fall of Hyperion* and *A Night on the Galaxy Railroad*

1. The common practice of Japanese criticism refers to the author by his given name (Kenji), although I do not follow it here.

2. It is far easier to point out some analogies in the lives of Keats and Miyazawa. Both authors came from the middle class, were vigorously prolific during short periods, saw their siblings succumb to tuberculosis, themselves died young of the same disease, and gained largely posthumous fame. Even in the biographical field, however, differences are more noticeable than similarities. Residing in the urbanity of London and being associated with literary personages such as Byron and Shelley, Keats was one of the prominent Romantics of the younger generation in England. He was quite at ease in the given circumstances of his life, without getting involved much with any other social group but his own. On the other hand, living marginally in the countryside and having little interaction with his fellow writers in Tokyo, Miyazawa regarded his writings as an important part of his lifetime enterprise to change people's lives, especially the living conditions of the poor peasants and farmers around him. In order to have direct contact with these people, he quit a comfortable, white-collar position and engaged himself in farming.

3. A translation of *Galaxy Railroad* is now available in English: Sarah M. Strong, trans., *Night of the Milky Way Railway* (Armonk, N.Y.: M. E. Sharpe, 1991). I owe the transcription of the name Bulcaniro to Strong's translation. I have one reservation about a few of the illustrations in her book. Those pictures show Giovanni and Campanella in garments which look like casual Japanese *kimono*. I do not think that Miyazawa created the figures of Giovanni and Campanella in specific Japanese cultural circumstances, particularly since he gave them European names.

4. For the deconstructive approach I have recourse to, among others, see Jacques Derrida, *Of Grammatology*, trans. Gayatri Chakravorty Spivak (Baltimore: Johns Hopkins University Press, 1976); Jacques Derrida, *Writing and Difference*, trans. Alan Bass (Chicago: University of Chicago Press, 1978).

5. Spariosu, 32. For this point, see further Spariosu, 6–7, 32.

6. Plato, *The Republic*, 391c.

7. Finley argues that, to a lesser degree, Hector is an Achillean figure, because the Trojan hero chooses his own "honorable death by combat, and the end of his city and his people" rather than the inaction of status quo and the surrender for peace (124). In this sense, as Spariosu puts it, "[t]he 'tragedy of Hector' . . . is no different from that of Achilles" (33).

8. Homer, *The Odyssey*, trans. Robert Fitzgerald (Garden City, N.Y.: Anchor Books, 1963), 261, 304, 347, 418. Odysseus' mere presence can be ominous to a community when he is referred to with the same epithet. An example is found at the beginning of book 8 when he wakes up as a guest in Alcinoüs' palace (125). The favor the Phaeacians give him brings a communal disaster and xenophobia on them later in the form of a boat petrified by angry Poseidon. Proud of the appellation, Odysseus himself uses it when he mockingly calls from his leaving boat to the Cyclops he blinded (160).

9. See Bowra, 33; H. Rushton Fairclough, "Life of Virgil," in *Virgil in Two Volumes*, trans. H. Rushton Fairclough, The Loeb Classical Library 63 (Cambridge, Mass.: Harvard University Press; London: Heinemann, 1916), xi.

10. Fairclough, xi.

11. *The Aeneid*, 6.1212, 1214–15, 1217–18.

12. Ibid., 6.1206–7, 1208–9, 1209–10.

13. *Paradise Lost*, 3.98–99, 104.

14. Adkins, 13. See further Adkins, 22–23, 25. In contrast, Milton was fully aware of the incompatibility of human free will with God's control over universal causation, and he had to offer some explanation.

15. Spariosu (30–35) explains the problematic ideality of the Homeric poems as stemming from the two conflicting sets of values they contain, given their transitional nature between the heroic archaic society they present and the civic median society in which they were written.

16. Ishimoda Shō, *Heike monogatari* (*The Tale of the Heike*) (Iwanami Shoten, 1957), 50. Because the author of the *Heike* is so "vigorous with a narrating spirit," Ishimoda calls him "an optimist," compared with his contemporaries who were increasingly pessimistic about life (48, 50). Unless otherwise indicated, all the references to Japanese works are my translation.

17. Keats to J. H. Reynolds, Winchester, 21 September 1819, *The Letters of John Keats: 1814–1821*, ed. Hyder Edward Rollins, 2 vols. (Cambridge, Mass.: Harvard University Press, 1958), 2:167. All the references to Keats' letters are to this edition.

18. Concerning the silence and statuesque imagery in *Hyperion*, see Anya Taylor, "Superhuman Silence: Language in *Hyperion*," *Studies in English Literature* 19.4 (1979): 673–87, and Nancy Moore Goslee, *Uriel's Eye: Miltonic Stationing and Statuary in Blake, Keats, and Shelley* (University, Ala.: University of Alabama Press, 1985), 96–133.

19. See Wilkie, 155–78.

20. See Wilkie, 154–55, 180–82.

21. John Keats, *The Fall of Hyperion*, 1.227, in *The Poems of John Keats*, ed. Miriam Allott (London: Longman, 1970). All references to Keats' poems are to this edition.

22. William Wordsworth, *The Prelude: 1799, 1805, 1850*, ed. Jonathan Wordsworth, M. H. Abrams, and Stephen Gill (New York: Norton, 1979), 1.35, 78–79, 129, 164–65. All references to this poem are to the 1850 version of the poem in this edition.

23. Wilkie, 89.

24. See M. H. Abrams, *Natural Supernaturalism: Tradition and Revolution in Romantic Literature* (New York: Norton, 1973), 90–94. See also Lukács, 29–30.

25. Wilkie, 71.

26. Lord Byron, *Don Juan*, 6.960, in *Byron*, ed. Jerome J. McGann (Oxford: Oxford University Press, 1986). All references to this poem are to this edition.

27. *Don Juan*, 1.1593–1616; 2.1725; 3.978; 5.1265–72; 7.57–60; 8.305–8; 8.718–20; 10.695–96; 14.543–44.

28. Ibid., 4.590; 5.1272; 6.960; 10.35–36; 14.430.

29. Ibid., 3.1.

30. Wilkie, 191.

31. See Lukács, 59; Bakhtin, 5–6, 23, 33, 35.

32. *Don Juan*, 1.1670.

33. See Wilkie, 211.

34. See *Don Juan*, 1.41–56.

35. *Don Juan,* 11.653–54.

36. Percy Bysshe Shelley, *Prometheus Unbound,* 3.1.31, in *Shelley's Poetry and Prose,* ed. Donald H. Reiman and Sharon B. Powers (Norton: New York, 1977). All references to Shelley's works are to this edition.

37. John Ower, "The Epic Mythologies of Shelley and Keats," *Wascana Review* 4.1 (1969): 67.

38. *Prometheus Unbound,* 4.533.

39. Ibid., 1.674.

40. Ibid., 4.424.

41. Ibid., 1.12–13.

42. Wilkie, 89.

43. Bloom, 6.

44. Giovanni's age is not stated in the story. Concerning this point, see Murase Manabu, *"Gingatetsudō no Yoru" to wa nani ka* (What is *A Night on the Galaxy Railroad?*) (Yamato Shobō, 1989), 32–37.

45. In this study, I do not translate the *ama no gawa* into English for several reasons. "The stream of heaven" would be confusing in relation to "heaven" to which the text refers, while "the river of the sky" greatly loses the poetic quality the Japanese phrase possesses. This is because the meaning of the archaic word *ama* ambiguously hovers between sky and heaven. For other reasons, see my further argument in the next chapter.

46. Concerning the textual change, see Nishida Yoshiko, *Miyazawa Kenji ron* (On Miyazawa Kenji) (Ōfūsha, 1981), 81–117, and Miyazawa Kenji, *Shinshū Miyazawa Kenji zenshū* (The new complete works of Miyazawa Kenji), ed. Miyazawa Seiroku, Irisawa Yasuo, and Amazawa Taijirō, 17 vols. (Chikima Shobō, 1980), 12:318–24, 334–36.

47. *Shinshū Miyazawa Kenji zenshū,* 12:300. Unless otherwise indicated, all the references to Miyazawa's works are to the twelfth volume of this edition.

48. Concerning Miyazawa's source of "telepathy," see Ono Ryūshō, *Miyazawa Kenji no shisaku to shinkō* (The speculation and faith of Miyazawa Kenji) (Tairyūsha, 1979), 256–57.

49. *Galaxy Railroad* (early), 300.

50. Concerning Miyazawa's use of astronomical knowledge in his works, Sugawa Chikara points out that "Kenji had the latest concept of

the universe at that time." Sugawa Chikara, *Hoshi no sekai: Miyazawa Kenji to tomo ni* (The world of stars: With Miyazawa Kenji) (Soshiete, 1979), 3.

51. Concerning these locational names in *Galaxy Railroad*, see Kusaka Hideaki, *Miyazawa Kenji to hoshi* (Miyazawa Kenji and stars) (Gakugei Shorin, 1975), 59–70. In Miyazawa's other stories, place names are sometimes coined from actual ones. Examples include Īhatovu from Iwate and Sendāto from Sendai.

52. Miyazawa's knowledge of botany is explained in detail in Miyagi Kazuo and Takamura Kiichi, *Miyazawa Kenji to shokubutsu no sekai* (Miyazawa Kenji and the world of plants) (Tsukiji Shokan, 1980).

53. Miyazawa's use of geological and mineralogical knowledge is explained in Miyagi Kazuo, *Miyazawa Kenji: Chigaku to bungaku no hazama* (Miyazawa Kenji: Between physical geography and literature) (Tamagawa Daigaku Shuppan bu, 1977). Sakai Tadaichi says that "the abundant use of mineralogical terms helps in framing Kenji's imagery." Sakai Tadaichi, *Miyazawa Kenji ron* (On Miyazawa Kenji) (Ōfūsha, 1985), 134. See also Yoshimoto Takaaki, "Miyazawa Kenji ron" (On Miyazawa Kenji), *Bungaku* 44 (1976): 1560–61.

54. See Ōoka Shōhei, "Miyazawa Kenji to Nakahara Chūya: Meiji izen no sekai" (Miyazawa Kenji and Nakahara Chūya: The world before names), in *Miyazawa Kenji*, Gendaishi Tokuhon 12 (Shichōsha, 1983): 216.

55. Other good examples of cultural mixture include *Polāno no hiroba* (The Polano square) and *Gusukō Budori no denki* (The biography of Gusukō Budori), both of which were continuously revised together with *Galaxy Railroad* until Miyazawa's death. The two stories are set in an imaginary country called *Īhatovu*, which Miyazawa spelled variously. In an advertisement he wrote for *Chūmon no ōi ryōriten* (A restaurant of many orders) (1924), Miyazawa locates *Īhatovu* "in the same world with the mirror land in which the girl Alice wandered," and continues to say that *Īhatovu* is "Iwate Prefecture in Japan [Miyazawa's native place] as a dreamland which existed in *the author's imagery* with such scenery." See Miyazawa Kenji, *Miyazawa Kenji zenshū* (The complete works of Miyazawa Kenji), ed. Amazawa Taijirō, Irisawa Yasuo, and Miyazawa Seiroku, 8 vols. (Chikuma Shobō, 1985–86), 8:600, 601. See also Tsuzukihashi Tatsuo, *Miyazawa Kenji: Dōwa no kiseki* (Miyazawa Kenji: The orbit of his children's tales) (Ōfūsha, 1978), 43. Miyagi (*Chigaku*, 80) suggests that *Īhatovu* could possibly refer to the whole Japanese nation.

56. The use of such Italian names echoes certain Italian works Miyazawa probably read in translation, such as *Cuore: Libro per i*

ragazzi (Heart: A book for the young) (1886) by Edmondo de Amicis and *La città del sole: Dialogo poetico* (The city of the sun: A poetical dialogue) (1623) by Tommaso Campanella. The former work is similar to *Galaxy Railroad* in several respects. It is a novel about an Italian schoolboy's daily life, and its themes are friendship, the loneliness of a poor boy, and self-sacrifice. One of its episodes deals with a boy who saves a friend from drowning, and another episode is about a shipwreck which involves two Italian children. The latter book, whose author has the same name as Giovanni's close friend, discusses communitarian production in agriculture, respect for labor, and equal opportunity of education, all of which are found in Miyazawa's *Polāno no hiroba*. Moreover, before they go to sleep, the citizens of Campanella's utopian city pray "for happiness both for themselves and for all the people." See *Shinshū Miyazawa Kenji zenshū*, 12:336; "Campanella" and "Giovanni," in Hara Shirō, ed., *Miyazawa Kenji goi jiten* (Glossarial dictionary of Miyazawa Kenji) (Tokyo Shoseki, 1989), 161–62, 351–52; Tommaso Campanella, *La città del sole: Dialogo poetico* (The city of the sun: A poetical dialogue), trans. Daniel J. Donno (Berkeley: University of California Press, 1981), 107.

57. Saitō Jun even considers Kaoru and Tadashi "foreigners," that is, non-Japanese despite their Japanese names. He also calls Giovanni *and* Campanella, who, unlike Giovanni, does not reveal his religious stance clearly, "pagans," that is, non–Christians. Saitō Jun, "*Gingatetsudō no Yoru* no monogatari toshite no kōzō: Shokikei kara saishūkei e no dainamizumu" (The structure of *A Night on the Galaxy Railroad* as a story: Dynamism from the early versions to the final version), *Miyazawa Kenji* 8 (Yōyōsha, 1988): 105.

58. Takao Hagiwara, "The Bodhisattva Ideal and the Idea of Innocence in Miyazawa Kenji's Life and Literature," *Journal of the Association of Teachers of Japanese* 27.1 (1993): 41–42.

59. *Miyazawa Kenji zenshū*, 8:601.

60. Concerning these points, see Hagiwara Takao, *Miyazawa Kenji: Inosensu no bungaku* (Miyazawa Kenji: Literature of innocence) (Meiji Shoin, 1988), 190–91, 233.

61. Concerning the problem of life in "Yodaka no Hoshi," see Yamauchi Osamu, "*Gingatetsudō no Yoru*" (A Night on the Galaxy Railroad), *Kokubungaku: Kaishaku to kanshō* 44.10 (1979): 98–99.

62. Tsuzukihashi argues that Miyazawa's children's tales "trace back to the contradiction with which life is fundamentally burdened," and "try to deal with various human and social problems from that point of view" (*Kiseki*, 45).

63. Spariosu, 1. Hagiwara calls this "cosmic autophagy" in a positive sense that, through the act of eating, the eater becomes identified with the eaten (*Inosensu no bungaku,* 176).

64. Vidaeus quotes these words from one of the radio audience who heard the Swedish version of "The Nighthawk Star" in the fall of 1977. Kerstin Vidaeus, "Miyazawa Kenji no dōwa ni tsuite" (On children's tales by Miyazawa Kenji), in *Shinshū Miyazawa Kenji zenshū,* 17:249.

65. Tsuzukihashi Tatsuo, *Miyazawa Kenji: Dōwa no sekai* (Miyazawa Kenji: The world of his children's tales) (Ōfūsha, 1975), 174.

66. Usami Eiji, "*Gingatetsudō no Yoru*" (A Night on the Galaxy Railroad), in Kusano Shinpei, ed., *Miyazawa Kenji kenkyū* (Research on Miyazawa Kenji), 2 vols. (Chikuma Shobō, 1958, 1969), 1:106.

67. Vidaeus, 248.

68. Ōmi Masato, "'Minna no saiwai' sagasu tabi: *Aoi Tori* to no hikaku o tōshite" [A trip to look for 'everyone's happiness': Through a comparison with *The Blue Bird*], *Miyazawa Kenji* 7 (Yōyōsha, 1987): 92.

5. The Epic Nature of *The Fall of Hyperion* and *A Night on the Galaxy Railroad*

1. Concerning the centrality of Dante's role in the *Divine Comedy,* Lukács observes:

> [J]ust as the totality of the transcendent world-structure is the pre-determined sense-giving, all-embracing *a priori* of each individual destiny, so the increasing comprehension of this edifice, its structure and its beauty—the great experience of Dante the traveller—envelops everything in the unity of its meaning, now revealed. Dante's insight transforms the individual into a component of the whole, and so the ballads become epic songs. (60)

2. *Hyperion,* 2.203.

3. Ibid., 2.206–15, 228–29.

4. Nietzsche, *The Birth of Tragedy,* 42–43.

5. *Endymion,* 1.1.

6. *The Fall of Hyperion,* 1.148–49.

7. Ibid., 1.154–60.

8. Ibid., 1.161, 163.

9. Ibid., 1.162, 169.

10. Ibid., 1.201–2.

11. Stephen Gurney writes that the Romantics "substituted imaginative perception for religious belief and denied the efficacy of external institutions as legitimate props for a fully developed humanity." Stephen Gurney, "Between Two Worlds: Keats's 'Hyperion' and Browning's 'Saul,'" *Studies in Browning and His Circle* 8.2 (1980): 57.

12. *Galaxy Railroad* (later), 96.

13. See Satō Michimasa, *Miyazawa Kenji no bungaku sekai: Tanka to dōwa* (The literary world of Miyazawa Kenji: His tanka poems and children's tales) (Tairyūsha, 1979), 278; Yamauchi, 98.

14. *Galaxy Railroad* (early), 262.

15. See Hagiwara, *Inosensu no bungaku*, 168, 171.

16. *Galaxy Railroad* (later), 135.

17. *Galaxy Railroad* (early), 302.

18. *Galaxy Railroad* (later), 114.

19. Ibid., 115.

20. Ibid., 153.

21. Ibid., 134–35.

22. Ibid., 148.

23. Ibid., 149–50.

24. For a support of this idea, see Saitō Jun, 104–6.

25. *Paradise Lost*, 8.382.

26. In relation to this point, Hagiwara explains that the fear the inhabitants of Miyazawa's "other world" in general have toward people "might have been a sign of protest by oppressed, innocent beings against the tyranny of self-righteous human 'reason'" (*Inosensu no bungaku*, 105).

27. Satō calls Miyazawa's idea of self-sacrifice for others "*kaisei*" (resuscitation) and finds the essence of his literature there (243).

28. "The festivity of existence" is translated from the subtitle of Mita Munesuke's *Miyazawa Kenji: Sonzai no matsuri no naka e* (Miyazawa Kenji: Into the festivity of existence) (Iwanami Shoten, 1984).

29. Miyazawa reportedly started writing his tales enthusiastically because he was advised by one of the leaders of Kokuchūkai, a Buddhist nationalist organization in Tokyo, to write *Hoke bungaku* (Lotus Sutra literature).

30. Tamura Yoshirō, *Hokekyō: Shinri, seimei, jissen (The Lotus Sutra:* Truth, life, practice) (Chūōkōron, 1969), 74, 77.

31. Miyazawa often used these religious terms in his personal life. For instance, see Sugawara Chieko and Gamō Yoshirō, "*Gingatetsudō no Yoru* shinken: Miyazawa Kenji no seishun no mondai" (A new view of *A Night on the Galaxy Railroad*: A problem of Miyazawa Kenji's young days), *Bungaku* 40 (1972): 962–68.

32. *Miyazawa Kenji zenshū*, 1:15–16; 1–10, 14–18, 23–28. See Giovanni's similar experience in *Galaxy Railroad* (early), 301.

33. See Hagiwara, *Inosensu no bungaku*, 86–87; Itaya Eiki, *Miyazawa Kenji no mita shinshō: Den'en no kaze to hikari no naka kara* (The images that Miyazawa Kenji saw: From the wind and light of pastoral) (Nihon Hōsō Shuppan Kyōkai, 1990), 204–5; Mita, 22–25.

34. Yoshimoto considers the "utopian world" of *Galaxy Railroad* "the Jōdo structure of Mahayanist Buddhism" (1567). But that world is not a religious paradise, and, as I argue later, it is not even a perfect utopia.

35. *Galaxy Railroad* (later), 155.

36. Ibid., 151–52.

37. *Galaxy Railroad* (early), 300–301.

38. Tanikawa Tetsuzō regards Miyazawa's idea of religion as "fundamental instinct and fundamental sentiment about the order and unity of the entire world," like what Einstein called "cosmic, religious sentiment." Tanikawa Tetsuzō, *Miyazawa Kenji no sekai* (The world of Miyazawa Kenji) (Hōsei Daigaku Shuppan kyoku, 1970), 109.

39. Concerning this view of a poet's role, Karl Kroeber thinks Keats and his contemporary poets believed that "in uttering beautifully their private visions they contribute to a better, a more fully human life for all men." See Karl Kroeber, "The Commemorative Prophecy of *Hyperion*," *Transactions of the Wisconsin Academy of Sciences, Arts, and Letters* 52 (1963): 204.

40. *The Fall of Hyperion*, 1.120.

41. Ibid., 1.107–8, 114–17; emphasis added.

42. *The Fall of Hyperion*, 1.122–31.

43. Ibid., 1.132.

44. Ibid., 1.141–43.

45. Charlotte Schrader Hooker, "The Poet and the Dreamer: A Study of Keats's *The Fall of Hyperion*," *McNeese Review* 17 (1966): 41.

46. *The Fall of Hyperion*, 1.247–48.

47. Ibid., 1.425–29.

48. *Hyperion*, 1.113–16, 121–24, 133–34.

49. Ibid., 2.14.

50. Ibid., 2.93–95.

51. Ibid., 2.96–98; emphasis added.

52. Kroeber regards "placidity" as "the characteristic quality of" the lost "Titanic rule" (194).

53. Taylor refers to the paradox of mortality within immortality with such phrases as "forever mortal" (679), "a metamorphic condition without name" (680), "intermediary states between being and non-being" (681), "supernatural beings who are in the act of returning to the natural forces" (682), and "divinities in absentia" (684). Concerning this point, see also Geoffrey H. Hartman, "Spectral Symbolism and the Authorial Self: An Approach to Keats's *Hyperion*," *Essays in Criticism* 24.1 (1974): 7; Wolf Z. Hirst, "'The Politics of Paradise,' 'Transcendental Cosmopolitics,' and Plain Politics in Byron's *Cain* and Keats's *Hyperion*," in *Byron: Poetry and Politics: Seventh International Byron Symposium, Salzburg 1980*, ed. Erwin A. Stürzl and James Hogg (Salzburg: Institut für Anglistik und Amerikanistik, Universität Salzburg, 1981), 252; Kroeber, 189–90.

54. *Hyperion*, 1.168.

55. Ibid., 1.169–70, 175–76, 182–89.

56. Ibid., 1.299.

57. Pierre Vitoux notes that this "primeval God . . . is not individualized into a mythical character, because his existence is hardly disengaged from his being as one of the natural elements." Pierre Vitoux, "Keats's Epic Design in *Hyperion*," *Studies in Romanticism* 14.2 (1975): 170.

58. *Hyperion*, 1.332–33, 334–35.

59. Ibid., 1.335–36.

60. Sherwin, 389.

61. In this tainted immortality, the Titans are comparable to Milton's Satan in *Paradise Lost*, who, although a spirit, is internally mortalized to experience various emotions such as anger, envy, hatred, and despair at the prospect of Eden. Gurney calls the Titans' lost happy state "mythical innocence and unselfconscious joy" (63).

62. Brian Wicker points out that the poet-narrator's rebirth is "not into immortality" but "[i]t merely 'dates on his doom.'" Brian Wicker, "The Disputed Lines in *The Fall of Hyperion*," *Essays in Criticism* 7.1 (1957): 41.

63. Kusaka (60–61) and Sugawa (5) mention a few instances from other cultures which regard the galaxy as a path of the dead.

64. Amazawa Taijirō shares this view about the passengers on the Galaxy Train. See Amazawa Taijirō, *Miyazawa Kenji no kanata e* (To the other side of Miyazawa Kenji), new ed. (Shichōsha, 1987), 61. On the other hand, Nishida presumes that the birdcatcher does not have a ticket to heaven because he "committed the crime of killing life in this world." See Nishida Yoshiko, "*Gingatetsudō no Yoru* no Giovanni" (Giovanni in *A Night on the Galaxy Railroad*), *Kokubungaku* 20.15 (1975): 225, and also Nishida, *Miyazawa Kenji ron*, 58–59. But her view is based on the ungrounded idea that the people who live in that strange space are reborn there because of their crimes on earth. These people seem to be simply native to the place.

65. Michael Ragussis suggests that the Titans "seem always on the verge of becoming the barren stones that surround them." Michael Ragussis, *The Subterfuge of Art: Language and the Romantic Tradition* (Baltimore: Johns Hopkins University Press, 1978), 45.

66. *The Fall of Hyperion*, 1.260, 258.

67. *Galaxy Railroad* (later), 129.

68. Ibid., 129. Hagiwara says that Giovanni's pass resembles a *mandala* and it is "a kind of magic carpet" (*Inosensu no bungaku*, 172). Concerning the religious significance of this special pass, see Nishida, *Miyazawa Kenji ron*, 30–75.

69. *Galaxy Railroad* (later), 129.

70. *The Fall of Hyperion*, 1.245.

71. Ibid., 1.290.

72. Ibid., 1.291–300.

73. Ibid., 2.49.

74. Ibid., 2.49–56.

75. Ibid., 1.247.

76. Irene H. Chayes says that what Moneta shows is "not a collection of facts or events in the abstract but concrete, pictorial 'scenes,' which she holds unchanged in her mind." Irene H. Chayes, "Dreamer, Poet, and Poem in *The Fall of Hyperion*," *Philological Quarterly* 46.4 (1967): 505.

77. *The Fall of Hyperion*, 1.282.

78. *Hyperion*, 2.191–201.

79. *The Fall of Hyperion*, 1.303–4.

80. Ibid., 1.384–99.

81. Ibid., 1.304–6.

82. Ibid., 1.248.

83. *Galaxy Railroad* (later), 157.

84. Ibid., 160.

85. Ibid., 118–19.

86. Ibid., 119.

87. Ibid., 108.

88. Ibid., 110.

89. Ibid., 115. Hagiwara suggests that, by not indicating whether Giovanni's journey begins in the morning and breaks in the afternoon or vice versa, Miyazawa "aims at an effect of the ambiguous atmosphere that the peripheral situation brings about" (*Inosensu no bungaku*, 167). In my opinion, Miyazawa does not have such an intention and does not have to indicate a.m. or p.m. for two obvious reasons. First, because Giovanni falls asleep in the evening, it is far more natural to assume that his dream journey starts in the darkness of that same night. Second, because Miyazawa's universe here is based on the precise physical movement of heavenly bodies, if Giovanni's trip begins in the morning, a bright sun would illuminate the cloudless sky, changing the story completely.

90. *Galaxy Railroad* (later), 115.

91. Nishida relates the train image to Miyazawa's religious aspiration: "For Kenji at that time, the vehicle by which to go to the true world had to be by all means the one, like a train, which 'carries many people,' a vehicle [*ichijō*] which 'heads straight' for the (Mahayanist) goal" (*Miyazawa Kenji ron*, 126). *Ichijō* (one ride) is another name for *myōhō* compared to "a vehicle that unifies all things and all laws" (Tamura, 74). Mita understands the railroad as "an apparatus of power that deprived communities throughout the nation of their imagination" and directed it toward Tokyo, that is, the illusory center of a rising "modern, capitalistic state" (46). From this viewpoint, Mita argues that, "by switching this rail," Miyazawa "liberates" the direction of the reader's imagination "from the closed space of 'Tokyo' . . . to the open space of 'space'" (46). See also Sarah Mehlhop Strong, "The Poetry of Miyazawa Kenji" (Ph.D. diss., University of Chicago, 1984; UMI microfiche 8417583), 292.

92. *Galaxy Railroad* (later), 127.

93. Discussing the phrase "the Four-Dimensional extension" in the prefatory poem of *Spring and an Asura*, Hagiwara proposes that, "not restrained by the number '4,' we assume the multi-, infinite-, or super-dimensional 'other space' in the context of Miyazawa's universe" (*Inosensu no bungaku*, 88).

94. *Galaxy Railroad* (later), 119–20.

95. Concerning the sense of sight in *The Fall of Hyperion*, see Paul D. Sheats, "Stylistic Discipline in *The Fall of Hyperion*," *Keats-Shelley Journal* 17 (1968): 82–83, and also Chayes, 509–10.

96. Tanikawa explains that Miyazawa took this term from *Kagaku Honron* (Main discourse on chemistry) by Katayama Masao, which was "one of the most advanced, introductory books on physical chemistry at that time," and which he closely and repeatedly read along with the *Lotus Sutra* (91–92).

97. See note 45 to the previous chapter.

98. See Hagiwara, *Inosensu no bungaku*, 147–48.

99. *Galaxy Railroad* (later), 92, 94.

100. Kuwahara Hiroyoshi, "Ijigen sekai o byōsha shite miseta *Gingatetsudō no Yoru*" [*A Night on the Galaxy Railroad* that showed us the hetero-dimensional world], *Miyazawa Kenji* 7 (Yōyōsha, 1987): 57.

101. See Hagiwara, *Inosensu no bungaku*, 182.

102. For instance, among many others, the lack of water, as well as the hope of getting it, is a central image in the final section of *The Waste Land* by T. S. Eliot.

103. *Galaxy Railroad* (later), 160.

104. Hagiwara, *Inosensu no bungaku*, 153, 181.

105. *Galaxy Railroad* (later), 127.

106. Ibid., 135.

107. Ibid., 154.

108. Ibid.

109. Ibid., 110.

110. Kuwahara considers the *ama no gawa* to be *kū* or emptiness in the Buddhist sense that is "not nihility but existent X, the maternal body of life, that is, light/energy, idea, and matter" (57).

111. *Galaxy Railroad* (later), 126.

112. Ibid., 124.

113. Ibid., 124, 141.

114. Ibid., 122.

115. Ibid., 106.

116. For instance, see Ogiwara Masayoshi, "Tenkirin no hashira: Ozawa Toshirō shi no setsu o ukete" (The Pole of the Weather Ring: In response to Mr. Ozawa Toshirō's argument), *Miyazawa Kenji* 1 (Yōyōsha, 1981): 59–71.

117. *Galaxy Railroad* (later), 107.

118. At the very end of the early version, upon waking up, Giovanni sees "the star of the Lyre shifted far to the west and again extending its leg like a mushroom" (303), suggestive of the same passage his dreaming self took on the way back from the night sky.

119. *Galaxy Railroad* (later), 108.

120. Ibid., 111.

121. Ibid., 114.

122. Ibid., 153.

123. Hagiwara (*Inosensu no bungaku*, 173–75) and Mita (4–8) regard an apple as an important symbol of Miyazawa's universe, the

two sides (this side and "the other side") of which are reversible through
the two holes. If that is the case, the holes of the apple that "induces our
sinful imagination directly toward the secret location of the core of existence" (Mita, 5) should symbolize not "the Coalsack" as Mita argues
(7–8) but the two unmentioned heavenly poles for three reasons. First,
the two actual Coalsacks (Northern and Southern) do not diametrically
correspond to each other as the imagery of an apple demands. Second,
the text has a reference only to the Southern Coalsack near the Southern Cross, while the Northern Coalsack is completely ignored even
though, in reality, it is situated in the constellation of the Cygnus or the
Northern Cross. Unlike the Southern Pole, it is not even textually
implied. Third, although the dark, unfathomable Coalsack might give a
viewer (not Giovanni) the impression of sucking him in, it has nothing to
do with the *ama no gawa* that should come from, and go back to, "the
secret location of the core of existence." If the Coalsack applies to the
symbolism of an apple as the universe, it should rather be regarded as
a dented stain on the peel.

124. *Galaxy Railroad* (later), 108.

125. Ibid., 106; Hagiwara, *Inosensu no bungaku,* 160–61. See also
Katori Naoichi, "Tenkirin no hashira to tōyō no seigaku: Senki Gyokkō
kō" (The Pole of the Weather Ring and an oriental astrology: A thought
on Senki Gyokkō), *Miyazawa Kenji* 6 (Yōyōsha, 1986): 152–56.

126. Ikegami Yūzō, "*Gingatetsudō no Yoru* no ichi: 'Fūrin' kara
'Shūkyō fū no Koi' made no keiretsu-ka to kōsatsu" (The position of *A
Night on the Galaxy Railroad*: A systematization from 'A Windy Grove' to
'Religious Love' and a thought), in *Miyazawa Kenji II*, ed. Nihon Bungaku
Kenkyū Shiryō Kankō kai (Yūseidō, 1983), 164.

127. See Miyazawa Seiroku, *Ani no toranku* (The trunk of my elder
brother) (Chikuma Shobō, 1987), 213–14, 237.

128. *Galaxy Railroad* (later), 95, 101.

129. Ibid., 103.

130. See Mita, 183, about one of Miyazawa's other stories "Yuki
watari" (Snow crossing).

131. Katori argues that, in spite of its appellations, the festive celebration is really about "the Big Dipper and the un-described North
Star" that indicates "the world pole: the cosmic pole" (156).

132. *Galaxy Railroad* (later), 102.

133. Ibid.

134. Ibid.

135. The early version includes the display scene with some differences, but it has exactly the same description of the owl. The owl, a traditional symbol for wisdom in the West, apparently stands for Dr. Bulcaniro, who watches over Giovanni's dream journey through his transmittal experiment. The presence of the stone bird in the later version might be an oversight from the revising process that deleted the scientist.

136. Hagiwara, *Inosensu no bungaku*, 153.

137. Hagiwara points out that the stream is in fact made of fires (stars) (*Inosensu no bungaku*, 154). Hagiwara also figures out a way of identifying the fireworks with "the dews of the Centaur." He considers a Greek myth according to which the half-human creature was born from the union between the man Centaur and a female horse of the Magnesia region. The mineral magnesium was produced there and was named after the locale (*Inosensu no bungaku*, 155). Unfortunately, there is no denying that, without convincing relevance to Miyazawa's story, the etymological association sounds far-stretched at best.

138. Hagiwara, *Inosensu no bungaku*, 181.

139. Ibid., 155.

140. *Galaxy Railroad* (early), 301–2.

141. See Hara, "Bō no kusari" (The chain of the Pleiades), 635.

142. Ibid.; Mita, 147.

143. See Hagiwara, *Inosensu no bungaku*, 175–76; Mita, 144, 147–48, 149–51.

144. Hagiwara, *Inosensu no bungaku*, 176.

145. *Galaxy Railroad* (early), 302.

146. *Paradise Lost*, 6.586.

6. The Self-Consciousness of Transitional Epic

1. *Galaxy Railroad* (early), 300.

2. Ibid., 302.

3. Ibid.

4. *The Fall of Hyperion*, 1.161.

5. Ibid., 1.166–69, 175–76.

6. Ibid., 1.148–49.

7. Ibid., 1.163.

8. Ibid., 1.242.

9. Ibid., 1.200.

10. Ibid., 1.201.

11. Ibid., 1.207–8.

12. Ibid., 1.205.

13. Concerning this point, Kroeber says that Apollo "is invoked, not as the god of poetry, but as the god of pestilence . . . to destroy not dreamers but bad poets" (203).

14. *The Fall of Hyperion*, 1.204.

15. *Galaxy Railroad* (later), 117.

16. Ibid., 136, 138.

17. Ibid., 127.

18. Ibid.

19. See Amazawa, 70.

20. *Galaxy Railroad* (early), 268.

21. *Galaxy Railroad* (later), 126.

22. Ibid., 137.

23. Nakamura Minoru, *Miyazawa Kenji* (Chikuma Shobō, 1972), 47.

24. In *Nōmin geijutsu gairon* (An outline of peasants' art) (1926), Miyazawa says that "[i]n all probability, the labor of primitive men is not at all different from play in form and content." He also asserts that artistic activities should be the driving force of agricultural production. See *Shinshū Miyazawa Kenji zenshū*, 15:5–22. Nakamura thinks that, with these words, Miyazawa suggests the ideal state of agricultural production in which labor is not a cause of pain. According to Nakamura's interpretation, agricultural labor is instead "free from any troubles, natural or artificial, which impede the production" and is "close to dancing" (47). Therefore, Nakamura regards the Illusory Four-Dimensional Space, where "labor productivity is extremely high" (47), as Miyazawa's ideal locus.

25. *Galaxy Railroad* (later), 144. See Murase, 83.

26. See note 24 above.

27. *Galaxy Railroad* (later), 137.

28. Hagiwara, *Inosensu no bungaku*, 76.

29. *Galaxy Railroad* (later), 137–38. One source of Miyazawa's food imagery is found in the Buddhist heaven (*Jōdo*). For instance, Mishima Yukio describes the diet in the Pure Land as follows:

> If one feels like having something to eat, there automatically appears before one's eyes a seven-jeweled table on whose shining surface rest seven-jeweled bowls heaped high with the choicest delicacies. But there is no need to pick up these viands and put them in one's mouth. All that is necessary is to look at their inviting colors and to enjoy their aroma: thereby the stomach is filled and the body nourished, while one remains oneself spiritually and physically pure. When one has thus finished one's meal without any eating, the bowls and the table are instantly wafted off.

Yukio Mishima, "The Priest of Shiga Temple and His Love," trans. Ivan Morris, in *"Death in Midsummer" and Other Stories* (New York: New Directions, 1966), 60.

30. "*Chūmon no Ōi Ryōriten* jo" (The preface to *A Restaurant of Many Orders*), in *Miyazawa Kenji zenshū*, 8:15–16.

31. *Galaxy Railroad* (later), 153. Hagiwara mentions two reasons for the symbolism of fruits and sweets: "their close association with children and festivals, and the 'pure' impression they give as the subsidiary food in compared with the staple food, such as meat and rice, which leads to putrefaction as excrements" (*Inosensu no bungaku*, 169). Hagiwara also points out the apple's origin in a northern climate (*Inosensu no bungaku*, 170). See also Mita, 218–19, 230–31.

32. In the self-imposed observance of Buddhist discipline, Miyazawa himself was a vegetarian. He even wrote a fragmentary story titled "Bijiterian taisai" (The great festival of vegetarians), in which vegetarian delegations from all over the world meet in a village in Newfoundland and discuss how their movement should develop.

33. *Galaxy Railroad* (later), 123.

34. Ibid., 126. See Murase, 61.

35. *Galaxy Railroad* (later), 129.

36. Ibid., 129.

37. Ibid., 119.

38. See Iwami Teruyo, "Shiroi kurayami e: *Gingatetsudō no Yoru* shiron" (To white darkness: A thought on *A Night on the Galaxy Railroad*), *Miyazawa Kenji* 7 (Yōyōsha, 1987): 85.

39. Hagiwara, *Inosensu no bungaku*, 91.

40. *Galaxy Railroad* (early), 302.

41. See Sakai, 149.

42. Following his Buddhist belief, Miyazawa disregarded his own welfare in order to improve the material, spiritual, and cultural conditions of the people around him, who were poor peasants in the poorest agricultural region of Japan. In the end, he fatally damaged his health. After a brief recuperation, greatly disappointed in his abortive attempt, he died at the age of thirty-seven. For more detailed English biographies of Miyazawa, see Takao Hagiwara, "The Theme of Innocence in Miyazawa Kenji's Tales" (Ph.D. diss., University of British Columbia, 1986; UMI microfiche 0560040), 9–61; Strong, "The Poetry of Miyazawa Kenji," 15–124.

43. Satō argues that the drama leading to Giovanni's resuscitation is "too heavy and tense" (275) for the setting in which his dream was induced by Dr. Bulcaniro and that the deletion of the scientist from the later version is reasonable. But it is doubtful that Giovanni has spiritually regenerated by the end of the later version.

44. In reference to this aspect in *Galaxy Railroad*, Fukushima Akira notes that in his later days when Miyazawa "was gradually overshadowed by darkness, . . . the ground and the sky, which had once been connected somewhere [in his early tales], were strictly distinguished." Fukushima thinks that, because of this pessimism, Miyazawa came to call his prose works not children's tales but "shōnen shōsetsu" (juvenile novels). Fukushima Akira, *Miyazawa Kenji: Geijutsu to byōri* (Miyazawa Kenji: His art and pathology) (Kongō Shuppan, 1970), 256. See also a similar view in Yamauchi, 101.

45. *Galaxy Railroad* (early), 301.

46. Amazawa, 71.

47. *The Fall of Hyperion*, 1.244–45.

48. Ibid., 1.276–79.

49. Ibid., 1.289–90.

50. Ibid., 1.256–62.

51. Warren U. Ober and W. K. Thomas, "Keats and the Solitary Pan," *Keats-Shelley Journal* 29 (1980): 117.

52. "Ode on a Grecian Urn," 45.

53. Ibid., 5.

54. Ibid., 1.

55. Ibid., 44–45.

56. *The Fall of Hyperion*, 1.264.

57. "Ode to a Nightingale," 70–71. Concerning this point, see Mori Masaki, "'Naichingēru ni Yoseru Ōdo' ni okeru jōshō to kakō" (Ascent and descent in Keats' "Ode to a Nightingale"), *Shiron* 24 (1985): 37–38.

58. *Galaxy Railroad* (later), 155.

59. *The Fall of Hyperion*, 1.265.

60. Ibid., 1.268, 271.

61. Hooker, 46.

62. *The Fall of Hyperion*, 1.78.

63. Ibid., 1.72–77.

64. Ibid., 1.194, 216.

65. Ibid., 1.243, 246.

66. Ibid., 1.102.

67. Ibid., 1.187, 282.

68. Ibid., 1.168.

69. Ibid., 1.201.

70. *Hyperion*, 2.228–29.

71. Concerning the transformation of Greek mythology by Keats in the Hyperion poems, see Tilottama Rajan, *Dark Interpreter: The Discourse of Romanticism* (Ithaca: Cornell University Press, 1980), 156–57.

72. *Hyperion*, 2.207, 206.

73. Ibid., 2.213.

74. Ober and Thomas claim that Keats intended for "the solitary Pan" (*The Fall of Hyperion*, 1.411), who is just once mentioned in the Hyperion epopea, a reconciliatory role between the two generations of gods in strife.

75. *Hyperion*, 3.68.

76. Keats to B. R. Haydon, 23 January 1818, *Letters of John Keats*, 1:207.

77. *Hyperion*, 1.105.

78. Ibid., 2.186.

79. Ibid., 2.132–36, 148–49.

80. Ibid., 3.113–16.

81. Concerning the oxymoronic nature of Apollo as a "creative process" in "his perfection," see Shiv K. Kumar, "The Meaning of *Hyperion*: A Reassessment," in *British Romantic Poets: Recent Revaluations*, ed. Shiv K. Kumar (New York: New York University Press; London: University of London Press, 1966), 317; Rajan, 160–61.

82. *Hyperion*, 3.130.

83. *The Fall of Hyperion*, 1.62–64.

84. Ibid., 1.83–86.

85. Ibid., 1.65–71.

86. Rajan, 203, 145.

87. *The Fall of Hyperion*, 1.288.

88. Ibid., 1.204.

89. With regard to "a literal or metaphorical excursion" in English Romantic lyrics in general, Jack Stillinger explains that the speaker of the poem visits an ideal world which stands for many things, such as heaven, immortality, eternity, spirituality, the unknown, and the infinite. The speaker eventually comes back to the actual world for various reasons, "but most often because he finds something wanting in the imagined ideal or because, being a native of the real world, he discovers that he does not or cannot belong permanently in the ideal." But the speaker does not simply come back, "for he has acquired something—a better understanding of a situation, a change in attitude toward it—from the experience of the flight, and he is never again quite the same person who spoke at the beginning of the poem." Jack Stillinger, *"The Hoodwinking of Madeline" and Other Essays on Keats's Poems* (Urbana: University of Illinois Press, 1971), 101–2. In *The Fall of Hyperion*, however, the space is not ideal. The acquired knowledge does not help the poet-narrator in understanding the situation better, because it is no more than a further acknowledgement of the transient world full of strife. He just feels more helpless in the dark irony inherent in Romanticism.

90. See Gurney, 67; Wicker, 41.

91. Shelley, "A Defence of Poetry," 508.

92. Keats to C. W. Dilke, 20, 21 September 1818, *Letters of John Keats*, 1:368–69; Keats to J. H. Reynolds, 22 (?) September 1818, *Letters of John Keats*, 1:370.

93. Keats to J. H. Reynolds, Teignmouth, 3 May 1818, *Letters of John Keats*, 1:281.

94. Chayes (500–501) situates *The Fall of Hyperion* in the dream-vision tradition of European literature, which includes such various works as *Roman de la Rose*, the *Divine Comedy*, and Chaucer's *House of Fame*.

95. Chayes (502) traces back this convention to Guillaume de Lorris' introduction to *Roman de la Rose* and Chaucer's proem to *The House of Fame*. Kroeber (199) points out the use of the word "dream" five times in the initial eighteen lines.

96. *The Fall of Hyperion*, 1.13–14.

97. Ibid., 1.15.

98. Ibid., 1.16–18.

99. Ibid., 1.1.

100. Ibid., 1.19, 21.

101. Curtius, 192–95. K. K. Ruthven calls this scene "a Spenserian *pleasaunce* which is an appropriate setting for those Golden Age festivities at which immortals preside." K. K. Ruthven, "Keats and *Dea Moneta*," *Studies in Romanticism* 15.3 (1976): 457.

102. *Paradise Lost*, 4.132, 217.

103. *The Fall of Hyperion*, 1.30–31.

104. See Wicker, 40.

105. See Chayes, 505.

106. Concerning Keats' reaction to Dante, see John Saly, "Keats's Answer to Dante: *The Fall of Hyperion*," *Keats-Shelley Journal* 14 (1965): 65–78.

107. *The Fall of Hyperion*, 1.1–2.

108. Ibid., 1.44–45, 42.

109. "Ode to a Nightingale," 16.

110. *The Fall of Hyperion*, 1.46.

111. Ibid., 1.47–54.

112. "Ode to a Nightingale," 16, 14–15.

113. *The Fall of Hyperion*, 1.55.

114. *Hyperion*, 2.14.

115. Ibid., 2.82–86.

116. Ibid., 3.3–12.

117. *The Fall of Hyperion*, 1.44, 29, 40.

118. *Hyperion*, 1.18–19.

119. Ibid., 1.10, 11, 18.

120. Ibid., 1.3.

121. Ibid., 1.7–14.

122. Ibid., 1.18, 17.

123. Chayes, 501.

124. Hagiwara explains Giovanni's fall into sleep by a process of accumulated dizziness caused by the abundant images of circles and gyrations before the boy reaches the hill (*Inosensu no bungaku*, 148–51).

125. *Galaxy Railroad* (later), 109.

126. Ibid., 144.

127. Ibid., 145.

128. For this reason, the Galaxy Station cannot be regarded as "at once the starting station and the terminal station" of Giovanni's trip as Hagiwara suggests (*Inosensu no bungaku*, 164). In disjunction with Hagiwara's further assertion (*Inosensu no bungaku*, 181), the boy's soul does not "travel the galaxy from the northern to the southern end," and the orbit it makes is not a complete circle that "symbolizes the unity and order of the entire universe" but an interrupted one that suggests the collapse of such an idealistic vision. His dreaming consciousness returns by necessity to the hilltop because his physical reality (i.e., body) is waiting there.

129. *Galaxy Railroad* (later), 153.

JAPANESE WORDS
IN THE TEXT

jojishi　叙事詩

Man'yōshū　万葉集

tanka　短歌

Kokin(waka)shū　古今(和歌)集

Ki no Tsurayuki　紀　貫之

Kojiki　古事記

Yamato Takeru　ヤマト　タケル

Heian　平安

Genji monogatari　源氏物語

Murasaki Shikibu　紫　式部

gunkimono(gatari)　軍記物(語)

Heike monogatari　平家物語

Genji, Heike　源氏、平家

Yoshinaka　義仲

Heian-kyō　平安京

biwa　琵琶

tenka　天下

Kiyomori 清盛

Jōdo-shū 浄土宗

Edo 穢土

Amida 阿弥陀

mujōkan 無常感

samurai 侍

Tsuginobu 嗣信

Yoshitsune 義経

Yashima 屋島

Shigehira 重衡

Nara 奈良

Yoritomo 頼朝

harakiri 腹切り

Gikeiki 義経記

Benkei 弁慶

Taiheiki 太平記

Kamakura 鎌倉

Godaigo 御醍醐

Ashikaga Takauji 足利尊氏

Soga monogatari 曽我物語

Genpei seisuiki 源平盛衰記

Nansō Satomi Hakken den　南総里見八犬伝

yomihon　読本

kanzen chōaku　勧善懲悪

shi-shōsetsu, watakushi-shōsetsu　私小説

Gingatetsudō no Yoru　銀河鉄道の夜

Miyazawa Kenji　宮沢　賢治

ama no gawa　天の川

Kaoru, Tadashi　かほる、タダシ

Chūmon no ōi ryōriten　注文の多い料理店

Yodaka no hoshi　よだかの星

Frandon Nōgakkō no buta　フランドン農学校の豚

Obbel to zō　オツベルと象

Nametoko Yama no kuma　なめとこ山の熊

Kojūro　小十郎

Bar(u)dora　バルドラ

Tegami 1　手紙１

minna　みんな

Kashiwa-bayashi no yoru　かしはばやしの夜

Hatake no heri　畑のへり

Myōhōrenge-kyō, Hokekyō　妙法蓮華経、法華経

Nichiren-shū　日蓮宗

bosatsu-gyō　菩薩行

Haru to Shura　春と修羅

inga　因果

tenkirin no hashira　天気輪の柱

Hyōga-nezumi no kegawa　氷河鼠の毛皮

Hanayasai　花椰菜

Fuyu to Ginga Station　冬と銀河ステーション

Toshiko　とし子

karasuuri　烏瓜

kowasu, kiru, hazusu, toku　壊す、切る、外す、解く

SELECT BIBLIOGRAPHY

Primary Sources

Ariosto, Ludovico. *Orlando Furioso*. Trans. Guido Waldman. The World's Classics. Oxford: Oxford University Press, 1983.

Byron, Lord. *Don Juan*. In *Byron*, ed. Jerome J. McGann, 373–879. The Oxford Authors. Oxford: Oxford University Press, 1986.

Camoens, Luis Vaz de. *The Lusiads*. Trans. William C. Atkinson. Penguin Classics. Harmondsworth, U.K.: Penguin, 1952.

Campanella, Tommaso. *La città del sole: Dialogo poetico* (The city of the sun: A poetical dialogue). Trans. Daniel J. Donno. Biblioteca Italiana. Berkeley: University of California Press, 1981.

Dante Alighieri. *"The Divine Comedy" of Dante Alighieri*. Trans. John D. Sinclair. 3 vols. New York: Oxford University Press, 1939.

De Amicis, Edmondo. *Cuore: Libro per i ragazzi* (Heart: A book for the young). Milan: Garzanti, 1959.

Gotō Tanji, Kamada Kisaburō, and Okami Masao, eds. *Taiheiki* (The chronicle of great peace). 3 vols. Nihon Koten Bungaku Taikei 34–36. Iwanami Shoten, 1960–62.

Hamilton, Rita, and Janet Perry, trans. *The Poem of the Cid*. Penguin Classics. Harmondsworth, U.K.: Penguin, 1975.

Hatto, A. T., trans. *The Nibelungenlied*. Penguin Classics. Harmondsworth, U.K.: Penguin, 1965.

Homer. *The Iliad*. Trans. Robert Fitzgerald. Garden City, N.Y.: Doubleday, 1974.

——— . *The Odyssey*. Trans. Robert Fitzgerald. Garden City, N.Y.: Anchor Books, 1963.

Keats, John. *The Letters of John Keats: 1814–1821*. Ed. Hyder Edward Rollins. 2 vols. Cambridge, Mass.: Harvard University Press, 1958.

——— . *The Poems of John Keats*. Ed. Miriam Allott. Longman Annotated English Poets. London: Longman, 1970.

McCullough, Helen Craig, trans. *The Tale of the Heike*. With an introduction by the translator. Stanford: Stanford University Press,
1988.

———, trans. *Yoshitsune: A Fifteenth-Century Japanese Chronicle*. Stanford: Stanford University Press, 1966.

Milton, John. *Paradise Lost*. Ed. Alastair Fowler. Longman Annotated
English Poets. London: Longman, 1968.

Mishima, Yukio. "The Priest of Shiga Temple and His Love." Trans. Ivan
Morris. In *"Death in Midsummer" and Other Stories*, 59–75. New
York: New Directions, 1966.

Miyazawa Kenji. *Miyazawa Kenji zenshū* (The complete works of
Miyazawa Kenji). Ed. Amazawa Taijirō, Irisawa Yasuo, and Miyazawa
Seiroku. 8 vols. Chikuma Shobō, 1985–86.

———. *Shinshū Miyazawa Kenji zenshū* (The new complete works of
Miyazawa Kenji). Ed. Miyazawa Seiroku, Irisawa Yasuo, and
Amazawa Taijirō. 17 vols. Chikima Shobō, 1980.

Sandars, N. K, trans. *The Epic of Gilgamesh*. Penguin Classics. Harmondsworth, U.K.: Penguin, 1960.

Sayers, Dorothy L., trans. *The Song of Roland*. Penguin Classics. Harmondsworth, U.K.: Penguin, 1957.

Shelley, Percy Bysshe. *Shelley's Poetry and Prose*. Ed. Donald H. Reiman
and Sharon B. Powers. Norton Critical Editions. Norton: New York,
1977.

Spenser, Edmund. *The Faerie Qveene*. Ed. A. C. Hamilton. Longman
Annotated English Poets. London: Longman, 1977.

Takagi Ichinosuke, et al., eds. *Heike monogatari* (The tale of the Heike).
2 vols. Nihon Koten Bungaku Taikei 32–33. Iwanami Shoten,
1959–60.

Tasso, Torquato. *Jerusalem Delivered*. Trans. Ralph Nash. Detroit:
Wayne State University Press, 1987.

Virgil. *The Aeneid*. Trans. Robert Fitzgerald. New York: Random House,
Vintage, 1983.

Wenders, Wim, dir. *Wings of Desire*. Prod. Antole Dauman and Wim
Wenders. 130 min. Paris: Argos Films; Berlin: Road Movies; Köln:
Westdeutscher Rundfunk, 1987. Videocassette.

Wordsworth, William. *The Prelude: 1799, 1805, 1850*. Ed. Jonathan Wordsworth, M. H. Abrams, and Stephen Gill. Norton Critical Editions. New York: Norton, 1979.

Wright, David, trans. *Beowulf*. Penguin Classics. Harmondsworth, U.K.: Penguin, 1957.

Secondary Sources

Literary History, Criticism, and Theory

Adams, Hazard, ed. *Critical Theory since Plato*. San Diego: Harcourt Brace Jovanovich, 1971.

Adkins, Arthur W. H. *Merit and Responsibility: A Study in Greek Values*. London: Oxford University Press, Clarendon Press, 1960.

Aristotle. *The Poetics*. In *Aristotle's Theory of Poetry and Fine Art*, trans. S. H. Butcher, 5–111. 4th ed. New York: Dover, 1951.

Atsumi Kaoru. *"Heike monogatari" no kisoteki kenkyū* (Basic research on *The Tale of the Heike*). Kasama Sōsho 95. Kasama Shoin, 1978.

Bakhtin, M. M. *The Dialogic Imagination: Four Essays*. Trans. Caryl Emerson and Michael Holquist. Ed. Michael Holquist. University of Texas Press Slavic Series 1. Austin: University of Texas Press, 1981.

Bloom, Harold. *The Anxiety of Influence: A Theory of Poetry*. London: Oxford University Press, 1973.

Boileau-Despréaux, Nicolas. *The Art of Poetry*. In *Boileau: Selected Criticism*, trans. Ernest Dilworth, 11–42. The Library of Liberal Arts. Indianapolis: Bobbs-Merrill, 1965.

Bowra, C. M. *From Virgil to Milton*. London: Macmillan, 1945.

Butler, Kenneth Dean. "The *Heike Monogatari* and the Japanese Warrior Ethic." *Harvard Journal of Asiatic Studies* 29 (1969): 93–108.

———. "The Textual Evolution of the *Heike Monogatari*." *Harvard Journal of Asiatic Studies* 26 (1966): 5–51.

Calin, William. *A Muse for Heroes: Nine Centuries of the Epic in France*. Toronto: University of Toronto Press, 1983.

Castelvetro, Lodovico. *Castelvetro on the Art of Poetry: An Abridged Translation of Lodovico Castelvetro's "'Poetica' d'Aristotele Vulgarizzata et Sposta."* Trans. Andrew Bongiorno. Medieval & Renaissance Texts & Studies 29. Binghamton, N.Y.: Center for Medieval & Early Renaissance Studies, State University of New York at Binghamton, 1984.

Curtius, Ernst Robert. *European Literature and the Latin Middle Ages.* Trans. Willard R. Trask. Bollingen Series 36. Princeton: Princeton University Press, 1973.

Derrida, Jacques. *Of Grammatology.* Trans. Gayatri Chakravorty Spivak. Baltimore: Johns Hopkins University Press, 1976.

——— . *Writing and Difference.* Trans. Alan Bass. Chicago: University of Chicago Press, 1978.

Fairclough, H. Rushton. "Life of Virgil." In vol. 1 of *Virgil in Two Volumes*, trans. H. Rushton Fairclough, ix–xi. The Loeb Classical Library 63. Cambridge, Mass.: Harvard University Press; London: Heinemann, 1916.

Fielding, Henry. Preface to *Joseph Andrews.* Ed. Martin C. Battestin. The Wesleyan Edition of the Works of Henry Fielding. Middletown: Wesleyan University Press, 1967. 3–11.

Finley, M. I. *The World of Odysseus.* New York: Viking, 1954.

Frye, Northrop. *Anatomy of Criticism: Four Essays.* Princeton: Princeton University Press, 1957.

Goethe, Johann Wolfgang von. "On Epic and Dramatic Poetry." In *Essays on Art and Literature*, trans. Ellen von Nardroff and Ernest H. von Nardroff, ed. John Gearey, 192–94. Vol. 3 of *Goethe's Collected Works.* New York: Suhrkamp, 1986.

Greene, Thomas. *The Descent from Heaven: A Study in Epic Continuity.* New Haven: Yale University Press, 1963.

Griffin, Jasper. *Homer.* Past Masters Series. New York: Hill and Wang, 1980.

Hegel, G. W. F. *Aesthetics: Lectures on Fine Art.* Trans. T. M. Knox. 2 vols. Oxford: Oxford University Press, Clarendon Press, 1975.

Ishimoda Shō. *Heike monogatari* (The Tale of the Heike). Iwanami Shinsho (Aoban) 294. Iwanami Shoten, 1957.

Ker, W. P. *The Dark Ages.* Periods of European Literature 1. Edinburgh: William Blackwood and Sons, 1904.

Ki no Tsurayuki. "Kanajo: The Japanese Preface." In *Kokinshū: A Collection of Poems Ancient and Modern*, trans. Laurel Rasplica Rodd and Mary Catherine Henkenius, 35–47. Princeton Library of Asian Translations. Princeton: Princeton University Press, 1984.

Lewis, C. S. *A Preface to "Paradise Lost."* London: Oxford University Press, 1942.

Longinus. *Longinus on the Sublime.* Trans. W. Rhys Roberts. Cambridge: Cambridge University Press, 1899.

Lukács, Georg. *The Theory of the Novel: A Historico-Philosophical Essay on the Forms of Great Epic Literature.* Trans. Anna Bostock. Cambridge, Mass.: MIT Press, 1971.

Merchant, Paul. *The Epic.* The Critical Idiom 17. London: Methuen, 1971.

Miner, Earl. *Comparative Poetics: An Intercultural Essay on Theories of Literature.* Princeton: Princeton University Press, 1990.

Morris, Ivan. *The Nobility of Failure: Tragic Heroes in the History of Japan.* New York: Holt, Rinehart and Winston, 1975.

Nietzsche, Friedrich. *The Birth of Tragedy or: Hellenism and Pessimism.* With "Attempt at a Self-Criticism" by the author. In *"The Birth of Tragedy" and "The Case of Wagner,"* trans. Walter Kaufmann, 15–144. New York: Random House, Vintage, 1967.

――――. *Twilight of the Idols or, How One Philosophizes with a Hammer.* In *The Portable Nietzsche,* trans. Walter Kaufmann, 463–563. The Viking Portable Library. Harmondsworth, U.K.: Penguin, 1954.

Pascal, Blaise. *Pascal's "Pensées."* Trans. H. F. Stewart. New York: Pantheon, 1950.

Plato. *The Laws.* Trans. Trevor J. Saunders. Harmondsworth, U.K.: Penguin, 1970.

――――. *Phaedrus.* In *"Phaedrus" and the "Seventh and Eighth Letters,"* trans. Walter Hamilton, 19–103. Harmondsworth, U.K.: Penguin, 1973.

――――. *The Republic.* Trans. Desmond Lee. 2nd ed. Harmondsworth, U.K.: Penguin, 1974.

Scaliger, Julius Caesar. *Select Translations from Scaliger's "Poetics."* Trans. Frederick Morgan Padelford. Yale Studies in English 26. New York: Henry Holt, 1905.

Schiller, Friedrich von. *Naive and Sentimental Poetry.* In *"Naive and Sentimental Poetry" and "On the Sublime": Two Essays,* trans. Julius A. Elias, 81–190. Milestones of Thought. New York: Frederick Ungar, 1966.

Sidney, Sir Philip. *"An Apology for Poetry" or "The Defence of Poesy."* Ed. Geoffrey Shepherd. London: Nelson, 1965.

Spariosu, Mihai I. *God of Many Names: Play, Poetry, and Power in Hellenic Thought from Homer to Aristotle.* Durham, N.C.: Duke University Press, 1991.

Tamura Yoshirō. *Hokekyō: Shinri, seimei, jissen (The Lotus Sutra:* Truth, life, practice). Chūkō Shinsho 196. Chūōkōron, 1969.

Tasso, Torquato. *Discourses on the Heroic Poem.* Trans. Mariella Cavalchini and Irene Samuel. London: Oxford University Press, Clarendon Press, 1973.

Tsunoda, Ryusaku, William Theodore de Bary, and Donald Keene, comps. *Sources of Japanese Tradition.* Records of Civilization: Sources and Studies: Introduction to Oriental Civilizations 54. New York: Columbia University Press, 1958.

Vico, Giambattista. *The New Science of Giambattista Vico.* Trans. Thomas Goddard Bergin and Max Harold Fisch. Ithaca: Cornell University Press, 1948.

Webber, Joan Malory. *Milton and His Epic Tradition.* Seattle: University of Washington Press, 1979.

Wordsworth, William. "Preface to *Lyrical Ballads, with Pastoral and Other Poems*" (1802). In *William Wordsworth,* ed. Stephen Gill, 595–615. The Oxford Authors. Oxford: Oxford University Press, 1984.

John Keats and Romanticism

Abrams, M. H. *The Mirror and the Lamp: Romantic Theory and the Critical Tradition.* London: Oxford University Press, 1953.

——— . *Natural Supernaturalism: Tradition and Revolution in Romantic Literature.* New York: Norton, 1973.

Barnard, John, ed. *The Complete Poems,* by John Keats. 2nd ed. Harmondsworth, U.K.: Penguin, 1977.

Bate, Walter Jackson. *John Keats.* Cambridge, Mass.: Harvard University Press, Belknap Press, 1963.

Chayes, Irene H. "Dreamer, Poet, and Poem in *The Fall of Hyperion.*" *Philological Quarterly* 46.4 (1967): 499–515.

Gittings, Robert. *John Keats.* Boston: Little, Brown and Company in association with Atlantic Monthly Press, 1968.

Goslee, Nancy Moore. *Uriel's Eye: Miltonic Stationing and Statuary in Blake, Keats, and Shelley.* University, Ala.: University of Alabama Press, 1985.

Gurney, Stephen. "Between Two Worlds: Keats's 'Hyperion' and Browning's 'Saul.'" *Studies in Browning and His Circle* 8.2 (1980): 57–74.

Hartman, Geoffrey H. "Spectral Symbolism and the Authorial Self: An Approach to Keats's *Hyperion*." *Essays in Criticism* 24.1 (1974): 1–19.

Hirst, Wolf Z. "'The Politics of Paradise,' 'Transcendental Cosmopolitics,' and Plain Politics in Byron's *Cain* and Keats's *Hyperion*." In *Byron: Poetry and Politics: Seventh International Byron Symposium, Salzburg 1980*, ed. Erwin A. Stürzl and James Hogg, 243–64. Salzburger Studien zur Anglistik und Amerikanistik 13. Salzburg: Institut für Anglistik und Amerikanistik, Universität Salzburg, 1981.

Hooker, Charlotte Schrader. "The Poet and the Dreamer: A Study of Keats's *The Fall of Hyperion*." *McNeese Review* 17 (1966): 39–48.

Kroeber, Karl. "The Commemorative Prophecy of *Hyperion*." *Transactions of the Wisconsin Academy of Sciences, Arts, and Letters* 52 (1963): 189–204.

Kumar, Shiv K. "The Meaning of *Hyperion*: A Reassessment." In *British Romantic Poets: Recent Revaluations*, ed. Shiv K. Kumar, 305–18. New York: New York University Press; London: University of London Press, 1966.

Mori Masaki. "'Naichingēru ni Yoseru Ōdo' ni okeru jōshō to kakō" (Ascent and descent in Keats's "Ode to a Nightingale"). *Shiron* 24 (1985): 21–42.

Ober, Warren U., and W. K. Thomas. "Keats and the Solitary Pan." *Keats-Shelley Journal* 29 (1980): 96–119.

Ower, John. "The Epic Mythologies of Shelley and Keats." *Wascana Review* 4.1 (1969): 61–72.

Ragussis, Michael. *The Subterfuge of Art: Language and the Romantic Tradition*. Baltimore: Johns Hopkins University Press, 1978.

Rajan, Tilottama. *Dark Interpreter: The Discourse of Romanticism.* Ithaca: Cornell University Press, 1980.

Ruthven, K. K. "Keats and *Dea Moneta*." *Studies in Romanticism* 15.3 (1976): 445–59.

Saly, John. "Keats's Answer to Dante: *The Fall of Hyperion*." *Keats-Shelley Journal* 14 (1965): 65–78.

Sheats, Paul D. "Stylistic Discipline in *The Fall of Hyperion*." *Keats-Shelley Journal* 17 (1968): 75–88.

Sherwin, Paul. "Dying into Life: Keats's Struggle with Milton in *Hyperion*." *PMLA* 93.3 (1978): 383–95.

Sperry, Stuart M. *Keats the Poet*. Princeton: Princeton University Press, 1973.

Stillinger, Jack. *"The Hoodwinking of Madeline" and Other Essays on Keats's Poems*. Urbana: University of Illinois Press, 1971.

Taylor, Anya. "Superhuman Silence: Language in *Hyperion*." *Studies in English Literature* 19.4 (1979): 673–87.

Vitoux, Pierre. "Keats's Epic Design in *Hyperion*." *Studies in Romanticism* 14.2 (1975): 165–83.

Ward, Aileen. *John Keats: The Making of a Poet*. New York: Viking, 1963.

Wicker, Brian. "The Disputed Lines in *The Fall of Hyperion*." *Essays in Criticism* 7.1 (1957): 28–41.

Wilkie, Brian. *Romantic Poets and Epic Tradition*. Madison: University of Wisconsin Press, 1965.

Miyazawa Kenji

Amazawa Taijirō. *Miyazawa Kenji no kanata e* (To the other side of Miyazawa Kenji). New ed. Shichōsha, 1987.

Fukushima Akira. *Miyazawa Kenji: Geijutsu to byōri* (Miyazawa Kenji: His art and pathology). Patogurafî Sōsho 3. Kongō Shuppan, 1970.

Hagiwara, Takao. "The Bodhisattva Ideal and the Idea of Innocence in Miyazawa Kenji's Life and Literature." *Journal of the Association of Teachers of Japanese* 27.1 (1993): 35–56.

——— . "The Theme of Innocence in Miyazawa Kenji's Tales." Ph.D. diss., University of British Columbia, 1986. UMI microfiche 0560040.

Hagiwara Takao. *Miyazawa Kenji: Inosensu no bungaku* (Miyazawa Kenji: Literature of innocence). Meiji Shoin, 1988.

Hara Shirō, ed. *Miyazawa Kenji goi jiten* (Glossarial dictionary of Miyazawa Kenji). Tokyo Shoseki, 1989.

Ikegami Yūzō. "*Gingatetsudō no Yoru* no ichi: 'Fūrin' kara 'Shūkyō fū no Koi' made no keiretsu-ka to kōsatsu" (The position of *A Night on the Galaxy Railroad*: A systematization from 'A Windy Grove' to 'Religious Love' and a thought). In *Miyazawa Kenji II*, ed. Nihon Bungaku Kenkyū Shiryō Kankō kai, 160–75. Nihon Bungaku Kenkyū Shiryō Sōsho. Yūseidō, 1983.

Irisawa Yasuo. "*Gingatetsudō no Yoru* no hassō ni tsuite" (About the conception of *A Night on the Galaxy Railroad*). In Kusano, 2:141–50.

Itaya Eiki. *Miyazawa Kenji no mita shinshō: Den'en no kaze to hikari no naka kara* (The images that Miyazawa Kenji saw: From the wind and light of pastoral). NHK Books 591. Nihon Hōsō Shuppan Kyōkai, 1990.

Iwami Teruyo. "Shiroi kurayami e: *Gingatetsudō no Yoru* shiron" (To white darkness: A thought on *A Night on the Galaxy Railroad*). *Miyazawa Kenji* 7 (Yōyōsha, 1987): 78–90.

Katori Naoichi. "Tenkirin no hashira to tōyō no seigaku: Senki Gyokkō kō" (The Pole of the Weather Ring and an oriental astrology: A thought on Senki Gyokkō). *Miyazawa Kenji* 6 (Yōyōsha, 1986): 146–56.

Kusaka Hideaki. *Miyazawa Kenji to hoshi* (Miyazawa Kenji and stars). Miyazawa Kenji Kenkyū Sōsho 1. Gakugei Shorin, 1975.

Kusano Shinpei, ed. *Miyazawa Kenji kenkyū* (Research on Miyazawa Kenji). 2 vols. Chikuma Shobō, 1958, 1969.

Kuwahara Hiroyoshi. "Ijigen sekai o byōsha shite miseta *Gingatetsudō no Yoru*" (*A Night on the Galaxy Railroad* that showed us the hetero-dimensional world). *Miyazawa Kenji* 7 (Yōyōsha, 1987): 51–63.

Mita Munesuke. *Miyazawa Kenji: Sonzai no matsuri no naka e* (Miyazawa Kenji: Into the festivity of existence). 20 Seiki Shisōka Bunko 12. Iwanami Shoten, 1984.

Miyagi Kazuo. *Miyazawa Kenji: Chigaku to bungaku no hazama* (Miyazawa Kenji: Between physical geography and literature). Tamagawa Sensho 46. Tamagawa Daigaku Shuppan bu, 1977.

Miyagi Kazuo and Takamura Kiichi. *Miyazawa Kenji to shokubutsu no sekai* (Miyazawa Kenji and the world of plants). Tsukiji Shokan, 1980.

Miyazawa Seiroku. *Ani no toranku* (The trunk of my elder brother). Chikuma Shobō, 1987.

Murase Manabu. *"Gingatetsudō no Yoru" to wa nani ka* (What is *A Night on the Galaxy Railroad*?). Yamato Shobō, 1989.

Nakamura Minoru. *Miyazawa Kenji*. Chikuma Sōsho 191. Chikuma Shobō, 1972.

Nishida Yoshiko. "*Gingatetsudō no Yoru* no Giovanni" (Giovanni in *A Night on the Galaxy Railroad*). *Kokubungaku* 20.15 (1975): 224–25.

———— . *Miyazawa Kenji ron* (On Miyazawa Kenji). Ōfūsha, 1981.

Ogiwara Masayoshi. "Tenkirin no hashira: Ozawa Toshirō shi no setsu o ukete" (The Pole of the Weather Ring: In response to Mr. Ozawa Toshirō's argument). *Miyazawa Kenji* 1 (Yōyōsha, 1981): 59–71.

Ōmi Masato. "'Minna no saiwai' sagasu tabi: *Aoi Tori* to no hikaku o tōshite" (A trip to look for 'everyone's happiness': Through a comparison with *The Blue Bird*). *Miyazawa Kenji* 7 (Yōyōsha, 1987): 91–103.

Ono Ryūshō. *Miyazawa Kenji no shisaku to shinkō* (The speculation and faith of Miyazawa Kenji). Tairyūsha, 1979.

Ōoka Shōhei. "Miyazawa Kenji to Nakahara Chūya: Meiji izen no sekai" (Miyazawa Kenji and Nakahara Chūya: The world before names). In *Miyazawa Kenji*, Gendaishi Tokuhon 12 (Shichōsha, 1983): 216–18.

Saitō Bun'ichi. *Miyazawa Kenji to ginga taiken* (Miyazawa Kenji and the experience of the galaxy). Kokubunsha, 1980.

Saitō Jun. "*Gingatetsudō no yoru* no monogatari toshite no kōzō: Shokikei kara saishūkei e no dainamizumu" (The structure of *A Night on the Galaxy Railroad* as a story: Dynamism from the early versions to the final version). *Miyazawa Kenji* 8 (Yōyōsha, 1988): 102–15.

Sakai Tadaichi. *Miyazawa Kenji ron* (On Miyazawa Kenji). Ōfūsha, 1985.

Satō Michimasa. *Miyazawa Kenji no bungaku sekai: Tanka to dōwa* (The literary world of Miyazawa Kenji: His tanka poems and children's tales). Tairyūsha, 1979.

Strong, Sarah Mehlhop, trans. *Night of the Milky Way Railway*, by Miyazawa Kenji. Armonk, N.Y.: M. E. Sharpe, 1991.

———— . "The Poetry of Miyazawa Kenji." Ph.D. diss., University of Chicago, 1984. UMI microfiche 8417583.

Sugawa Chikara. *Hoshi no sekai: Miyazawa Kenji to tomo ni* (The world of stars: With Miyazawa Kenji). Soshiete Bunko 35. Soshiete, 1979.

Sugawara Chieko and Gamō Yoshirō. "*Gingatetsudō no Yoru* shinken: Miyazawa Kenji no seishun no mondai" (A new view of *A Night on the Galaxy Railroad*: A problem of Miyazawa Kenji's young days). *Bungaku* 40 (1972): 954–69.

Tanikawa Tetsuzō. *Miyazawa Kenji no sekai* (The world of Miyazawa Kenji). Sōsho: Nihon Bungakushi Kenkyū. Hōsei Daigaku Shuppan kyoku, 1970.

Tsuzukihashi Tatsuo. *Miyazawa Kenji: Dōwa no kiseki* (Miyazawa Kenji: The orbit of his children's tales). Ōfūsha, 1978.

——— . *Miyazawa Kenji: Dōwa no sekai* (Miyazawa Kenji: The world of his children's tales). Ōfūsha, 1975.

Usami Eiji. "*Gingatetsudō no Yoru*" (A Night on the Galaxy Railroad). In Kusano, 1:106–12.

Vidaeus, Kerstin. "Miyazawa Kenji no dōwa ni tsuite" (On children's tales by Miyazawa Kenji). In *Shinshū Miyazawa Kenji zenshū*, 17:247–54.

Yamauchi Osamu. "*Gingatetsudō no Yoru*" (A Night on the Galaxy Railroad). *Kokubungaku: Kaishaku to kanshō* 44.10 (1979): 98–101.

Yoshimoto Takaaki. "Miyazawa Kenji ron" (On Miyazawa Kenji). *Bungaku* 44 (1976): 1559–71.

INDEX

The number in the parentheses that follow the number of a note refers to the text page on which the note number is originally printed.